Praise for THE BIG MISS

"While *The Big Miss* is many things—a coach's story; an account of a collapse; a deep dive into the swing mechanics and the art of golf—it also offers a welcome and unvarnished look inside. Books about major athletes are often authorized pabulum or arm's-length agglomerations. Haney's recollections are his own, and subject to dispute, but this is **a rich and compelling rendering of a complicated athlete undone less by embarrassing details than by a self-inflicted, unsustainable myth."**

—Jason Gay, *Wall Street Journal*

"I learned more about Tiger in *The Big Miss* than I have in eleven years of covering him on the PGA Tour. . . . I actually thought the book was very fair; it was honest."

—Damon Hack, senior writer, *Sports Illustrated*

"The first real crack in the armor, someone in the inner circle who is no longer in the inner circle actually telling about life inside the Tiger camp. **I applaud what Hank has done. I'm reading the book now and loving it."**

—Michael Bamberger, senior writer, *Sports Illustrated*

"An alarming look at an athlete whose public glories masked a day-to-day existence of profound superficiality . . . Even more revealing than the swing material is evidence of Woods' emotional blank wall: his indifference to people around him, his inability to empathize, and an obsession with military training and the Navy SEALs that, according to Haney, probably led to the leg injuries which have hampered Woods' golf career."

—*Golfweek*

"Incredibly interesting—especially if you play golf . . . Haney does a great job of simply telling it like it is. . . . The 'why' behind the mystery of Tiger's perplexing personality weaves its way through the entire book."

—David G. Kindervater, featured columnist, *Bleacher Report*

"After flying through this 247-page, mostly breezy and fascinating look into the life of a champion, I suspect most readers will ultimately have a newfound respect for Woods. I know I do. . . . For the first time in the history of golf literature, we get a behind-the-scenes look at how an all-time great works. Many times the details are not pretty, but most of the journey Haney takes us on reveals a relentless passion to thrive in an era when so many professionals appear content to occasionally contend and collect healthy checks. **If I were asked to recommend a book for an aspiring young golfer, *The Big Miss* would be the first title I'd select, if for no other reason than most of today's Tiger-wannabes will be motivated to work much harder than they currently do."** —GeoffShackelford.com

"A worthy read that'll continue the debate whether anyone can endure and survive a long relationship with Woods . . . Ultimately, *The Big Miss* is an insightful account of dealing with a demanding superstar and the suffocating expectations."

—*Avid Golfer*

The Big Miss

The Big Miss

MY YEARS COACHING TIGER WOODS

HANK HANEY

THREE RIVERS PRESS
NEW YORK

Published in the United States by Three Rivers Press, an imprint of the Crown Publishing Group, a division of Random House, Inc., New York.
www.crownpublishing.com

Three Rivers Press and the Tugboat design are registered trademarks of Random House, Inc.

Originally published in hardcover in the United States by Crown Archetype, an imprint of the Crown Publishing Group, a division of Random House, Inc., New York, in 2012.

Cataloging-in-Publication Data is on file with the Library of Congress.

ISBN 978-0-307-98600-9
eISBN 978-0-307-98599-6

Printed in the United States of America

Cover design: Michael Nagin
Cover photographs: © Timothy A. Clary/AFP/Getty Images

First Paperback Edition

To my loving wife, Suzanne

CONTENTS

1. The Last Time 1

2. Beginnings 8

3. Coaching Tiger 37

4. Greatness 84

5. Distraction 134

6. Highest Mountain 167

7. Quitting 193

8. Adding It Up 229

Acknowledgments 249

Tiger Woods's Worldwide Performance Record While Hank Haney Was His Coach 251

Glossary of Golf Terms 255

Index of Names 259

1

The Last Time

Finally, a moment of truth.

Less than an hour before he'll tee off in the final round of the 2010 Masters, Tiger Woods walks onto the far corner of the Augusta National's vast practice range.

The other players and caddies sneak looks. A cheer rises from the packed grandstands, and the rowdier people squeezed together behind the green gallery ropes yell encouragement from short range. "Go, Tiger! You're the man!" He might be disgraced, he might be a punch line, but he's still iconic.

As he puts on his glove, the force of the collective gaze that always makes me feel uncomfortable when I'm walking with Tiger at a major championship is more penetrating. He's become more than just the greatest player alive. He's the human being who's fallen farther faster than anyone else in history. The haters, the sympathizers, the commentators—everyone—want to see what it's done to him.

So do I. Yes, he's been different since returning from an addiction-treatment facility six weeks ago—more subdued, possibly shell-shocked—but I've been waiting to judge whether he's changed as a golfer. Tiger has always been able to go to a special place mentally in the majors, and I'm eager to find out if he still can. Will he still be Tiger Woods? Passing golf's excruciating Sunday tests has always been what he does best. But this one feels most like a reckoning.

Tiger is in third place, four strokes behind Lee Westwood and three behind Phil Mickelson. Without saying so—he's said little about anything all week—he knows that a good round today will regain him respect. And it's in the air that a victory would be even bigger than the 2008 U.S. Open at Torrey Pines, when he won on a broken leg; finishing on top here might legitimately be judged the most dramatic win in golf history. It would mean redemption, a goal that suddenly seems more important than surpassing Jack Nicklaus's record of 18 major championships.

Now it's go time. Tiger's Sunday warm-ups are traditionally works of art, especially when he's in contention. After three competitive rounds, he's usually distilled what is working to its essence, and using a mix of adrenaline and focus, he can go through the whole bag without missing a shot. Despite having watched Tiger hit thousands of balls, I still feel that thrill that comes with seeing him with full command at close quarters. His swing begins with serene poise at address, continues with a smooth gathering of power, and then, with the coordinated explosion that announces a supreme athlete, uncoils in a marriage of speed and control, the ball seemingly collected more than hit by the clubface. As he relaxes into his balanced finish, the look Tiger gets on his face as he watches his ball fly is more peaceful than at any other moment.

But something is wrong. After a few balls, I can see Tiger is strangely detached. He's taking too little time between swings, barely watching where the balls go, sometimes even taking one hand off the club before completing his follow-through. The flush yet cracking sound of his impact that for years has announced his superiority over other players isn't quite the same. He's having a terrible warm-up, almost as if he's not really trying. Other than a few quick grimaces of disgust, his face remains eerily stoic.

I'm about ten feet away, standing behind him along his target line, checking to see if his club shaft is on plane, marking his head movement, assessing the ball flight, weighing whether to say something or continue to stay quiet. It's what I've done as his coach during countless practice sessions over the past six years, but he's acting as if I'm not there. I wait for some eye contact from Tiger, some words beyond a mumble, some sense of partnership in this warm-up and this moment. I get nothing. Since emerging from his meal in the clubhouse, he's switched on that cold-blooded ability to leave a person—even someone close to him—hanging. Amazingly, right here, right now, Tiger is blowing me off.

This is the treatment. I got my initiation the second time I ever officially worked with him, on the practice range at Isleworth in March 2004. I'd stood my ground then, and I'm standing my ground now. Tiger doesn't respond well when underlings ask him if something's wrong, or worse, when they've done something wrong. His longtime but now former trainer, Keith Kleven, was always fretting about whether Tiger was mad at him. Rather than taking Keith's concern as a show of loyalty, Tiger saw weakness. In his world of testosterone-fueled heroics and military hardness, that's unacceptable.

He's never done this at a major championship when he's been in contention, so I'm not sure what he's thinking. My best guess is that he's carried over his aggravation from the night before, when the raw numbers on the scoreboard forced a realization that winning will be a long shot. He's probably telling me in a passive-aggressive way that he doesn't like the golf swing I've given him for this week. His swing problems could also be attributable to pain in his chronically injured left knee or some other body part, but he hasn't complained about anything like that all week. Ultimately, there may be a far simpler reason for the chill I'm feeling from him: He's firing me in the nonconfrontational way that's more common to a breakup than a professional relationship.

Whatever is going on, I know one thing: He's not going to explain.

I react clinically. Tiger is Tiger, in all his complexities, and my job is to adjust and adapt to him and keep finding ways to get his best. That's always been a lot harder to do than people think. It turned out to be a lot harder than I thought. But since he's returned from the Mississippi clinic where he followed a psychologically brutal program of self-examination, it's gotten harder still.

He's playing in this Masters after his most rushed, most erratic, and poorest preparation for a major championship ever. Five days before the first round, his game was so ragged it forced me to suggest a limited swing that has cost him distance and shot-making versatility but kept his misses playable.

It's been a theme of my work with Tiger for much of our time together. Although it's commonly thought that Tiger plays go-for-broke golf and tries the most difficult shots with no fear, it's a false image. Tiger is, above all, a calculating golfer who plays percentages and makes sure to err on the safe side. What he abhors, and has built his career on avoiding, are the kinds of mistakes that produce bogeys or worse and kill both momentum and confidence—wild tee shots that produce penalty strokes, loose approaches that leave no chance to save par, blown short putts. These blunders are the stuff of high scores, and after such a round, a tour player or caddie will often lament "the big miss." Avoiding the big miss was a big part of what made Ben Hogan and Jack Nicklaus so great, and it's a style that Tiger has emulated. Until recently, his entire life seemed free of the big miss. But things change.

It's why the game Tiger has brought to Augusta has been less powerful, less versatile, and less likely to shoot a low number than his A game. But it's fulfilled its purpose by producing consistent scores of 68, 70, and 70 to stay in contention.

Now Tiger knows that he'll almost certainly need something in the mid-60s to have a chance to win, and I'm getting the sense he's unhappy that the style of play we've prepared is going to lack the kind of firepower such a round usually requires. He's also aware that he's never come from behind on a Sunday to win any of his 14 major championships. In his current state, the odds are against his making that breakthrough, and it's not helping his mood.

I have the feeling that Tiger is most aggravated that he's spotting three strokes to Mickelson. Tiger has always had a chilly relationship with Phil. Some of it is personality, but most of it is that Mickelson possesses the kind of talent that has made him a legitimate threat to Tiger's supremacy. Phil's popularity with the fans and gentle treatment from the media add to Tiger's annoyance. For years Tiger reveled in the idea that Mickelson had trouble playing in his presence. But Phil adjusted, and in recent years he's outplayed Tiger down the stretch in several tournaments. His increased confidence against Tiger, along with the positive energy of the gallery, has flipped the psychological advantage in their matchup in his favor. Phil has won two of the last six Masters, both victories coming on the lengthened and narrowed Augusta course that has given Tiger—who won three of his four on the earlier design—trouble. I sense that Tiger has begun to press against Mickelson, making today's mountain that much higher.

Then again, at this Masters, Tiger has already accomplished a great deal. In the first tournament he's played in five months—a period in which he's suffered public humiliation, the painful, regimented program designed to look into a psyche he never before questioned, the ordeal of his televised February 19 public apology, which was so anticipated that it preempted network programming, and the certainty that his wife will soon file for divorce—he's battled furiously and played amazingly well. He's made more mistakes than usual but nearly offset them with short bursts of truly spectacular golf. By the end of the tournament, he will have made a total of 17 birdies and a record four eagles in 72 holes, a 25-under-par barrage that will exceed his sub-par holes in 1997, when he won by 12 and set the tournament record on a much shorter golf course. Considering where he was a few weeks ago, I consider having a part in where he is my best job of short-term coaching ever.

In my mind, Tiger is playing with house money. As a person who has lost so much, he should be feeling that this final round presents him with everything to gain. But as I watch him rake another ball out of the pile without looking up, there's zero indication he sees things that way. He hasn't been going through our practice progression of the Nine Shots—in which he hits the nine possible ball flights with each club—in a regimented way. Somehow, his devotion to excellence, the quality that most identifies him to the world, is missing.

But what I've learned at close quarters is that excellence, year after year, is exhausting. Late at night, I've been wondering if the 2010 Masters would mark the moment Tiger didn't want to be Tiger Woods anymore. It's not something I've said to many people, because it sounds so absurd, but I've often thought, even when Tiger's game was at its peak, that because of insane expectations that even he can't fulfill, there is no harder person to be in the world than Tiger Woods.

I look over at Steve Williams, standing a few feet away next to Tiger's bag. He's carried it for 13 major-championship victories since 1999, which, without even counting his long and very successful stints with Greg Norman and Raymond Floyd, make him the greatest caddie in history. He's been in my corner from the beginning, in part because he'd been in favor of Tiger leaving his former swing coach Butch Harmon and wanted Butch's successor to do well. Steve has his hard-ass game face on and hasn't said a word, but we're brothers in arms, and when our eyes meet, so do our thoughts.

What is going on? Scandal or no scandal, aren't these the moments Tiger has always said he worked for? Lived for? The times when his ability to hyperfocus and be mentally bulletproof give him his most important advantage over the competition? The times he's always said he relishes the most?

But Tiger, tellingly, is not relishing this. His attitude is straight-up horrible. Now, at the moment of truth, it's a defining signal.

I doubt anyone has a greater appreciation for how great Tiger is than I do. He's a genius in the most exacting sport there is—physically, technically, mentally, emotionally. Nicklaus might have the greatest overall record, but no one has ever played golf as well as Tiger Woods, and no one has ever been better than his competition by a wider margin. He's the greatest.

But life is about loss. With the cold part of my mind that keeps any sadness momentarily walled off, I make the call. He's become less of a golfer, and he's never going to be the same again.

2

Beginnings

Tiger Woods is sullen the first time I meet him. Maybe even a little rude. But also, without a doubt, fascinating.

It's May 1993, and Tiger is a 17-year-old amateur who has come to Dallas to play in the PGA Tour's Byron Nelson Classic on a sponsor's exemption. He and his father, Earl, are staying in the home of Ernie and Pam Kuehne, whose three kids—Trip, Hank, and Kelli—are all successful junior golfers I teach. Ernie, Hank, and Kelli have brought Tiger and Earl to the Hank Haney Golf Ranch—it's a former horse farm with converted barns and stables—in the North Dallas suburb of McKinney to show them where they practice and introduce them to the coach who helps them with their games.

I'm giving a lesson when I see the five of them appear from

behind one of the barns. I think, *Wow, that's Tiger Woods!* Like everyone in golf, I've heard a lot about Tiger and am excited to see him in the flesh. More than any junior golfer ever, he's famous. He's won his age group at the Optimist Junior World tournament almost every year since he was eight. He's won the U.S. Junior Amateur twice, and in a few months he'll make it three in a row. No male player has ever done those things.

I take a break to walk over and say hello. Tiger is gangly from a recent growth spurt, about six feet but weighing less than 150 pounds, and the bagginess of what has to be an XL-size golf shirt only accentuates his lankiness. But skinny as he is, he looks golf strong. His is a body built for clubhead speed.

I tell Tiger what a pleasure it is to meet him, and congratulate him on his accomplishments. He seems sleepy, and when I put out my hand, he takes it weakly. It reminds me of the light grip you get from older touring pros who believe a regular shake might mess up their touch. I notice that Tiger's hand seems kind of delicate, the fingers long and thin.

I greet Earl and compliment him on the job he's done with his son. Based on what I've read, I'm expecting a talker, but Earl is only slightly more responsive than Tiger.

Ernie, an extroverted bear of a man, fills the silence, but the whole encounter is a little strained. My first thought is that there's a natural reason for the wariness. Tiger is a black kid in a white sport, visiting a Southern state, where he's not wrong to assume that a lot of people who'd rather not see him rise to the top of the game are going to be nice to his face. I remember reading his account of "the look" he's gotten at some country clubs, and how he's been schooled by his dad on the subtle forms of racial prejudice.

My second thought is that this slouching, bored teenager projects a powerful presence. I'd heard about Tiger's focus, his intensity, and his will, and in a strange way he's demonstrating it all with his insolence. I'm an adult, a trusted friend of his hosts, and own the establishment he's visiting, but he doesn't care enough to engage me in the least, and it makes the vibe uncomfortable. Most young people—most people, *period*—would be able to stand the awkwardness for only so long before saying something. Tiger doesn't.

I don't take it personally. Instead, I think, *I'm not sure what all this is about, but I'm pretty sure it's got something to do with why he always wins.* I also remember thinking that, while there was a good possibility Tiger was going to be out on the tour and that I'd be around him again, I probably was never going to be friends with him.

It becomes clear that the group is just passing through, so Tiger won't be hitting balls. I'm a little disappointed, because as a coach, I would value the opportunity to ask Earl about how he's guided his son. I don't really feel a great need to watch Tiger swing. I've seen enough on television to know he's got a beautiful action, graceful and impossibly fast, and I know he can hit it a mile. But honestly, a lot of junior prodigies can do those things. I'm sure Tiger isn't as long as Hank Kuehne, who is the same age and will soon be the biggest hitter in the entire game. And to this day I've never seen a junior golfer who swung better or hit the ball as well as Trip Kuehne, whom I've been teaching since he was 11. But the swing of any kid at 17, no matter how impressive to the eye, is still in the embryonic stage as measured against what it must evolve into for a competitive career.

The things that make the difference in whether a young player progresses are intangibles: toughness, work ethic, self-confidence, desire, a sense of how to score, and most of all, true passion for the game. Of the Kuehne siblings, it's five-foot-three Kelli—who will go on to win a U.S. Girls' Junior, two U.S. Amateurs, a British Ladies Amateur, and an LPGA event—who possesses these qualities to the greatest degree. Hank will win the 1998 U.S. Amateur but, mostly due to a back injury, will have limited success on the PGA Tour, and Trip will lose an incredible U.S. Amateur final to Tiger in 1994, resist turning pro, and finally win a USGA title at the 2008 Mid-Amateur. The Kuehne boys have as much physical talent as Tiger. On meeting Tiger, though, I know in an instant—in that kind of flash Malcolm Gladwell talks about in his book *Blink*—that he possesses the right intangibles to the highest degree.

Our chat lasts only about five minutes, and if not for Ernie, it would have been shorter. But it's enough. As I walk away, I mentally file Tiger under "ultimate case study." And I know I'll be studying him for a long time.

I saw Tiger quite a bit over the next few years. I became the golf coach at Southern Methodist University (SMU) in 1994, the same year Tiger entered Stanford. Whenever our teams were at a tournament, I'd run into him and show interest in his progress. Having sized me up in Dallas, he became friendlier, though still guarded. We might kibitz about the Kuehnes, but mostly it was me encouraging and complimenting and him nodding his thanks.

When I had the chance, I'd watch him from afar, either on the practice range or on the course. Although he was still pretty thin, I could see he was both growing into his body and putting on some weight-room muscle, and under his teacher, Butch Harmon, his swing was becoming less willowy and more stable.

By his sophomore year, Tiger had won two U.S. Amateurs and was on his way to another unprecedented three-peat. I kept telling Mark O'Meara, my longtime student and a multiple winner on the PGA Tour, about how incredibly good this kid was. Mark was skeptical, as touring pros tend to be about prodigies. He'd point out that Tiger had never had a high finish in the several PGA Tour events in which he'd received a sponsor's exemption. Most pros were stars in childhood, and they all remember the kid who was better than they were who was projected for professional stardom but never made it. Mark would mention Doug Clarke, who beat the heck out of him, John Cook, and everyone else around

Southern California growing up, but who flamed out. Pros distrust early success.

There are fewer sure things in golf than any other sport. Even as good as the Kuehne boys turned out to be, neither fulfilled his promise in golf. But there was something very different about Tiger that made me sure he'd continue to be historic.

He definitely had a sense of mission, and you couldn't help thinking that it had something to do with belonging to a minority. No black player had come out and stuck as a regular on the PGA Tour since the late 1970s, and Tiger knew he was carrying a lot of hopes on his shoulders. At the same time, I already had the sense that he wasn't going to let societal pressures become extra baggage. The way he'd blocked me out at our first meeting told me he'd be able to build a wall around his game. As I observed him, I began to see him as a lone wolf. Nobody else in golf was like him: the son of an African American father who was a career soldier and an Asian mother who was a devout Buddhist, both of whom had poured all they had into their only child together. They'd raised an outsider and sent him on a singular journey.

The X factor was Earl Woods. Skeptics thought Earl wasn't doing Tiger any favors by predicting Tiger's future importance to sports and society. But I didn't sense in Tiger the resentment and rebellion I often saw in kids with pushy fathers. He and Earl were clearly really close. Earl was Tiger's rock and the source of his confidence.

Tiger shared his dad's grandiose vision. I could tell by the way he talked about himself after his victories. In 1996, in his last year at Stanford, Tiger won the NCAA individual championship at the Honors Course in Tennessee. It was an extremely difficult Pete Dye layout, but Tiger shot 69-67-69 the first three days to take a nine-stroke lead with one round to go. He struggled on the final day to shoot 80, but the course was so hard, he still won by four strokes. He looked as though he could blow it after a triple bogey on the ninth hole followed by four bogeys, but he kept his poise and finished it off. I told Mark that if the U.S. Open had been played that week at the Honors Course, Tiger would have definitely led after three rounds and might well have found a way to win it. I remember reading Tiger's quote afterward: "People will never know how much it took out of me," he said. Tiger saw himself—at least as a golfer—as doing and feeling things on a scale other people just couldn't understand.

Later that year, *Golf Digest* published a piece asking leading teachers how they thought Tiger would do in his first year as a pro. Most offered some variation of him keeping his tour card, perhaps garnering a victory. I said that in his first full year Tiger would be the leading money winner.

Tiger noticed my comment. He mentioned it the next time I saw him, again when he actually became the leading money winner in his first full season, and he brought it up a few more times over the years. I realized that while Tiger seemed to be ignoring things, he was actually paying close attention: watching, weighing, and figuring out whom he could trust. I know that quote had something to do with his eventually picking me to coach him.

At the time Tiger joined the tour, I never in a million years thought that I'd ever be his coach. He and Butch had a great relationship that seemed destined to last for Tiger's entire career. I was an experienced instructor with a good name. I ran three golf centers in the Dallas area, had been chosen the 1993 PGA of America Teacher of the Year, and was mostly known for coaching Mark, who'd developed into a top player on the PGA Tour. But Mark had yet to win majors, so our partnership didn't get the attention of David Leadbetter's work with Nick Faldo, or Butch's with Greg Norman.

Still, I was very much living my dream. I'd wanted to be a golf instructor from the time I was a teenager. I was born in 1955 and grew up in Deerfield, Illinois, in the northern suburbs of Chicago in an upper-middle-class neighborhood. My dad was a successful advertising salesman. My mom stayed at home, where she always stressed hard work. She was also very inquisitive, which I think helped me be curious about people, especially successful ones. She also told me at a young age that patience would be my greatest virtue.

As a kid, I noticed my parents seemed most proud of me when I did well in sports. I always wanted to excel, I was willing to do what it took to be good enough, and it used to bother me that so many of the guys on my teams in hockey or baseball just didn't want it as bad as I did.

I'm sure that's part of what appealed to me about golf. It was just me, and I could work at it as hard as I wanted to. Our family had a membership at Exmoor Country Club, and my dad started taking me to the course when I was 11. I'd played a lot of hockey, and that probably helped me make pretty good contact with the ball right away. I enjoyed batting it around the range and the practice green. When I started going out on the course, I did so mostly alone. But I didn't mind, because I was really intrigued by the challenge of the game.

When I was 13, I went to a summer golf camp in Indiana, with a couple of good instructors, Sam Carmichael and Joe Campbell, the latter an old touring pro people remember for the cigar that was always in his mouth when he played. They fixed my slice in a way that I could understand, and that process encouraged me to become very analytical about the swing and the game. I found that what I liked most about golf was that you could diagnose a problem and try to correct it technically, and then see if the changes held up on the course.

I worked hard at my game and had a bit of success in local tournaments, but even as I dreamed of the future, I never really envisioned myself becoming a touring pro. I remember playing in the biggest high school tournament in the state, the Champaign Invitational at the University of Illinois golf course, when I was 16. I shot 73-72 in windy conditions, the best I'd ever played. I finished second, 11 shots behind the winner, Jay Haas, who is now winning tournaments on the Champions Tour. That told me something.

In high school I was probably better at hockey, but golf became my sport. I wasn't recruited, so I wrote letters to colleges inquiring about golf scholarships. I got one answer, from the University of Tulsa, whose golf coach, an education professor named Carl Oliver, invited me to come down for a visit. I flew down there on my own, talked to Coach Oliver, was given a tour of the campus, and even practiced with the team. I took the round with them really seriously and performed well, shooting a 73 on a tough course called Cedar Ridge. In doing so, I beat everyone but one player, another future touring pro, Ron Streck. Right on the spot, I was offered a scholarship, and I very proudly took it. It was a great day.

With teaching golf in mind, I chose education as my major. I roomed with Ron, who was a phenomenal golfer and an amazing athlete who could dunk a basketball even though he was just six feet tall. I remember I beat Ron only once in a match, on an easy par-70 municipal course, when I shot a 61 and he shot 62. And he got so pissed that he wouldn't talk to me. It was my first exposure to how crazily competitive really good players can be.

In March 1974, my freshman year, I decided to go home to Chicago for a long weekend. I got into my Camaro, drove 12 hours, and went straight out to Exmoor, which had a new head pro named Jim Hardy. The temperature never got higher than the low 30s that day, and the place was pretty deserted. In the golf shop I met Jim, a dynamic guy who couldn't have been nicer. I asked him if I could use one of the holes near the clubhouse to practice with my shag bag, and he said to go ahead, and that he might come out to watch me. To my surprise, Jim came out soon after and worked with me on my game for a good four hours.

Jim had played on the PGA Tour, where he'd been known as a very long hitter, a good ball striker, and a terrible putter. He had a beautiful action reminiscent of Ben Hogan, whose books he'd studied as the basis for his teaching. Jim was and remains a tremendous communicator, and when he started talking and demonstrating, I was overwhelmed by his knowledge and how well he conveyed it. And as much as I was having a blast, I also noticed how energized he was by helping me. I thought, *This is so cool. This is really what I want to do.* It was one of those moments that change your whole life.

When I got back to school, my studies included teaching golf at recreation centers in Tulsa, and I found that I got a lot of satisfaction from the challenge of getting a complete beginner to execute the fundamentals and become a golfer who could enjoy the game. As a player, in a couple of tournaments I rose to number-two man on the team and made all-conference my junior year, but I knew I wasn't going to try to play competitively. I wanted to teach.

After graduation, I worked at MeadowBrook Country Club in Tulsa, where I was mostly responsible for changing the batteries in a fleet of more than 100 carts. I wasn't given the opportunity to teach, so after six months I headed back to Chicago, where John Cleland, the new pro at Exmoor, gave me a chance to give lessons.

It was the break I needed. Jim Hardy had left Exmoor to help run the John Jacobs' Golf Schools, but we stayed in touch, and after about a year he asked me to work with him at some winter schools. I was the low man on the totem pole at the Jacobs schools, basically charged with grunt work like setting up the range, picking up balls, and getting drinks for the students. But I got to watch Jim and John Jacobs teach, and it was a revelation.

John is the most important teacher in golf history, the man whose ideas and system of diagnosis, demonstration, and correction have influenced more teachers than anyone else. Butch Harmon, David Leadbetter, Jim McLean, Jim Hardy, myself, and so many others all owe a huge debt to John. As I write, he's 86 years old and remains an amazing man. He's generous, patient, dedicated, and, with that movie-star face and big personality, still charismatic. As a professional he played in the Ryder Cup and 14 British Opens, and won several events. Like Jim, his quest to become a better player led him into a study of the golf swing, and he came up with maybe the best sentence in the history of teaching: "Golf is what the ball does." In other words, the flight of the ball tells the teacher where the student's club was at impact. From there, the teacher can make the appropriate corrections to grip, posture, alignment, ball position, plane, club path, or clubface angle. It's a sound formula and basically all I do, whether it's with a beginner or Tiger Woods. A lot of teachers know much more about the biomechanics and physics of the swing than I do. When it comes to terms like ballistics and the kinetic chain, they can talk circles around me. But I feel very secure in my ability to fix ball flight.

Sitting around a table at night listening to John, Jim, and other respected golf instructors hold court was one of the most valuable experiences of my career. I remember one discussion in which John was talking about how, contrary to conventional wisdom, so many of the most consistent and enduring ball strikers had a slight "over the top" move, rather than the more classic "inside-out" path, in which the shaft flattens out on the downswing. John clicked off the names of Bobby Locke, Sam Snead, Arnold Palmer, and Bruce Lietzke as just a few examples of players who started down with their arms a bit farther from their body, the club taking something close to the "outside-in" path that slicers are always warned against. John said that way of hitting the ball held less danger for good players than dropping the club down and hitting from inside to out. "Hitting too late from the inside with an open face not only misses the fairway, it can miss the golf course," he said. "A little over the top never misses by too much. In competitive golf, it's not so much where the good ones go. It's where the bad ones go. You've got to build a swing that will eliminate the *big miss.*" It was a concept that stayed with me.

After a few months, I was teaching in the Jacobs schools in the winter and Exmoor in the summer. In 1980, the Pinehurst resort asked the Jacobs people to teach at one of their schools. While we were at Pinehurst, their director of golf, Mike Sanders, asked me if I'd be interested in taking a permanent position as the head of instruction for the Pinehurst Golf Advantage Schools. I was 25 years old, single, really ambitious, and willing to work for a modest salary in the remote Sandhills of North Carolina. Mike took a chance on me, and I was soon running the schools at the biggest golf resort in the world as well as teaching every day.

I was getting a lot of confidence in my ability to correct ball flight, and I was slowly developing some of my ideas about the swing. I also got to keep furthering my teaching knowledge because sometimes the Golf Digest schools would also come to Pinehurst, and we got to watch those instructors teach. It allowed me to pick the brains of such men as Bob Toski, Jim Flick, Davis Love Jr., Paul Runyan, and Peter Kostis. Toski and Flick in particular had great presentation skills. I'd try to take a little from everyone and keep improving.

It was a matter of timing. I had another life-changing event—and the most fortunate single moment of my career—occur in October of 1982, my second year at Pinehurst. The PGA Tour's Hall of Fame Tournament was being played at the resort, and on Friday evening one of the pros who missed the cut, Mark O'Meara, was on the iconic practice range, known as Maniac Hill, desperately trying to find a swing that would work.

After winning the 1979 U.S. Amateur, Mark had been the PGA Tour's Rookie of the Year in 1981. But he'd fallen into a deep slump, and with just three tournaments to go was 120th on the money list and in danger of falling out of the top 125 and losing his exemption for the next year. He was desperate, so when he saw one of the assistant pros on the range, Ken Crow, he asked if he'd watch him. To my everlasting gratitude, Ken said that he'd get the head of instruction.

When Ken came into the teaching center and asked me to come out and watch this young pro, I confess I didn't really want to. It was late in the day, and I suspected that the student was one of Ken's local assistant pro buddies. I reluctantly went out on the practice tee.

I was shocked when I saw it was Mark O'Meara. I said hello, and Mark barely looked up. He was clearly agitated and said sort of sharply, "Would you watch me and tell me what you see?" I said, "Sure." Mark was the first touring pro I'd ever helped, but I wasn't intimidated. I could see that his swing was built on feel and talent but not good technique. He got the club way too upright at the top, forcing him to drop the club sharply to the inside of the target line on the way down and then flipping his hands at impact to square the club. When he was on, he could get away with it. But when he was off, he was lost. For players with poor mechanics, the week-to-week grind of the PGA Tour is a brutally exposing place.

After about ten minutes, Mark asked, "Well, are you going to say something?" I kind of took my time, wanting Mark to calm down a bit, and said, "I'm just thinking about what you're going to need to do." I suggested we go inside to the clubhouse and talk about it over a Coke. Mark looked up and said harshly, "I'm about to lose my card. I don't have time for a Coke." But after a few more swings, he agreed to go inside.

What I formulated for Mark was a plan to get better. I explained the parts of his swing that needed to improve and the sequence of the steps ahead. I made it clear that achieving the ultimate goal was going to take time and a lot of discipline, but that in the short term I could give him something that would help him in the next few tournaments. He didn't know me, but something told him it was time to trust, and he said, "OK, let's get started." We practiced all weekend, and then he left for the next tournament. Mark made the next three cuts and kept his card. We kept working together, and the next year he finished 76th on the money list. In 1984, he won his first tournament and was second on the money list.

Mark's swing very quickly looked dramatically different. By virtue of getting the backswing and downswing on the correct plane, it became flatter in angle and rounder in shape. Mark made a bigger swing change—with success—than any other pro I've ever seen. Much greater than what Tiger did under Butch Harmon or me. Bigger even than Nick Faldo's reconstruction under David Leadbetter in 1985, which culminated in Nick's victory at the 1987 British Open and his subsequent rise to number one in the world.

In fact, in 1983, Nick, knowing what Mark had gone through, asked his advice about committing to an overhaul with David, and Mark told him he should go for it.

Both Mark's and Nick's success marked a shift in golf instruction. Prior to that, the best-known instructors built their reputations helping average golfers. At times, they'd work with touring pros, but never on any sort of full-time schedule. For example, Jack Nicklaus's lifelong teacher, Jack Grout, would see Jack only two or three times a year and spent most of his time helping the members at Scioto in Columbus and La Gorce in Miami Beach. Harvey Penick never went out on the tour with Ben Crenshaw or Tom Kite. He just stayed put at Austin Country Club and gave thousands of lessons to average players. But the publicity given to overhauls of pro players' swings, especially the attention paid to the success David had with Nick, changed the model. Not only did it drive more tour players to seek full-time teachers; it led more instructors to travel the tour looking for business and developing stables. Whereas previously the only "lessons" on tour practice ranges had been one pro passing a quick tip along to another, soon there were so-called swing gurus walking the practice tee with video cameras, often serving multiple players at once.

I did only a little of that with Mark because I preferred working with players at my facility or at their home courses away from tournaments. When I moved to Sweetwater Country Club outside Houston, it was then the headquarters of the LPGA Tour, so I worked with over a dozen women pros there. Later, when I moved to Dallas, I bought the golf ranch, where I worked with the Kuehnes, eventually expanding to four facilities.

Although I was following my calling, before I could really excel, I had to conquer a personal issue. For about a dozen years, from the mid-1970s to 1986, I drank too much.

My grandfather was an alcoholic, and my father was an alcoholic. He was never abusive to me. Rather, he was distant. He was a functional alcoholic. My parents argued a lot, but growing up

I was never aware of my dad's addiction. Eventually he and my mother divorced when I was in college, and he got treatment and stopped drinking. I admire that he finally got help and is living a better life. I only wish I'd been more aware of his problem before I started to develop one of my own.

Growing up in a home with an alcoholic left a mark on me. Although I've never gone through therapy for my problem, I've done a lot of reading on the subject and have spoken to a lot of experts in the field. I know that children of alcoholics are vulnerable to certain syndromes like approval-seeking, perfectionism, overwork, sensitivity to criticism, a desire to rescue others, inability to enjoy success, and, most fundamentally, repeating alcoholism. They tend to have trust and self-esteem issues. I know that to varying degrees all those patterns have been part of my life.

I never drank in high school. But when I got to college, I quickly fell into the culture of kegger parties and began drinking beer. I consumed a lot. Looking back, my excuse was that it was just "partying" or "growing up." I had some good times, in part because under the influence I was more open with people than I might have been otherwise. But even then, I was aware that the whole deal wasted a lot of time and energy and didn't leave me feeling very good physically or psychologically.

Drinking was an even bigger part of my life when I entered the golf business. In those days, it was common for golf pros to hang out in the club bar after work to drink and talk. At Pinehurst, the social life seemed to revolve around a few favorite local bars. I'd drink six or seven nights a week and have as many as ten or twelve beers at a time.

When I became director of golf at Sweetwater in Houston in 1984, I had more responsibility and not as many cronies. I was still drinking, but it was becoming an empty experience. I was getting tired of the cycle of waking every day with a hangover and a headache, taking all morning to feel better, and then starting the whole thing over again at night. I considered cutting back but didn't take a decisive step until one day in 1986. I woke up with another headache after another long night. And that's when I told myself, out loud, "I don't want to feel this way anymore. And I'm never going to have another drink the rest of my life."

At first, my approach was simply "just make it to tomorrow." I strung enough individual days together to make it to a year without a drink, and then two years, and then 20. Today when I'm with friends at a party, I'll get the urge to have a beer. But now I have a streak of more than 25 years. I can't break it.

Until now, I haven't talked about my path away from alcohol because I don't want to send the message that people don't benefit from professional help. Although I'm proud of where I got to, there's part of me that wishes I'd gone through therapy, both for the self-knowledge and to be able to better help people I've cared about in their battles with addiction. Still, to some extent, I feel like I've been there.

Ultimately, I think I made it because I've always been a very hard "tryer" with a strong will. I want to excel, and I like being recognized for success, not failure. I realize that the drive to prove myself carries its own issues, but life's complicated. I've learned everybody has issues, and the solution, if there is one, is to keep doing the best you can with who you are and who you want to be.

Having dealt with a lot of high-achievers, I've learned that anybody who is really successful at anything has an incredible passion that is basically an obsession. My mother and my sister used to complain that all I ever talked about was golf, that all I ever wanted to do was practice. My college teammates would make fun of me for constantly standing in front of the mirror looking at my swing, always trying to figure it out. But that's what it takes to separate yourself. No doubt it carries a cost, but so does every life decision.

It was probably the biggest similarity Tiger and I shared, perhaps even a big part of why we ended up working together. He never said so, but to me it was part of our bond.

The hard work led to more good things happening in my

career. A couple of the most rewarding were small moments that connected me to two icons. In the mid-1980s at Sweetwater, I was giving my first lesson to a man from Fort Worth. I always asked people why they'd decided to try a lesson with me, and this gentleman said a fellow member at Shady Oaks had told him that I knew what I was talking about. When I asked who the member was, he said, "Ben Hogan." A few years later, a father brought his young son to me. When I asked why, he said, "Byron Nelson told me the best thing you can do for your son is take him to Hank Haney for golf lessons." I'd never met Hogan or Nelson, but they knew of my reputation. Whenever I've gotten a little down from criticism, I think of those validations and feel better.

I got a lot of gratification coaching Emilee Klein, who had a successful career on the LPGA. Her dad had brought her to me as a six-year-old when I was Director of Instruction for Landmark Land Company at PGA West in La Quinta, California, in the early 1980s. Emilee was undersized and not really physically gifted beyond having good eye-hand coordination, but she was a great listener and did everything I told her. At age 14 she won the California Women's Amateur, and at 17 she won the U.S. Girls' Junior. In 1996, she won the Women's British Open. All told, students of mine, in the period that I worked with them, have won 17 USGA and R&A championships. That's not counting the nine Tiger got before 2004, or Mark's U.S. Amateur.

The thing that *wasn't* working was my golf game. As I got very busy teaching in the mid-'80s, I found very little time to play. I'd always loved playing the game, and the less I played, the more I lost my proficiency. In particular, I'd experience helpless moments with my driver. I'd be especially prone to spraying the ball way right, though I could throw in a bad snap hook just as easily. Things went from bad to worse, eventually balls to the right starting out at almost comical 45-degree angles and ending up as much as 100 yards off line. I got to where I couldn't play nine holes without losing at least one sleeve of balls, and usually two.

Swing instructors always have to deal with the fact that a student expects his or her teacher to play or demonstrate impressively, so perhaps my problem was a reaction to anxiety I might have had about my reputation as a teacher being on the line every time someone saw me hit a ball. I'm not completely sure. I hit bottom at an off-season pro tournament at Pebble Beach in 1985. I'd practiced a bit for the event and hoped I had my problem under control. But instead, I was all over the course. Somehow, I lost only a couple of balls, got a lot of fortunate bounces, and made absolutely everything on the greens. Mark was playing behind me, saw a lot of the shots I hit, and after the round asked sympathetically what I shot. I said 73, and he couldn't believe it. Frankly, neither could I. I'd taken only 21 putts. But I knew that if I'd made a couple of big numbers early instead of some lucky saves, I probably would have shot in the high 80s at least. Right after the round, I was so exhausted from all the stress that I basically stopped playing golf.

For the next 15 years, I played no more than once or twice a year, and never in any sort of competition. I had a serious problem, one that was extremely frustrating because while I could fix others, I couldn't fix myself. Out of stubbornness and because I missed the game, I'd wait until the end of the day, when every customer and employee had left my facility in McKinney, and go out alone to hit hundreds of balls. I don't like to use a lot of video when I teach, but because it was the only way I could see myself, I would film my swing constantly. Actually, it looked all right. Its biggest flaw was the "good player" tendency to flatten the club out coming down, causing the disastrous "late from the inside" miss that John Jacobs had talked about. A closer examination began to reveal that I'd sometimes flinch with my forearms and hands in the impact zone.

What I came to understand is that I had the full-swing yips. The putting yips were an accepted phenomenon, and there was even new medical research at the time that classified the problem as focal dystonia, a motor-sensory disorder in which the motor-skill commands from the brain get distorted or blocked. The study of focal dystonia hadn't really been extended to the full swing, but I'm convinced it's what happened to Seve Ballesteros and Ian Baker-Finch, and later to David Duval, particularly when they were hitting a driver. It definitely happened to me.

There is still a lot of mystery about the driver yips. In my case, I found that they were not necessarily pressure- or anxiety-induced. I was as likely to hit one off the map while alone on the practice tee as I was in a competition. I came to think of the driver yips as more of a physiological than a psychological problem. However, anxiety tended to make them worse.

A key moment in finding a solution came about in the late 1990s when I was doing a clinic for a pretty large group, an experience that had become terrifying for me. When it came time to demonstrate a few shots, rather than take a deliberate stance and risk hitting embarrassing and credibility-killing shots, I sort of faked this casual approach where I'd begin swinging while still looking up at the students. Knowing they'd see this as a less than serious attempt to hit the ball, I felt less pressure. But amazingly, without looking at the ball, I'd hit much better shots than I did when I went through my normal preshot routine and swing.

What I subsequently learned from this experience and further trial and error is that the only thing that cures the yips is radically altering technique so that new pathways from the brain are created. This is why big changes—like the long and belly putter, the claw grip, or other variations on conventional putting—often work so well for people who have problems on the greens.

Following the same idea, I basically went with the opposite of what I'd incorporated into my old swing. It started with the grip. Rather than hold the club in my fingers, where it felt most comfortable and which is the way the grip is commonly taught, I decided to experiment with a grip that I'd read the master ball striker Moe Norman used—more in the palms. I also came up with a wacky preshot routine in which I'd exaggerate a takeaway that started the club way outside, tracing a path that, if retraced coming back down, would give me the sensation that it was impossible to hit the ball from the inside. When it was time to hit the ball, I'd look at the underside of my cap so I couldn't see the ball during the backswing, and then on the downswing turn it back to the left so that my eyes again never settled on the ball but were directed only at the intended target. My swing path was decidedly outside-in, and whereas I'd always played a pretty powerful draw (curving the ball from right to left), now I was hitting a weak slice (moving the ball from left to right).

It didn't matter, because my goal was to simply make any kind of swing that wasn't a yip. I was like a hacker who'd hit crappy shot after crappy shot but could always find his ball. As long as that was the case and I avoided yipping, I was happy and knew I could gradually work on improving the path of the swing. The swing that eventually evolved was kind of short and quick, producing a low cut that carried a lot of backspin—far from ideal and at least 25 yards shorter than I used to hit it—but I became a very straight driver. I did almost all this rehab work on the practice range, but in 2002, when I got up the nerve to start playing regularly again, I was astounded to find that I was soon a significantly better player than I'd ever been. I started to occasionally shoot in the 60s, but the best part was that I stopped fearing the big miss. At one point I played 156 straight rounds without a penalty stroke with my driver. When I'd play with Mark, he'd laugh at my contortions and funky ball flight, but he also gave me props for having pulled my game off the trash heap.

The experience taught me that life—both as an instructor and as a person—is better when I'm able to play golf, because I truly love the game. Long-term, the real significance of what I went through is that it helped me teach Tiger.

As luck would have it, I was being brought closer to Tiger. After he won his third straight U.S. Amateur in August 1996, he turned pro and signed with IMG. Tiger had been introduced to Mark O'Meara, also an IMG client, when the management group was courting him. Mark is a very easy guy to get along with, and he and Tiger shared Southern California roots. Tiger had decided to make Orlando his base when he turned pro, in part because he liked Mark's situation at Isleworth. He bought a place there, and he and Mark soon became regular practice partners and friends.

When I went to Isleworth to work with Mark and stay at his house, I began to see a lot of Tiger. He'd sometimes come over for breakfast before a practice session or dinner after one, and perhaps stay to watch a game on TV. He was still quiet but also comfortable with Mark and his wife and two kids. He was just 21 when he won the 1997 Masters, living on his own for the first time, and he appreciated the normalcy to be found at Mark's home during a time that his life outside the gates was being hit by the gale force of Tigermania.

Tiger didn't discourage the media's playing up the big brother/ little brother dynamic between Mark and him. It was a feel-good story, and it also got the press off his back, because Mark began answering a lot of Tiger questions. At first Mark enjoyed the attention, and he was deft at portraying Tiger as a great young guy without giving away anything private.

Meanwhile, Tiger would present Mark as a confidant to whom he could talk about anything. But the reality was that Tiger was guarded even with Mark. Tiger might sound out Mark on business matters, because Mark is very shrewd about career management. But usually the talk was about sports teams and other guy stuff, with some tour gossip thrown in. There were no big discussions about life that I can remember. I know Mark really cared about Tiger. But for all the talk of how close they were, he also felt that Tiger kept a certain distance. It was a space Mark wished he could close, but never really did.

The golf course was where the relationship really worked. Mark, who'd been going through a career lull in which he was fighting to find motivation, was definitely energized by Tiger. He liked being identified as an important influence in the formative years of a player he believed would be one of the best in history. But he was also a prideful competitor who, just because he hates getting drilled, stepped up his game to hang with Tiger in practice. Though it's not widely known, Mark has one of the best records for turning third-round leads to victories and is very tough to beat head-to-head, mostly because he makes very few mistakes. In their matches—which were usually for something like $10 three ways, with Tiger rarely paying when he lost—Mark used all his guile and skill. In fact, his excellent putting often enabled him to win.

The new regimen really raised Mark's confidence and enthusiasm. He won twice in 1997, and in 1998, at age 41, Mark had the greatest season of his career. He not only won his first major by taking the Masters with a last-hole birdie, but three months later captured the British Open. He was voted PGA Tour Player of the Year, and he closed out the season by beating Tiger in the final of the 1998 World Match Play, 1 up. In that match, Tiger made some late mistakes and kind of gave it away, but rather than being angry, he was genuinely happy for Mark. It was the only time I ever saw him react to a tough loss that way, and as much as he hates to lose, it said a lot about how he felt about Mark.

Tiger's end of the deal was just as good. In the course of their play together, Mark, in the manner of a wise and caring friend rather than a would-be rival, passed along many lessons to Tiger. In particular, when the two were home, Tiger got nearly daily demonstrations on the nuances of saving shots. Mark has never had a visually spectacular game—he's neither particularly long or straight off the tee, and his iron shots don't paint beautiful lines in the sky—and Tiger would sometimes be left wondering, *How did that guy just beat me?* Figuring out the answer made Tiger a better, more complete golfer.

My role was chiefly one of privileged observer. It was already apparent that Tiger really valued the solitude he found at Isleworth, and the last thing he wanted was anyone breaking that up. So whenever I was around Tiger, I stayed in the background.

I didn't ask a lot of questions, didn't bring people around to say hello, didn't ask for autographs or memorabilia. I knew he had enough of that everywhere else, and there was no part of it that he liked. I put my focus into working on Mark's game, and whenever that intersected with his contact with Tiger, I went with the flow.

I was also very cognizant of Tiger's relationship with Butch Harmon, whom I've always respected as a great teacher. Regardless of which of us happened to be Tiger's coach over the years, we've always been on good terms. Our philosophies on the physical swing differ a bit, but not as much as people might think. Butch, too, acknowledges John Jacobs's principles as a huge influence. Butch has a big personality and he's fun to be around. With his tour players, what I admire most is how he connects with them as people. He's great at both inspiring and relaxing his players so that they're ready to perform with confidence. That's a huge part of coaching, and he certainly did that with Tiger.

When Butch was with Tiger at Isleworth and I was there with Mark, we always worked on separate sides of the range. It made good sense. Because Tiger and Mark were friends, it was a way of avoiding banter that could end up being distracting. The four of us all got along, but I don't remember a time when we sat around and had a bull session about the golf swing. If Mark finished his session before Tiger, I never went over and watched Butch and Tiger work. It was just professional courtesy. Butch knew I was sometimes around Tiger when he wasn't, and I wanted him to feel confident that I wasn't doing anything behind his back. We never talked about that; it was just understood.

In spite of having to be careful, I really enjoyed getting to know Tiger in those early days. He was a little more innocent, a little less guarded, and a lot less cynical than he'd become. I got a sense of his life and a feel for the pressure he was under to reach a ridiculously high level and be a role model at the same time. For a kid in his early 20s, he got points with me for handling it all without screwing up. Sometimes I even felt a little sorry for him.

But I also realized my attraction to Tiger was about his being "Tiger Woods"—something bigger and more mythic than the young man himself. What drew me to him was his being potentially the greatest golfer of all time, not his personality. Because of my passion for understanding the game, Tiger was going to be interesting to me no matter what he was like. What he clearly understood and never had to say was that anyone who was brought into his world was lucky and would be playing by his rules. Those were never spelled out, but anyone with any sense could tell that the wisest course was to err in the direction of invisibility. At the same time, even at a young age, he had to know that the eagerness to be around him was not about him as a person but about who he was and what he could do. It was another reason he had a hard time developing trust and friendships.

The most concentrated time I spent around Tiger in his first six years as a professional was during practice rounds at the four major championships. In those days, Mark and Tiger routinely played 18 holes together on Monday, Tuesday, and Wednesday. That was 12 rounds a year where I walked every hole inside the ropes with the players and their caddies, and perhaps a few more at the odd overseas events that Mark brought me to in which Tiger also played. Butch might have been there for half of those rounds, for he had other players to coach, as well as a commitment to commentate for Sky Sports.

At the beginning of this period, after his first Masters victory, Tiger embarked on some key swing changes with Butch. Perhaps the most important was altering his position at the top of his swing, an effort that Tiger would continue when I became his coach. Tiger knew my ideas on that position from observing and talking to Mark, but for more than a year he never asked my opinion about his goal or his progress, and I certainly never volunteered anything. If I'd been asked, I would have said what I believed, which was that he and Butch were working on the right thing.

The first time I had a conversation about technique with Tiger was at the 1998 Dunhill Cup at St. Andrews, where Tiger, Mark, and John Daly represented the United States. The eleventh hole at the Old Course is a short par 3 that usually plays into a hard left-to-right wind to a green that slopes sharply the same way. The proper shot in such conditions is a low draw without much spin, and Mark was really good at it. Tiger marveled at the way Mark's ball stayed under the wind without upshooting, then admitted it was a shot he didn't have. Tiger's method at the time for hitting a short iron low was to play it back in his stance and pound down on it. But such a strike would produce a lot of backspin on the ball, which would invariably lose penetration and be carried off target by the heavy wind. He startled me by looking my way and asking how Mark hit that shot. I explained that it came from hitting a less lofted club and relaxing the arms into an abbreviated finish. He tried a shot, didn't like the results, and declared, "No way I can do that." But I knew he'd file it away.

Early 1999 was the first time something substantive passed between us in terms of technique. Tiger was working alone at Isleworth on the other side of the practice tee from Mark and me. At that time, one of his biggest problems remained controlling the distance on his short irons. He and Butch had been working on it, and I'd been noticing Tiger's progress. At the time, Tiger was coming off a 1998 season in which he'd won only once on tour. Tiger insisted he wasn't discouraged because he knew his swing changes would take some time to pay off, but as the new year started, the pressure on him to perform as he had in 1997 was increasing.

I was as interested an observer as anyone, and during a break in our practice, I said to Mark that I thought Tiger, in golf-speak, had the club "shut and across the line." And Mark kind of surprised me by saying, "Why don't you tell him?" And I said, "I'm not going to tell him. It's not my business." And Mark said, "No, he wants you to. He wants to know."

This suggested that Tiger and Mark had discussed what I taught, and that Tiger was curious. So when Tiger came over to where Mark and I were hitting, I made my first comment a joke, saying, "Tiger, you look like the pizza-delivery guy, where you've got the club at the top." This was touchy territory. Over the years several of Butch's most successful students—most notably Greg Norman—had the club in a position most teachers considered across the line at the top of their swing.

Tiger was sensitive to being across the line—it was the area he most wanted to fix with Butch. He looked at me and said, "No, that just happens when my backswing gets long. I just need to keep it short of parallel." Though I knew I would be close to encroaching on someone else's student, I decided to voice my honest disagreement. "Well, even though it's short of parallel, the club can still be across the line," I said, and then demonstrated what I thought was the proper top-of-the-backswing position. "That club should be over here," I said, pointing the club more to the left. He kind of took it in and went back to his work, and Mark and I left him alone.

In the next few tournaments, including the Masters in which he finished in a disappointing tie for 18th, I noticed that Tiger had altered his club position more toward what I'd demonstrated. I have no doubt that this was something he and Butch worked on, and I'm also sure it was the key reason his swing came together in early May when he won in Dallas and started on a tear. Tiger won seven more official tournaments before the end of the year, and would get even hotter in 2000. What was interesting was that several other golf instructors came up to me during this period, and knowing that I was often around Tiger through Mark, asked, "Hey Hank, are you working with Tiger? Because at the top he's starting to look like what you teach." I always said no, that it was a position Tiger had worked on with Butch. But David Leadbetter, along with Butch the biggest-name instructor at the time, was telling people that Tiger didn't get that swing from Butch Harmon, he got that from Mark O'Meara, who got it from Hank Haney.

That was unfair to Butch. It's hard to imagine that Tiger's

thinking about the swing wasn't influenced by being around Mark, but Mark wasn't Tiger's teacher; Butch was. Talking about an idea like his position at the top, as Mark and I had, and actually working with a student to implement that position are two very different things. The other thing is that Butch and I didn't see Tiger's swing all that differently. Although everyone questioned why Tiger wanted to make swing changes after being so dominant at the 1997 Masters, those changes made good sense. From what I could tell, Butch was trying to get Tiger to the same place in his swing that I would have tried to take him, even though we might have used different drills and terminology. Those first big changes Tiger made with Butch were the most dramatic of his career up to that time. The transition was quite difficult because rather than taking some time away from competition to really ingrain the changes, Tiger decided to incorporate them while still playing a full schedule of tournaments. Most players don't have the talent to pull that off, and even for Tiger, it might have been a slower way to go. But because the changes were right, they ultimately paid off.

In 2000 and 2001, Tiger played better than he ever had. At the same time, he was showing signs of getting tired of Butch. Tiger particularly disliked Butch's habit of holding court on the practice tee, drawing a lot of people into the area where he did serious work. Tiger hadn't minded when he was young and the stories were new, but after he became the world's most famous athlete, he craved quiet. During one of our practice rounds, at the 2000 British Open at St. Andrews, Mark told me that Tiger had gestured toward me and said, "I wish Butch would be a little more like Hank. Just kind of blend in, instead of bringing people around and being loud."

Butch was being himself, and he wasn't about to change his approach, especially after he and Tiger had had so much success. I suppose that Tiger was willing to put his annoyance aside while he and Butch were winning five out of six major championships through the 2001 Masters, but after that came the beginning of a long good-bye. Even while Tiger was winning the 2002 U.S. Open at Bethpage, they seemed a little distant, and it was at the PGA at Hazeltine a couple of months later that Tiger told Butch he wanted to work alone on the practice tee.

I think what really turned the tide was Butch's belief that the best approach with Tiger after he solidified his swing changes was maintenance. This is definitely an old-school view that has a lot of merit. It holds that a person's swing is basically that person's swing and that once the big issues have been resolved, refinement rather than more reconstruction is the wisest policy. Golf history is littered with good players who got worse trying too hard to get better, and Butch didn't want Tiger to fall prey to the same syndrome. But such an approach went against Tiger's grain. He wanted to always be consciously doing something to get better. It was as if he needed the stimulation and the challenge to stay motivated. It was a compulsion. Certainly in some ways it was a strength but perhaps also a weakness. Tiger didn't grow tired of Butch the person as much as he grew tired of what Butch was teaching him.

Late 2002 is when Tiger entered a shadowy period. He basically started working on his own, in part with Mark as his eyes. There was speculation that I was working with him, but that's simply not true. I wasn't even seeing him as often. Mark himself had stopped playing and practicing with as much intensity, and my trips to Isleworth were becoming fewer. Sometimes I'd ask Mark how Tiger was doing, and Mark would give me a summary of what he was working on. I knew that Tiger had a lot of knowledge about the golf swing, and so did Mark, but neither had ever demonstrated much success working on his own. Very simply, they were players, not teachers. That's usually not a problem when a player is "maintaining," but making real swing changes is another matter.

Tiger won a couple more times in 2002, but he'd dropped off slightly from his high level. His left knee started to really bother him, requiring painkillers, and that undoubtedly led to a worsening of certain bad swing habits, such as dropping his head to the right on the downswing. In December, he had arthroscopic surgery on his left knee to remove some benign cysts and drain fluid. During the procedure, it was determined that his anterior cruciate ligament was fraying. The surgery took place in Park City, Utah, where Mark and I both owned condos that we'd try to get to every year for a ski trip. Tiger's surgery coincided with our trip, and Mark was present when Tiger was taken into surgery and when he came out. I met them later, and Tiger told me that because of the condition of the ACL, which he estimated was only about 20 percent intact, "I'm going to have to change my swing."

The recovery required Tiger to miss the first five tournaments of 2003. Then he won three of the first four he played, including an 11-stroke victory at Bay Hill. But Tiger would later say he did it mostly with superb putting, and that year he didn't win a major for the first time since 1998. Worse, he didn't really come close, his tie for fourth at the British Open being his only top ten. It would later come out that the last time Tiger worked with Butch was during a visit to Las Vegas a week before the 2003 U.S. Open at Olympia Fields, where he finished tied for 20th.

I'd occasionally hear rumors that I'd be Tiger's next coach, or that in fact I was already secretly working with Tiger, but I never paid much attention to them. I honestly believed that Tiger was determined to work things out on his own, that he liked the notion of not having a coach, and felt that he was at a point in his career where he could essentially fix himself. Even if he was looking for a new coach, there were several bigger names than mine. My approach was to keep working hard on the tasks at hand, which included coaching Mark and running my golf schools. I didn't drop any hints to Mark, and he never talked about what he thought Tiger might do in the future. I'm sure Mark would have liked me to become Tiger's coach, but the subject was such a touchy one with Tiger that Mark never even talked about it to me away from Tiger. I definitely didn't make any comments about Tiger in the press or respond to any of the rumors, because that would have only been perceived, by everyone from Tiger on down, as angling for the job. As 2003 ended, I had no more reason to think I'd ever work with Tiger than I had when the year began.

But things changed when Tiger accepted that, despite his best efforts, he wasn't getting better on his own. He won the WGC Match Play in early 2004 but wasn't happy with the way he hit the ball. A week later he traveled to the Dubai Desert Classic. There Mark won for the first time since 1998. He'd been fighting a case of the yips, and he finally switched over to an unconventional "saw" putting grip that I'd encouraged him to try at the end of 2003. He putted like his old self and held on to win by one over Paul McGinley. Tiger, who finished five strokes back, waited for Mark off the eighteenth green to congratulate him, something I never saw him do for another player. According to Mark, Tiger told him, "I'm as happy for you as I'd be if I'd won myself."

Everyone was in a good mood when they boarded Tiger's leased Gulfstream 550 (nicknamed TWA, for Tiger Woods Airlines) for the ride back to the States. Mark later told me that when the subject of Tiger's game came up, he was feeling so good about his victory and his friendship with Tiger that he just decided to stop holding back. First Mark said, "Tiger, you've got to get someone to help you with your game." Tiger answered, "OK, who should I get?" Mark said that Tiger mentioned Butch's younger brother, Billy, who was Jay Haas's coach and whom Tiger liked, but then dismissed the idea because the sibling connection would probably cause complications. A couple of other names came up before Mark finally said, "Tiger, I know Hank's my friend and I've been with him for years, but Hank's the best teacher in the world. Besides that, he's the one who suggested you make the big change in your swing in the first place."

Tiger paused for a moment and said, "Yeah, I know. I'm going to call him tomorrow."

When the plane landed in Orlando, I got a call from Mark's agent, Peter Malik. "Hey, Hank," Peter said. "Stay loose. You're going to be getting a phone call."

3

Coaching Tiger

The next day, March 8, 2004, I'm having dinner at Bob's Steak & Chop House in Plano, Texas, with my father, Jim, who's in town for the day. It's the kind of traditional Chicago-style steak place from my dad's expense-account days, all mahogany and white linen. I rarely eat steak, but I order a New York strip, medium rare. The waiter has just brought us our food when my cell phone rings.

I've told my father I might be getting a call from Tiger sometime in the next few days but that I'm not really holding my breath. I don't have Tiger's number, but when I look down and see the 407 area code on my screen in front of a number I don't recognize, my stomach jumps. "Excuse me," I tell my dad, "I gotta take this call."

I walk quickly toward the entrance, and answer. "Hey, Hank," I hear on my cell, "this is Tiger." I give my normal "Hey, bud" greeting, but there's no small talk. Barely pausing, Tiger says, "Hank, I want to know if you'll help me with my golf game."

My mind flashes on that winter day at Exmoor with Jim Hardy, and as I stand on the sidewalk watching the valet-parking guys running around and people going in and out of the adjoining shops, I feel disoriented. Everything around me is normal, but I know my life has just changed forever. I'm talking to Tiger Woods, the greatest golfer who's ever lived, and he's asking me to be his coach.

Because of Tiger's tone, I try to hide any excitement from my voice. "Sure, Tiger. Of course," I say, adding, "Thank you for the opportunity." Tiger stays all business, asking, "What do you think of my game?"

I kind of surprise myself with how easily I snap into professional mode. I don't say, "Tiger, I think you have the best game of all time," which is what I believe. I realize he is a tour pro asking a tour teacher to measure him purely against his own abilities. I say very straight, but aware of how odd it sounds, "I think your game is pretty good."

The next question isn't a surprise. "What do you think I need to do better?"

I'm in my wheelhouse now, and I tell him exactly what I've observed in him for over a year. "Looking from the outside, and not knowing everything, it looks like you're working on a lot of great things," I say. "It looks like you know a lot about the swing. But it's hard for me to tell what your plan is. It doesn't look like you have a real step-by-step plan. I think when you're trying to improve, the most important thing is to always have a plan."

I leave it there, without going into specifics, and Tiger doesn't ask for any. I feel confident I've hit on the central issue. Certainly Tiger followed a plan with Butch early on, just as he followed a plan as an adolescent with John Anselmo. Indeed, I know that one of Earl's stock responses whenever he's asked about Tiger's progress has long been "It's all part of the plan." But it looks to me that since the end of Tiger's time with Butch—who said his emphasis was maintaining the swing changes Tiger had made—the plan has become less clear.

I know Tiger has a lot of knowledge about the golf swing, but a lot of players do. Sometimes that can make it even easier to become aimless, because an active and especially an impatient mind can lurch from idea to idea and go off on experimental tangents. Left to their own devices when practicing, talented players tend to go back to swing thoughts or feels or drills that have brought success in the past, and when one doesn't seem to work, they try another. The upshot is that whether or not the player hits on something successful, he or she is likely going in a circle, rather than working toward something. With this haphazard approach, it's very difficult for players to say at the end of a day of practice or play that they got better. With the right plan, even if things didn't go well, there is the confidence that improvement is taking place. That's what I believe Tiger needs, and I think—recognizing that he's been in relative limbo for many months—he's called me mainly to deal with this issue.

Tiger had tried it on his own, with Mark O'Meara sometimes watching him or suggesting things. But players, even great ones, aren't trained teachers. They tend to impart the things that *they're* working on, which an experienced teacher might conclude are exactly the wrong things. Mark certainly knows my ideas, but he doesn't know the best way to impart them, and he probably doesn't know which parts are best for Tiger.

Because I've done it so often, I'm very confident in my ability to make the right diagnoses and then give the cure in the right sequence, in the right portions, and at the right pace. As much as having knowledge, doing all that involves knowing the student. And even in my excitement, I know the thing I'm looking forward to most is getting the opportunity to intimately understand Tiger Woods.

Our phone call lasts no more than three minutes. It ends with Tiger saying he wants me to come work with him at Isleworth the following Monday. He doesn't follow with any small talk or pleasantries, so after a last quick thanks from me, we say good-byes.

After hanging up, I stand on the sidewalk, stunned. Besides sheer amazement, my mind is filled with all sorts of thoughts. As a golf instructor, I feel as though I've won the lottery. I'm going to gain in stature. I'm going to be famous. I'm going to get to try out all my ideas on the ultimate student, and he's going to prove them so right. And then I think, I won't even have to tell him anything. This guy is going to win no matter what I tell him. He's done it all his life, he's so good. I've just landed the easiest job in golf.

After a long few minutes, I walk back into the restaurant. I tell my father I'm now Tiger's coach. It feels kind of funny, because my dad's the biggest Jack Nicklaus fan who ever lived, and I know he isn't going to want Tiger to break Jack's record. He chuckles at that, and I can tell he's proud. But he also has a sense of the pressures ahead, and he says, "You know, that's going to be a hard job. Are you sure you want to do it?"

I appreciate the question. But yes, I'm sure. To be able to teach the best player—that's always been my dream. I'm going to give Tiger as much as I've got for as long as I can. And somehow I already know he's going to be the last touring pro I teach.

The next Monday, as I would about fifty times over the next six years, I took the six a.m. American Airlines flight from Dallas to Orlando. It was the week of the Bay Hill Invitational, played at a course about three miles from Isleworth. Tiger was attempting to win the tournament for the fifth straight time, which would be a PGA Tour record for consecutive victories at one event.

My early euphoria had been followed by a reality check. I knew that Tiger craved improvement, but I wondered if he could improve on what he'd accomplished with Butch Harmon. From the Tiger Slam, to being number one in the world by the widest margin ever, to his streak for consecutive cuts made, to his incredible record of holding final-round leads—all of it. I felt I had a good conception of Tiger's swing from observing him, and I thought I could help him make it better. But I also worried that there was a decent possibility Tiger had already reached his peak, from which the only place to go was down. If that was true, I'd be associated with his decline, probably even be blamed for it. From that shifting perspective, the greatest job ever could become a no-win.

I was also aware that Tiger hadn't played that well in 2003, even though he'd won five times. His performances in the majors had, for him, been poor. Three weeks before, he'd won the World Golf Championships–Accenture Match Play Championship, but he hadn't won a stroke-play event in 2004.

I wondered how Tiger and I would get along. Sure, we always had, but I knew things would be different now. I'd be accountable based on his performance. Tiger had sounded almost corporate on the phone. I knew that over the years Tiger had replaced a lot of people on his team. I could be entering a very cold and unforgiving world.

After landing, I got a rental car, which would also become the regular routine. I drove the 15 miles west toward the Lake Butler area of Orlando, went through the gate at Isleworth, and made the slow drive along the winding entranceway lined with ponds and tropical flora. I was keyed up, but as I made the three turns required to get to Tiger's house, I felt myself go calm. I thought, *Whatever happens, enjoy the opportunity.*

I'd been to Tiger's house a few times with Mark. It would eventually be photographed from the air as often as O. J. Simpson's house, and a lot of people have been surprised that it wasn't more of a set-apart mansion. Even though Tiger went on to build such an edifice near Palm Beach, I never sensed that he cared that much about opulence. Outside, his Isleworth house didn't stand out.

Inside, the decor was more functional than luxurious. There were a lot of TVs, and his trophies were prominently displayed.

When I drove in, I was startled to see him right there in the driveway swinging a club, wearing shorts and appearing very relaxed. His bag was on his golf cart, which had spinner wheels with a TW logo, a stereo system, and a top speed of 28 miles per hour, factory altered to go about twice as fast as a normal cart. Tiger certainly spent more time in his golf cart than in his street car, so these improvements weren't really extravagant.

Whenever I saw Tiger, I had a dual reaction. On some level he was still that kid who was originally self-contained and standoffish but who gradually let down some of his guard. But he was also a worldwide icon, maybe the most famous athlete in the history of sport. To me, he always remained more of the first guy. Even when I was around him off the course in places like New York or Las Vegas and all around us people were agog and doing everything for him and it was all very A-list, he was never quite that other guy. Probably, I thought, because he really didn't want to be.

As I got out of the car, he came over to greet me, but there was no welcome-aboard hug. It was as if I was still primarily Mark's coach and we were just meeting before another practice round. But when I opened the conversation by saying, "I'm looking forward to working with you," Tiger went into boss mode. Starting with the words "OK, now," he wanted to be clear that there were a couple of things he'd observed me teach Mark that he didn't agree with.

The first was my idea of limiting his head movement to the right on the backswing, which would never get completely resolved. He also reviewed the moment on the eleventh hole at St. Andrews where into a hard left-to-right wind Mark had demonstrated how to hit an iron shot on a low trajectory with little spin so that it didn't balloon in the wind. Tiger said that the method was too foreign to what he was used to. I'd eventually win him over on that one.

His objections almost didn't matter. I realized that he was

marking his territory, showing the new dog that he was the alpha. That was fine; I wasn't going to argue with him. He didn't yet know enough about what I teach or the plan I had to help him achieve his best golf.

I told him I understood his concerns, and that we'd work on those things in different ways. I realized right away that he was going to be a difficult student, that he wasn't going to just accept everything I said. I knew his trust would have to be hard-earned, and that there would be tests ahead. But I was also thinking, *I like this. This is going to be a challenge. This guy is different, and that's part of why he's great. This is going to be an incredible learning experience.* I felt energized.

We got into the cart and drove across the street to the more secluded corner of the range that Tiger favored. On the way over, he spelled out an overall goal. "I want to get more consistent in every phase, so I have the kind of game that at majors will always get me to the back nine on Sundays with a chance," he said. "I don't want to just have a chance on the weeks when I'm hot. I want to have a chance all the time. Always putting yourself in the mix, that's the only way you can win a lot of them." Helping him build that kind of game, one that he could keep at a high level even when he wasn't at his best, became my mission.

We continued our discussion as he hit balls. It was clear his big priority was ridding himself of "getting stuck" on the downswing. This position occurred when—for a combination of reasons—Tiger got his lower body too far ahead of his arms on the downswing, causing the club to drop behind his hands. From that position, he couldn't simply let his upper body rotate and carry his arms along to effortlessly square the clubface at impact. Instead, the only way to become "unstuck" was to compensate with some quick arm and hand action. Tiger was very adept at saving shots in this manner, but it was not a reliable way to achieve consistency.

From the stuck position, Tiger's most common tendency was to leave the ball to the right, a shot that could be identified by the way his right shoulder finished high as a result of a too-late effort to overuse his upper body and arms to square the face. It was also possible from the stuck position for Tiger to use too much hand action and hit a hook to the left, but this was a shot he abhorred and avoided.

Eventually I would see that getting stuck was simply one of Tiger's individual tendencies, so ingrained that he'd always have to fight to keep it suppressed. His goal was to get rid of getting stuck forever, but though I thought that was worth trying for, I knew the probability was that the tendency would always lurk, ready to come back when he didn't take specific measures against it, especially under pressure. That's golf, even at the highest level. Every player has his or her set of chronic mistakes that are as personal as a fingerprint. Teachers don't give players these mistakes. Their role is to provide ways to control them.

The other priority was preserving the health of Tiger's left knee. I'd already known this from talking to Tiger in Park City, Utah, in late 2002, the day after his clean-up operation had revealed that his ACL was damaged. I'd later overhear him complain to Mark that he'd hurt the knee by following Butch's advice to snap it straight at impact when he wanted extra distance. There was really no way of knowing if the damage had been caused by that action. A lot of players hyperextend their lead leg and never suffer knee injuries, which are actually pretty rare in golf compared to hand, wrist, elbow, and shoulder injuries. Part of me thought that blaming the knee on Butch was a way for Tiger to justify leaving him for other reasons. Still, there was no doubt that the knee was a problem, and protecting it was of great importance. "I've got to do everything I can to make it last," Tiger told me at Isleworth.

As he hit balls, my first lesson was fairly gentle. I wanted Tiger to get his eyes to stay "level" throughout the swing. When Tiger let his head move to the right on his backswing, he had a tendency to simultaneously let his chin tilt to the right. Then on the downswing, he'd tilt his chin back to the left. This would help him drop his head behind the ball, which contributed to his getting stuck. I was sure that if he recognized this action/reaction move and corrected it, it would make him better.

I was focused on Tiger's progress, but I also had moments—especially when we first started working together—in which I'd just admire how good he was. Beyond his technique, his swing was mesmerizing for displaying the sheer grace that only the most special athletes possess. But besides exhibiting impressive coordination and explosiveness, even in practice Tiger had a focus and intensity that were beyond anything I'd ever witnessed. I could feel his love for what he was doing: his thrill at controlling the ball, his enthusiasm for learning how to do it better.

Tiger was a receptive student for the two days we worked together before I returned to Dallas. I stayed in his house with him and Elin, to whom he was engaged and was scheduled to marry in October. I'd met Elin when she and Tiger started dating in 2002, and I'd gotten along well with her. I gave her some golf lessons at Isleworth even before I began working with Tiger, and she was a good athlete and careful listener who improved quickly and was capable of breaking 90. She had a nice swing, and Tiger had fun helping her with it. They both really liked tennis, and they enjoyed occasionally going to tournaments to watch their friend Roger Federer play. Elin is naturally quiet, but her personality became more outgoing and feisty when she played sports. She could hold her own against Tiger in tennis, Ping-Pong, and even running. She even liked to talk trash, saying stuff like "I'm going to take you down," and celebrating with a yell when she won a point. I know Tiger really liked her competitive streak, and seemed to enjoy treating her like one of the guys, needling her and even telling raunchy jokes around her, which Elin didn't seem to mind.

But as life became more complicated, I thought Elin changed. By the time she and Tiger married, she remained friendly but had become more guarded, even in her own home. She and Tiger developed a calm, almost cool relationship in front of other people, and conversations with them tended to be awkward and strained. I never saw them argue, but they weren't openly affectionate either.

I went home on Wednesday. In Thursday's first round at Bay Hill, Tiger shot a 67 that left him only a shot out of the lead. When he called me that night, he was excited, saying he'd really hit the ball well and believed that what we'd worked on had made a difference.

However, he followed with three poor rounds of 74, 74, and 73. As we talked after each round, he said he was still getting stuck with the driver, missing wide right a lot, worried about missing left, and generally putting the ball in places off the tee from where it was difficult to hit an approach shot close to the hole. Without saying he'd worked with me, he told the media that he'd been "so excited about the things I was working on Tuesday and Wednesday." He said that 90 percent of his game was good, "it's just the other 10 percent that is off the charts." When he got pressed on where the problems were, he gave the sort of answer that was meant to maybe create a humorous sound bite, but which would also close the subject. "Yeah," he said, "the takeaway, the backswing, and the downswing."

I would soon learn that what Tiger told the media about his round was way different from what he'd later tell me in private or on the phone. In his television and press interviews, he mostly answered in generalities, usually putting an overly positive spin on how he'd played. Then when we talked, he'd go into detail about the real issues in his round, and was often quite self-critical. There were also times he would tell the media he hit it badly but then tell me he'd hit it well. I never knew what to expect after a round, but he was good at explaining how he felt on the course, and what thoughts or moves he felt he could handle or couldn't handle under the heat of competition. I encouraged him not to talk about his swing changes with the media. It would just open up a new line of scrutiny, put him in a situation of always explaining, and set him up to be criticized. No previous player had ever undergone so much public swing analysis, and it wasn't going to do him any good. It would likely mean my name wouldn't get mentioned, and certainly for the short term, I was fine with that.

When we talked on Saturday, he said he wanted me to see him at Isleworth again on that Monday, to prepare for the next week's Players Championship. Following what would become my routine, I met him around ten a.m. on the practice range, looking forward to putting more of my plan into place.

But Tiger was completely different than the first time we worked. When I arrived, he was already out on the range, fully warmed up, and he barely acknowledged me after I approached. As he proceeded to keep hitting balls, I commented on a few things I saw in his swing, complimenting him on doing better with keeping his eyes level, but he sort of ignored me.

I didn't react, but inside I was shaken. I thought, *Man, this is weird. Am I getting fired before I've even started? Here I've barely told you anything, basically just given you a sugar pill to get off to an easy start together, and now you're acting like I screwed you up?*

It was my first test. The message Tiger wanted to send was clear: "When I play bad, when I don't win, it's your fault." He was reminding me that his expectations were going to be incredibly high, and I thought of the motto of Al Davis, the owner of Tiger's favorite NFL team, the Raiders: "Just win, baby."

I stayed calm and made a decision that I couldn't let him just run over me now. I felt I had nothing to lose, because if he truly didn't want me, there was no point in going forward anyway.

"Tiger," I said, breaking the silence, "I'm not sure what you're doing here, but I guess you're trying to knock me off my spot. I know what you need to do to get better. I know what your plan needs to be. So if you're trying to knock me off my spot, it's not going to happen."

He didn't say anything. I'd called him on the cold shoulder, but he didn't acknowledge that in any way. He just kept the same blank expression while the wheels turned behind it. I proceeded to introduce some drills to get his club on a better plane, and he carried them out with full effort. Overall, we had a good session, and an even better one on Tuesday morning before he drove to Ponte Vedra.

As I headed home again, I felt more accepted, but I also realized that I was never going to be able to relax with Tiger Woods. He was going to be complicated, and he was going to surprise me with his moods. I was just going to have to adapt on the fly. We were just starting, so he'd probably cut me a little slack, but that wouldn't be the case indefinitely. It was my nature to always be thinking about my teaching and my students, but with Tiger, I had a feeling that my mental absorption would be at a new level. And in fact, there wouldn't be a morning in the next six years that I wouldn't wake up thinking about how I could help Tiger Woods improve.

Throughout that time, I never lost any confidence in my ability to teach Tiger. I believed in my training, my ideas, and my ability. I also took strength from the fact that Tiger had picked me. He was comfortable with me as a person and my work ethic. He liked my low-key public style, appreciated that I didn't bring people around to play show-and-tell and wasn't going to take credit for his success. But more than anything, he was intrigued by what I taught, and he wanted that knowledge.

Underlying my instruction was a unifying principle: All good things in the golf swing flow from achieving the correct swing plane. I'd studied all the ways to correct ball flight, and it was that revelation that enabled me to make a giant leap as a teacher.

The importance of swing plane was especially true at the highest level, where players do so many things right and are trying to address the very few things—or even one thing—they do wrong. I found that getting a tour pro's club on the correct plane got them hitting more good shots, but more important, made their bad ones better. There are very few perfect shots hit in golf, even by experts. It's above all a game of managing misses.

Briefly, my concept is this: The plane of the swing is established by the angle of the clubshaft in the address position. When the shaft retains the angle of that plane as it moves through the swing, a player has the best chance to hit good shots.

I'd gotten the idea of the correct plane in the early 1980s after years of studying videos of the best players in history executing their swings. Not all of these players kept the club on plane throughout the swing, but the best and most versatile ball striker among them—Ben Hogan—did. Jim Hardy was hugely influenced by Hogan, always talked about him, and even swung a lot like him. I'd read Hogan's classic instruction book *Five Lessons* many times over but had never quite understood all of it. In the book there is a famous illustration in which Hogan is pictured at address with an imaginary pane of glass that tilts from the ball and rests on his shoulders, with a hole in it for his head to poke through. It was one of Hogan's tenets that the club should always stay under the pane of glass and never break it.

But as I looked at the illustration, the angle of the plane seemed too upright because the club wasn't on that plane at address. I thought the correct plane should go more through the sternum, at least at the start of the swing. The breakthrough for me came around 1981, when I was at Pinehurst. For probably the hundredth time, I was studying Hogan's 1964 match against Sam Snead at Houston Country Club on *Shell's Wonderful World of Golf,* when both of them were 52 years old but still incredible swingers of the golf club. Hogan's swing was so correct, with no mid-swing compensations, the club seemingly grooved inside a tilted wheel that went from the top of the swing to the finish. I started making lines on the video screen, and the constant tilt of that wheel followed the angle of the shaft at address. Hogan's swing, and the shots it produced, were my proof that I was correct with my unifying principle. The next year, when I met Mark on the range at Pinehurst, I had the opportunity to try out my ideas to change his too-upright swing, and I found that they worked.

When the proper swing plane is achieved, the shaft of the club is always swinging on, or parallel to, the angle the club established at address. At the top of the backswing, the club should point straight down the target line when it is parallel to the ground. A small but important distinction is that it should point not at the target itself, but parallel to the target line that goes through the ball to the target. When the club points at the target, especially if it has not yet reached parallel to the ground, it is actually "across the line."

For me, the club is either on the plane or off the plane. This was the biggest difference between Butch and me when it came to Tiger. As Tiger explained to me, Butch believed a correct plane could exist within a range, a gray area with about 10 percent latitude above or below what I considered the ideal plane. I believed the goal should be more precise.

When Butch began working with Tiger, there is no doubt that at the top of his swing Tiger's club was above his proper plane. Also, when his club reached parallel at the top of his swing, a view of him from behind and down the target line would reveal that the shaft was pointed to the right of the target. Tiger, as a right-handed golfer, was indeed "across the line." Meanwhile, the leading edge of the clubface when it reached the top of the swing did not match the plane angle of the shaft, with the toe not pointing down sufficiently. In this position, the clubface is closed relative to the swing plane, or "shut." So in golf parlance, Tiger was "across the line and shut."

It wasn't much. Tiger had obviously accomplished a tremendous amount playing from that position, as have other players who've been across the line. When his timing was on, as it was when he won by 12 strokes at the 1997 Masters, he could completely neutralize the flaw. But when it wasn't, he hit too many shots that were either far off-line or went the wrong distance. Although many top players, from Bobby Jones to Fred Couples, have played their entire careers from "across the line," Tiger's habits made him particularly prone to dropping the shaft "under the plane" on the downswing, creating an approach to the ball that was too much inside the target line—rather than along it—to be optimum. Tiger's incredible eye-hand coordination could save a significant number of "stuck" swings, but the across-the-line position put a big demand on even Tiger's gifts. When he was off, he'd usually go wide right with the driver out of fear of hitting a hook, and long and left with the shorter clubs because of the closed clubface. Either way, the misses were too often bigger than even he could manage.

It was why Tiger asked Butch to implement some fairly big changes shortly after that historic Masters win. Butch improved Tiger's plane, making it slightly flatter and less across the line, while getting his clubface to rotate more clockwise, or open, on the backswing so that it was closer to being parallel with the plane at the top of his swing. He also shortened Tiger's backswing with the driver, which gave the appearance of the club not "crossing the line."

But in his practice rounds with Mark, Tiger was seeing an approach to the plane that went even further than Butch's teaching, and they occasionally discussed the theory of the correct plane during practice. I got included in the conversation in early 1999 at Isleworth when, at Mark's urging, I told Tiger his backswing was too upright. Mark told me later that Tiger took the observation seriously and soon adjusted his backswing accordingly. My guess is that the change merely accelerated what Butch had in mind for Tiger, but there's no question that he was ready for it. Beginning with the PGA Championship of 1999, Tiger won five of the next six major championships.

After curtailing his work with Butch in 2002, Tiger continued to work on his swing plane. But though he wouldn't admit it, he got a little lost and actually regressed, producing, by his standards, a poor year in 2003. With me, Tiger would again have a plan. My goal was to get Tiger into a position at the top that would allow him to return the shaft more "in front" of his body, rather than behind him, which caused the stuck position.

I would later be criticized for "overfixing" Tiger into a "laid-off" position in which the club actually pointed to the left of the target at the top of the swing. It's true I wanted Tiger to err more toward having the club point to the left rather than the right. That was because Tiger was much less likely to get "stuck" from a laid-off position than from across the line. The laid-off position also guarded against a miss to the left and allowed Tiger to play with the comforting thought that he could eliminate one side of the golf course.

After Bay Hill, Tiger played better but still not well enough. He tied for 16th at The Players Championship on the tight TPC Stadium course, where he's won only once. He then spent most of the next week at Isleworth, where we prepared for our first major together, the 2004 Masters.

I quickly sensed the extra effort and focus that Tiger gave a major championship. In his professional career, his emphasis has been on being totally ready four times a year, and because of the way the schedule was constructed, he had more preparation time for the Masters than any of the other majors.

It was not a great week at Augusta. Tiger opened with a 75 in which his short game was sloppy, came back with 69, but another 75 in the third round took him out of it. He finished tied for 22nd, 11 strokes behind the winner, Phil Mickelson, who won his first major championship. Though Tiger hadn't hit the ball near his best, I felt good that his ball striking was not really the problem at the Masters. Probably all the work on our swing changes had taken some time from practicing his putting and short game, and those areas hadn't been sharp. In the big picture, though, I felt he was building.

It was also at the Masters that I saw Butch for the first time since I'd begun working with Tiger a month before. In fact, it was at Augusta that Butch for the first time publicly acknowledged that he was no longer Tiger's coach, although whether Tiger was working alone or with a new coach remained unknown to the public. At the Masters, I'd made a point of working most closely with Mark on the practice tee, though there were times when Tiger would be working right next to him.

When Butch saw me, he gave me a warm greeting and took me aside for a moment. He knew that I'd succeeded him as Tiger's coach and graciously congratulated me. Then he said, "Hank, good luck. It's a tough team to be on. And it's harder than it looks." His voice was sincere, from one swing coach to another. His words didn't chill me, but they did give me pause. Tiger and I hadn't had any success yet, and I hoped there was a long road ahead. But even with success, I was starting to realize that it was never going to be easy.

Certainly, the difficulty didn't lie with the other members of Tiger's team. I'd known one member, physical therapist Keith Kleven, for almost 20 years through Keith's association with Mark O'Meara. Keith, who'd worked with many top athletes, including former heavyweight champion Larry Holmes, is a sweet soul who would show his devotion to Tiger many times, never more than when Tiger overcame a torn ACL and two stress fractures in his left leg to win the 2008 U.S. Open.

Keith tried to regulate Tiger's workout schedule, but it became very apparent that he frowned on the intensity and style of some of the exercises Tiger was doing, especially the heavy weightlifting he favored to build up his upper body.

The point man for Team Tiger, agent Mark Steinberg, was Tiger's closest confidant. In his days at the University of Illinois, Mark made the basketball team as a walk-on guard, and he still gives off the tightly wound vibe of an overachieving athlete. I understand that mentality, and I always got along well with Mark, who was supportive of me. Besides being very loyal to Tiger and a trusted advisor on business matters, Mark could read Tiger better than anyone else, especially when Tiger went into silent mode. I think Mark considered Tiger a good person trapped in a very complicated and demanding life, and he cut Tiger a lot of slack when he was being uncommunicative or stubborn. After I'd been Tiger's coach for only a few months, Mark would make a point of telling me that I was one of Tiger's best friends. That always took me aback a bit, because though I felt a bond with Tiger over our obsession with golf, I always sensed he wanted me to stay at a distance. But as I was beginning to figure out, Tiger really didn't let anyone in. It was interesting that Mark also advised that when it came to Tiger, the best policy was "Don't get too close."

I suppose the compensation I was offered as Tiger's coach could be considered stingy, but I was thrilled at the opportunity. The truth is I probably would have paid Tiger just to teach him, it meant that much. I knew from a *USA Today* article that Butch had been paid $50,000 a year, so when I was offered the same thing I wasn't surprised. Considering that I'd end up spending more than 100 days on the road a year with Tiger, either at his home or at tournaments, plus talking to him on the phone another 100-plus nights, it wasn't a lot. But I also received a $25,000 bonus for every major victory, and I thought Tiger could win quite a few of those. I was doing fine financially with my four golf facilities in Texas, and I knew that my reputation and brand would be enhanced by my connection with Tiger. I'm sure that, from Tiger's perspective, that residual success would be my main compensation. I figured if things worked out, the contract would improve over time. I never spoke to Tiger about the arrangement, but I always felt that he was generous to give me the chance to be his coach, and I was happy with the deal.

I knew I'd be more appreciated if I stayed under the radar with my public profile. There had been rumors that I'd been working with Tiger since Bay Hill, but no one asked me about it directly until the fall. A lot of that was because of what Tiger told the media at the Byron Nelson in May, as he wove a pretty elaborate and believable fib at a press conference that went like this:

> QUESTION: Could you clarify your relationship with Hank Haney? Is he a friend? Is he a teacher? Is it Mo's [nickname for Mark O'Meara] guy who happens to look at you on the range at Isleworth or here?

TIGER WOODS: Well, he's my friend. He's always been a friend ever since college golf, actually [back when he was] the coach at SMU, it was a time I was still in college playing, and Hank and I were talking about the golf swing—I love picking guys' brains, whether it's Hank or Butch or Lead [David Leadbetter] or anybody. I love Bob Torrance [a Scottish swing coach], always got good stories about the golf swing from him. It's always nice to be able to pick someone's brain about the golf swing, and Hank has always been that since college for me. There are different ways of looking at the same things. That's one of the things that you get from all the different teachers. They're trying to accomplish the same thing in a different way of wording it, and it was nice to hear something that Hank said about my golf swing . . . some of the stuff I throw out, some of the stuff I'll try, and it either works or I'll throw it out later.

Q: This labeling him as your so-called new teacher is inaccurate?

TIGER WOODS: No, no. I will bounce things off of him, I'll bounce things off of him. Cookie [John Cook], he's at home all the time. We're always asking questions. Whether or not we actually go ahead and use it is a different story. One of the things I've always said, even when I was working with Butch at the time, ninety percent of the things I hear, I'll throw out. Five percent of the things I hear I'll try and throw out, and then five percent I'll try and I'll use. It's just one of those things where you try to get a feel for what's going to work. Some of the things Butch and I would work on, I would say, "That's not going to work," and I'd throw it out. That's not going to work on the back nine on Sunday.

The last question had to do with Tiger having joined Mark and me for a practice session at my home course, Vaquero. The media understandably saw this as evidence that I was in some way helping Tiger. Tiger was on the spot with his answer, but he defused things so well it was almost scary.

> Q: You guys played nine at Vaquero. Was that more of just him as a teacher or a friend going along that day?
>
> TIGER WOODS: I was just playing with Mo and looking at Mo's swing. Mo has been working on a few things and hasn't been feeling all that comfortable with his game. I asked Hank one question about my takeaway, where it was, and that was it.

At that time, most of the media believed that Tiger was basically truthful, even when he wasn't being candid. All the detail Tiger added in this case made his lie more believable. He wouldn't officially admit that I was his coach until the Tour Championship in early November.

After Mark Steinberg, the next-closest person to Tiger was Steve Williams. Without a doubt, Steve is the best caddie I've ever seen. His greatest gift is that he stays completely calm and retains a commanding presence under the greatest tournament pressure. His former boss Raymond Floyd once said that Steve is the only caddie he ever had who didn't choke. He proved it many times with Tiger, either by saying the right thing at a nervous moment, staying solidly silent in a moment of crisis, or calling Tiger off a shot if he believed it was the wrong one. Steve prided himself on being able to read Tiger's mind, and Tiger respected Steve's guts, judgment, and instinct. He also relied on Steve's ability to be gruff and intimidating so that fans and media would give him a wider berth. Steve is certainly a rugged New Zealander who didn't have a hard time playing enforcer, but there's definitely a warmer and more personable side to him. Privately, I found him a very honest person who was easy to talk to and very loyal to people he trusted. He always knew what Tiger and I were working on, and he had a good eye for helping Tiger when I wasn't at a tournament. He would also give me really useful insights about Tiger's rounds. Steve wanted me to succeed in part because he and Butch had clashed, Steve feeling that Butch's extroverted personality distracted Tiger. After Tiger's Masters victory in 2005, Steve sent me an e-mail saying he believed I could take Tiger to heights no other golfer had ever reached. He also said he was personally relieved by the Masters victory because since the split with Butch, he had been growing more uneasy the longer Tiger had gone without a major victory. With the win at Augusta, Steve said he felt like "the sky is the limit from here."

The toughest guy on the team was Tiger. I knew going into the job that Tiger had a strict goal of constant improvement. I accepted that and really believed that, given his ability, youth, and passion, I could help him with that goal for a number of years. There was always the assumption that Tiger's best golf was ahead of him, but he and I knew there was no guarantee that would be true. His stated vow to keep getting better made for a whirring machine of effort and pressure.

More difficult, though, than offering the correct instruction was playing the perception game. The fans and the golf media and other insiders considered Tiger as near to perfect as any athlete in history. The image he created from 1999 through 2002 was so pervasive that my work was going to be judged not against his relatively poor play in 2003 and early 2004, but against the very best he'd ever done, that incredible period when he won seven of eleven majors, including that streak where he won four professional majors consecutively, one by 15 strokes and another by 8.

Intellectually I understood this. Everyone in golf naturally wondered why Tiger would leave Butch. Because the only logical conclusion was that Tiger was pursuing a method that he figured might be better, there was great eagerness to see if Tiger's Hank Haney swing was superior to his Butch Harmon swing. I resolved to try to live up to the expectations. As good as Tiger swung it in his best years with Butch, I knew there still was room for improvement, and I think Tiger's record ultimately showed that the swing he developed with my help gained in soundness and consistency.

But Tiger's swing in 2000 and 2001 was better than the swing he had when I began with him in 2004, and his performance was way better. In recent years, Tiger had become a different golfer, with a bigger body, a less sound knee, and some swing habits that had ingrained themselves for the worse. When I began working with Tiger in 2004, my immediate goal was to make him better than he'd been in 2003, not 2000. I hoped I would receive the same kind of grace period for Tiger to master what we were working on that Butch received when Tiger implemented changes in late 1997 and 1998.

I couldn't talk about any of this, of course. It would only have sounded like whining, and besides, it would have put Tiger under even more of a microscope.

To begin making real changes in Tiger's game, I also had to lose some of my awe. Though my first reaction to landing the job was that Tiger would continue winning while I'd barely have to tell him anything, I soon found that this wasn't true. After a few weeks I came to see not only that he was far from a perfect player, but also that he wasn't quite as good as I'd thought. That didn't mean I stopped thinking of him as the greatest ever to play, but when I looked at him, I had to stop seeing a myth and deal with the actual player.

Earl used to have a saying after Tiger did something historic: "Let the legend grow." The legend did, and it led a lot of people to believe stuff about Tiger that just wasn't so. One misconception was that he knew more about the golf swing than any other modern player. Though Tiger definitely possessed a great deal of knowledge, he'd proved that he didn't have enough to fix himself.

The fact was, purely self-taught guys like Lee Trevino and/or idiosyncratic swingers like Jim Furyk probably knew more about how to correct their games than Tiger did about correcting his. Another misconception was that Tiger was a "sponge" who could assimilate and apply new information seamlessly. In reality, he was something of a chronic experimenter who could get off track without guidance, as the previous couple of years had showed. He was generally very stubborn when it came to my proposed changes, as opposed to ideas he'd come up with himself, forcing me to devote a lot of thought to coming up with ways to convince him to try things, many of which involved making the change seem like his idea.

His short game and putting weren't as good as I'd expected. He was incredible with difficult shots around the green, those that required a lot of height or a lot of spin and precise contact. But surprisingly, by touring-pro standards he was mediocre to poor on straightforward chips. He tended to overplay them with too much spin, instead of getting the ball on the ground and letting it run. This was always Steve Williams's pet peeve, in part because he'd caddied for two of the best chippers ever in Floyd and Norman, but also because he couldn't convince Tiger to stop putting so much backspin on his standard chip shots.

As good a putter as Tiger was—and I think the level he attained on the greens when he won seven of eleven majors has never been equaled—he had too many careless three-putts. They didn't come from lack of touch or poor short putting. Invariably, the cause was taking overly bold runs at birdie putts of 20 feet or more. It took me a while to convince Tiger that the percentages simply weren't in favor of making many putts over 20 feet, and that the smart play was to make sure to leave an easy second putt, if not a tap-in, rather than having to constantly make energy-draining five-foot comebackers. Steve was always pointing out that, according to the statistics he kept, when Tiger went through 72 holes without a three-putt, he won 85 percent of the time.

As for Tiger's swing, sometime in the murky period when he began working less with Butch, he'd picked up a bad habit of getting his arms out too far away from his body on the takeaway. I think this was born of trying to keep width in his backswing—one of Butch's main tenets—and create a path away from the ball that if simply retraced on the way down would keep the club "out in front of him" rather than "stuck." But the problem was that such a path created an unstable "disconnected" position at the top, from which Tiger's very strong and fast lower-body movement would actually cause his arms to drop even more on the downswing, encouraging more stuck swings and more foul balls.

In short, Tiger had become a diminished golfer who'd lost many of his old advantages over the other top players. If that continued, as it did during several winless months in 2004, I knew that as his new coach, I was going to get the blame. I decided that if I was going to get the blame anyway, I'd teach him not as some untouchable icon but as a real player with real problems and not hold back. To be true to Tiger and to myself, I had to truly coach him.

That meant making some noticeable changes, which I knew could potentially make me the man who tried to remodel the Taj Mahal. As Butch had predicted, what I thought would be an easy job had turned into something much harder than it looked.

Tiger's swing situation and the changes required were complicated by three issues.

The first was his left knee. Protecting Tiger's knee during the swing and still getting performance wasn't a simple thing. Although Tiger said Butch had encouraged him to snap his left knee at impact to gain distance, the move had another, more positive purpose. Basically, the fast and dramatic clearing of the hips that caused the hyperextension was a way to "hold off" club rotation and not hit a hook, even when Tiger's plane was slightly across the line. Hyperextending, or "snapping," his leg allowed Tiger to more easily hit a power fade with his driver, as well as controlling his irons with shots he knew had little chance of curving left.

Essentially, snapping his knee allowed Tiger to eliminate one side of the golf course, a hallmark of great players from Hogan and Locke to Nicklaus and Trevino.

But now to preserve his knee, Tiger wanted some flex in his left leg at impact. This meant not turning his hips as aggressively through the ball, making it easier for Tiger to turn his hands over in the hitting area and hit a hook. It was the shot he most dreaded, because with a clubhead speed of more than 125 miles per hour, a hook for Tiger could easily turn out to be a big miss.

The second issue was the movement of Tiger's head. Tiger was very attached to the idea of moving his head to the right on the backswing and leaving it there on the downswing. It was a move that had served him well as a skinny junior golfer trying to keep up in distance with the bigger kids. By staying behind the ball, Tiger could produce a "slinging" action with the club that, though not consistently accurate, generated a lot of speed and gave him the distance he believed he needed to win. Even as he got older and longer off the tee, he felt he needed to keep his floating head position to continue to outdrive the majority of other pros.

He wasn't completely wrong. It was just that in his case, the head movement had developed into a contributing cause of getting stuck. He could have gotten away with moving his head to the right if, on the downswing, he had put it back where it started. But with the longer clubs and especially the driver, he usually didn't. Instead it stayed to the right and lowered. There were periods in which I won this argument with Tiger, and in my opinion it's when he produced his best golf. But it was an ongoing battle.

The third issue was the biggie. Simply put, Tiger played the driver with a lot of fear.

It was a shocker for me. One of the adjectives most often used to describe Tiger Woods was *fearless.* But the more I observed him close up, the more it became clear: He wasn't. We never talked about it directly. I didn't want to say anything that could undermine Tiger's confidence, which was more important than any technical improvement. Sometimes, to make it less of a big deal, he'd remind me that he had never considered himself a particularly good driver, at least in comparison with the rest of his game. "That's why my name is Woods," he'd joke. "Maybe it would have been different if I'd been named Fairway."

I'd seen signs of driver anxiety before I became Tiger's coach. I knew that Tiger tended to struggle on courses with tight fairways like Southern Hills, the TPC Stadium Course, or Harbour Town at Hilton Head, which he took off his schedule early on. I remembered in Germany in 1999 or 2000, when he was playing a practice round there with Mark, there was a par 4 with water down the right side, but the target area looked pretty wide to me. Tiger hit a 3-wood off the tee, which surprised me, and I asked him why. "Oh, that water really cuts in tight," he said. More telling was the first hole at Isleworth, which didn't present a lot of problems from the tee and where in practice Tiger always hit a driver and almost never missed the fairway. But when the Tavistock Cup was played at Isleworth in 2005, which was the first time Tiger had played the course in an actual competition, he hit a 3-wood off the first tee. When I asked him about not hitting a driver, he said, "That out-of-bounds comes in tight on the left side." I was amazed because I had never seen him come close to hitting it out-of-bounds.

The most persuasive evidence of Tiger's fear with the driver was the shot pattern of Tiger's warm-up versus his competitive rounds. Near the end of his practice session before each round, Tiger would commonly hit a series of long, straight bombs, sometimes putting on a veritable driving clinic before heading to the first tee. Then, as soon as his name was announced, he would fire one way right, or even worse, way left. For the rest of the round, he'd play defensively off the tee, intentionally playing away from trouble even if it meant putting the ball in the rough, and usually in the right rough. It also meant he'd be less committed to swing changes we were trying to install, which had worked so well in practice.

Steve and I would wonder to each other before his rounds, "Is this the day he finally commits to his swing?"

Over my years with him, Tiger got better with the driver, but it was a gradual, hard-earned improvement with no big breakthroughs. We tried a lot of different strategies, including coming very close to developing a driver "stinger"—a low-flying shot intended to increase accuracy that would in theory be easier to repeat. He could execute it flawlessly in practice but never trusted it enough to put it into competition.

I can now admit I never felt totally comfortable when Tiger was standing over a drive in competition. When he hit a good one, I felt relieved. I was always worried about the big miss. And I know that most of the time, he was too.

Tiger's basic strategy with the driver was to play away from the side of the hole with the most trouble, even if it meant going into the rough. Generally, he favored missing to the right, because a pushed or faded shot would land more softly than a hook and have less chance of bouncing into a really bad spot. He knew that from a reasonable lie in the rough, he was good enough to get the ball on or around the green most of the time and avoid bogey. Indeed, it was his incredible ability with the other 13 clubs that made him so conservative with a driver. All Tiger needed was a shot, and he could not only survive but even go on to win. One of his playing thoughts was to capitalize on holes where he hit good drives, especially on par 5s, to shoot low scores.

Because of this strategy, the fairways were in effect half as wide for him as they were for most other players. He played to one side of the middle of the fairway, to defensively compensate for where the trouble was. He was good enough to afford half a miss, but even he couldn't afford a big miss.

His fear was really only with the driver. It might have been because it was the one club with which he was more concerned with distance than control. The biggest flaw in his swing—a tendency to let the shaft get too flat on the downswing—was more exposed with the longest club, which comes into the ball on a flatter plane. It's probably no coincidence that Tiger was a better driver early in his career, when he still used a steel shaft that was 43½ inches long. When, around 2003, he finally joined other players in using 45-inch graphite shafts, which were also lighter and could be swung faster, he had more problems. Ironically, for a lot of lesser players, the drive, teed up invitingly, was the easiest shot to play. For him it was the hardest.

It wasn't a unique phenomenon. Driver problems had attacked many top players after years of competing, among them Seve Ballesteros, Ian Baker-Finch, and David Duval. Typically issues began with a flaw in technique, and then became as much mental as physical. Although Tiger's mental strength seemed to make him the most unlikely candidate for such a problem, after a few weeks of working with Tiger I came to believe that he had the beginnings of such an issue as well. To deal with it, without ever mentioning it to him, I drew on my own experience with the driver yips.

From studying the problem, I learned that only a very small percentage of the golfing population was even a candidate for the driver yips. It was definitely a good player's issue. The power and speed to hit massive blocks and big hooks are possible only with certain swing characteristics: across the line at the top, powerful lower-body motion, inside-out swing path, and an overreliance on hand action to square the club in the hitting area. Such players also tend to grip the club with their left hands in a "stronger" position—turned more clockwise—as well as hold the club more in the fingers than in the palm. Those had been *my* tendencies, and Tiger had them as well—though to a much smaller extent.

Just as I'd done with myself, with Tiger I started to apply some opposites. It was basically Golf 101. To correct his getting the shaft across the line and stuck behind him, I began to give him drills that exaggerated getting the shaft pointed to the left of the target at the top. On the way down, I wanted him to not only feel the club more in front of him but actually come across the ball from outside the target line. This is the swing path of about 95 percent of all golfers; it produces the slice that is the signature of the hacker. But it was the fix for Tiger.

I knew that if he mastered this feeling, it would give him a bail-out shot when he got uncomfortable on the course. He could "saw off" a cut by exaggerating the feeling that he was swinging from the outside. By teeing it low and accepting that he was going to lose some yardage, he could hit a playable "spinner" that at worst would go into the right rough. When we played together after I began coaching him, he'd noticed me hitting this shot. It didn't go anywhere, especially compared to his drives, and he'd make fun of me for such a "wuss" shot. But he also noticed that I almost never missed the fairway.

The shot served the further purpose of not requiring him to straighten his knee to keep the club from turning over. What he'd done with superaggressive lower-body action he could now do with the path of the club. It cost him a bit of distance, but it helped preserve the knee.

I also implemented an opposite fix for his head movement. I suggested that he let his head turn toward the target on the downswing so he was not even looking at the ball as he hit it. It was the signature move of Annika Sörenstam, one of the straightest drivers in history. Annika had picked up the habit from a drill her teacher, Henri Reis, gave her as a teenager to essentially keep her from getting stuck. She found it helped so much that she put it into her competitive swing. A lot of good drivers had a similar move, including one of the perennial leaders in driving accuracy and greens in regulation on the PGA Tour, Joe Durant. Not looking at the ball had helped me conquer my driver issues by reducing anxiety, and I thought a less drastic variation would help Tiger.

I knew I was taking quite a risk in giving Tiger so many compensations. The golf world was expecting me to make changes that would bring him back closer to perfection, and here I was, at least temporarily, giving him a swing that was going to look less than classic—a little flatter and closer to his body, with a bit of a quicker tempo. Of course, once it became clear I was coaching Tiger, people thought that I was imposing my version of the ideal swing on him. I wasn't. I know what textbook looks like, and that was my ultimate goal for Tiger. But in the short term, with a slightly unorthodox technique, he would be better off hitting more spinners into the right rough, even though it would tag me as the guy messing up the world's greatest player. I began to think of the popular notion of Tiger as the perfect player—who was sure to display his awesomeness if not tampered with—as the Tiger Trap.

What nobody else knew was that if Tiger looked more orthodox—more upright, less laid off, and employing his old hip release—he wouldn't perform as well. In his time with me, whenever he'd start to do things that made him look more as he had with Butch in 2000, the worse he hit it. That might sound absurd, but swings are about more than how they look. They change in imperceptible ways over time, often internally more than externally, and what has always worked begins to fail and needs adjustment. My opinion is that the accumulated pressure Tiger played under began to make it difficult to use a swing that required the compensations he had relied on as a younger player.

I believed in what we were doing, and so did Tiger. Gradually the wild drives started to lessen, but the process was going to require steps through the different levels a touring pro faces. First there would be fewer wild drives on the practice tee at Isleworth, then in practice rounds at Isleworth, then on the practice tee at tournaments, then in practice rounds at tournaments, then in practice sessions before competitive rounds, then in competitive rounds, and finally in competitive rounds at majors. That's a tour player's progression, one of the hardest things about the profession.

After the Masters, Tiger finished tied for third at Charlotte on the Quail Hollow course, which is demanding off the tee. It was a good sign, but at his next tournament in Dallas, I decided to try to install one more significant change. The setting was right because I was at home and Tiger could work with me in private at Vaquero. (Though the media had found out about our practice round with Mark there, no one asked about this session.) Tiger had played well in the first two rounds, shooting 65-67 to take the lead. Normally, I wouldn't have tried to show him anything new at such a juncture, but I knew Tiger would be in a good mood and I felt an inspiration, so after Friday's round I asked him if he'd put in some practice with me at Vaquero.

Tiger was staying at the Four Seasons at the golf course, so he followed me in his courtesy car the ten miles to my place. On the way I had to decide how to introduce the idea in a way that he wouldn't immediately dismiss. I'd heard his quote about throwing out 90 percent of what he heard from teachers and keeping maybe 5 percent, so when we got to Vaquero, I said, "Tiger, I want you to try something that I think might make that five percent you hear from teachers that you actually keep." He laughed, and his good mood seemed to continue as we drove a cart out to the back of the range.

Basically, I believed Tiger would be better off with one more safeguard against the big miss. I'd found that pros who suffered from driver wildness invariably held the club more in the fingers. In my own case, I'd altered my grip so that the club was more in the palms. I had gotten the idea from studying Moe Norman, a Canadian whose competitive career had been hampered by his autism but who was legendary for the repetitive accuracy of his shots. Norman's simple swing was notable for its relative lack of hand action.

I'd noticed that when I held the club out with just my left hand, if the grip was in the fingers, the club head would quiver and shake with any change in grip pressure. But when I held it in my palms, the club was much more stable and would barely twist.

Grip changes are huge decisions for pros, because in the short term they're uncomfortable and greatly affect feel. So I told Tiger,

"Look, I just want to show you something. Just keep an open mind and try it for me, OK?"

He looked at me skeptically. I demonstrated the grip I wanted him to try, then put his left hand on his 5-iron and showed him how I wanted him to hold the club more in his palm. He immediately said, "I can't do this." I quickly said, "Yeah, I know it feels weird, but just try it." He took the new grip, placing his right hand also with more of his palm, and waggled the club. "There is no way," he said. I repeated my urging, putting a ball in front of him to hit. He got over the ball and complained, "I can't even cock my wrists." I said, "Just hit one." He stood over the ball for a longer time than usual, then swung.

The sound of the impact was distinctive. Tiger's shots always made a great sound, but this was even more "flush." The ball flight was ideal as well. Tiger was visibly astounded that he'd hit such a perfect shot with such an uncomfortable feeling. He looked at me and said, "Show me that grip again." I put his hands on the club and he once again said, "I can't hit the ball with this grip." I answered, "You just did." He flushed two more shots solidly and went, "Wow." After about a dozen more balls, he looked at me and said, "I'm going with it."

And just like that, he did. He used the grip the next two rounds at Dallas, and though he shot 70-69 to finish in a tie for fourth, he never complained about it. It was the fastest Tiger accepted any change I ever proposed to him, and the astounding thing is that it was probably the biggest change we ever made. Even though it was a grip that cost him some distance because it slightly restricted his hand action, Tiger never complained about the sacrifice and continued to hold the club more in the palm the entire time I coached him. The whole weird way it happened remains improbable to me and is a good example of how Tiger was simply different. I can't imagine another player adjusting to a grip change so quickly.

Off the course, I was also getting to know Tiger better. I stayed at his house about thirty days in 2004, the amount I'd average per year while we worked together. I tried to be a low-maintenance guest. I obviously knew by now that Tiger was allergic to people who even faintly crowded him, so I demurred on all things except his golf game.

Probably the least satisfactorily answered sports question of the last twenty years is, "What's Tiger Woods like?" The reason is that even for those who are actually around him a lot, never mind his millions of observers, he is very hard to know. There is a lot going on behind those eyes, but very little is shown.

I saw Tiger in many modes. He could be very gracious in public when he chose. But when the mood struck him, he could be coldly aloof with media, autograph seekers, or even officials. In private, I found that he could either be good company—conversational and intelligent in a way that made you wish he'd allow that side of himself to come out all the time—or completely distant.

As I'd learned from being around Tiger before coaching him, his public persona forced him to operate in a very tight box. Whereas some athletes and celebrities could actually enhance their images by behaving badly, Tiger could never do any wrong in public without it being pointed out that he was betraying the ideal Earl had promoted and that his endorsement contracts were built on. It made him wary of being in public or engaging with people other than the few in his inner circle. Whenever I was with him in a restaurant or a hotel or a casino, he was eerily good at avoiding eye contact. He acted impervious to his surroundings, but it struck me that he wished it could have been different, and that on some level he resented his situation.

I never sensed that Tiger wanted to be treated like a king. He never had a big entourage. He never bragged about what he'd won or how much money he had. Tiger didn't big-time. The most entitled I ever saw him act was when he drove around Orlando. It wasn't that he favored fast cars. He owned a McLaren and a Porsche that were basically race cars, but they stayed in the garage from what I could tell. Mostly he just drove his Escalade, but in a way that reflected an impatient guy who wasn't going to follow the silly rules of regular schlubs. He'd go over the speed limit, but not by a lot. Mostly it was rolling stops, turns over double lines, parking in a restricted spot—time-saving stuff he thought was worth the risk. When I was in the passenger seat, sometimes I'd say "Nice" after one of his illegal moves. That would draw a smile from Tiger as he enjoyed the rare feeling of breaking rules. But I never saw him get a ticket or even get pulled over.

I remember once reading something John Cook, who played a lot of practice rounds with Tiger at Isleworth, said about him that I thought rang true: "Tiger knows his place." What I think John was saying is that Tiger knew he was special, but with so much certainty that he never had to talk about it. He knew everyone else knew it as well, and he was content to let them make all the noise. He felt no need to prove it or revel in it or lord it over people. He never pulled rank with a "Do you know who I am?" routine in public places. When he walked into a restaurant, the red carpet was rolled out, a special room was provided, and the owner came by to pay homage. But all he cared about was that the meal came right away, and he'd try to slip in and out unnoticed. He might have needed indulging from those around him, but he didn't need attention from them. I guess he'd had too much from too young an age.

It always struck me that Tiger was at his most outgoing with kids at clinics. The few times I saw him in one of those situations, he took a lot of time helping individual kids with their games and talked with them freely. During the Q&A sessions, he answered 10-year-olds much more completely than he did the media. Being around youth seemed to relax him, which made me wonder if it was because he missed his.

At Isleworth, he played a lot with Mark and John, veterans who'd helped him when he first turned pro and whom he trusted, but he was loosest with a group of much younger guys, several of them teenagers. They were all good players, but Tiger liked to work with them on their games, encourage them with needling and prods during their rounds, or just listen to their jargon and expressions. Sometimes he'd play the best ball of a couple of them and me; sometimes everyone would just play his own ball. Or Tiger would bet them that they couldn't make a certain shot, and the payment would be push-ups, which might leave Tiger's victim sore for days afterward. The push-up bet had started after Tiger admitted he couldn't feel nervous playing for money. But the pain from hundreds of push-ups raised the stakes. Tiger's most intense push-up matches came against Corey Carroll, the son of a member at Isleworth, who is 11 years younger than Tiger. Their matches would be stroke play, with Corey getting a few shots. The standard bet was 150 push-ups per stroke, with payment to be completed by midnight. Tiger loved to "collect," usually laughing as he stood over the loser. But he sometimes lost, once having to pay Corey with 600 push-ups.

Overall, Tiger wasn't much of a bettor on the golf course. He had a habit, if he lost, of asking to play more holes, double or nothing. Mark would occasionally make jokes about it, even telling the media that Tiger was "kind of slow to go to the hip." In his rare high-stakes games against non-pros, Tiger set bets that would be very hard for him to lose. Former baseball pitching great John Smoltz came to Isleworth once to play with Tiger and Mark. Smoltz is a good golfer, maybe scratch or plus-1, and Tiger said he'd give him three strokes a side at stroke play. Even though Isleworth is one of the hardest courses in Florida, especially at the maximum length of 7,700 yards that Tiger played it from, Tiger's par was about 66. That meant Smoltz had to shoot around par to be competitive, a very tall order because according to the course rating, par for a scratch player from those tees is about 77. My recollection is that they were playing for $10,000. On the first hole, Smoltz pumped one out-of-bounds, and I heard Mark needle him with, "No big deal, Smoltzie. Normally a round with Tiger is worth at least six figures. You're getting off cheap."

There has long been a lot of talk about Michael Jordan and Charles Barkley being close to Tiger, but I didn't see those two guys that much. Each visited Tiger once at Isleworth that I know of, and Tiger met them in Las Vegas a few times. Tiger clearly admired Michael for what he'd accomplished as an athlete, and I think Michael gave him advice on how to handle fame. Charles cracked him up, but he also gave him some brotherly advice. But I got to know Charles well, and I know he was baffled by Tiger being closed off and keeping him at a distance. Someone else who's been identified as a confidant, Notah Begay, I saw just a couple of times when he stayed at Tiger's house when he was coming through Orlando. I know they'd been teammates at Stanford and that Tiger plays in Notah's charity event, but Tiger never talked about Notah.

I don't mean to imply that Tiger *didn't* consider these guys friends. Rather, I'm saying that Tiger didn't let anybody very close.

In my experience, the person Tiger shared the most with was Corey. They met on the practice range at Isleworth in 2004 after Tiger noticed how hard Corey worked on his game. Corey is an academically brilliant kid who did stuff like build computers and study quantum physics. He told me he missed one question on his SAT. Corey wanted to become a tour player and, even as a teenager, knew a lot about the golf swing. Tiger liked debating technique with him, especially because Corey was deep into the very complex cult instruction book called *The Golfing Machine* when they first met. Corey shared Tiger's work ethic, and they practiced and played together a lot. Corey also became Tiger's workout partner in the weight room.

Corey was a little nerdy, but I realized that for all the superjocks whom Tiger is said to be friends with, nerds—smart, diligent straight arrows—are the guys he most relates to. That's the way I'd characterize two of his long-standing friends, Bryon Bell and Rob McNamara, who also work for him. It seemed to me that on those rare occasions when Tiger sought advice, it was those guys, along with Mark Steinberg—who had that same buttoned-down character—whom Tiger confided in most.

In private, Tiger's humor was young. Sometimes he was clever or droll, but often what tickled him was something as mindless as belching. The larger the group, the more he stayed on the sideline, offering asides but never taking the stage to tell a joke or share a story on himself.

One example of Tiger's humor that he told me about occurred a month before the 2006 Ryder Cup. U.S. captain Tom Lehman thought it would be a good bonding experience for the team to go to the K Club in Ireland to spend two days together. Rather than give each player his own room, Lehman paired up roommates, putting Tiger with Zach Johnson. Knowing that Zach is a devout Christian, Tiger, when he got to the suite first, immediately purchased the adult-movie 24-hour package and turned the television on. When Zach walked in, he saw the sights and sounds, but presuming that it was what Tiger wanted to watch, didn't change the channel or turn it off. Tiger never commented on the movies, nor did Zach. "It was so funny watching him acting like everything was normal," Tiger told me. "I got him pretty good."

He'd put on a different face in public, offering nothing more risqué than a reference to "my farmer's tan." His favorite one-liners for the media were of the Clint Eastwood/Terminator variety. Before their first-round match at the 2006 WGC-Accenture Match Play Championship, Stephen Ames irritated Tiger by telling the reporters who asked him about his chances, "Anything can happen, especially where he's hitting it." Tiger put on a birdie blitz that got him 9 up and ended their match after 10 holes, the fewest holes required to win an 18-hole match. Asked to comment on the round, Tiger with a deadpan expression simply repeated the lopsided score: "Nine and eight." He liked ending interviews with similar getaway lines.

Although he didn't let any of them get close, Tiger's relationships with other players were mostly good. He enjoyed the team competitions for their camaraderie, especially the Presidents Cup, where there was less pressure than the Ryder Cup and the structure was looser. He definitely felt a kinship with those who knew firsthand what it was like to succeed and fail in the arena. He also liked the exalted status he held with the other players. Tiger never seemed to feel the need to say much, in part because what he'd done spoke for itself. With the players, he could just be.

Those he genuinely liked tended to be quiet, modest, hard-working guys like Jim Furyk and Steve Stricker, whose ability he respected but whose talent didn't elevate them to the position of serious rival. He kept the supertalented at a distance. He didn't want players who could be a threat to feel comfortable around him.

He was averse to loud and cocky players, especially if he felt their records didn't warrant all the talk. He wasn't a fan of Ian Poulter, for example. A couple of weeks before the 2007 U.S. Open at Oakmont, a few players drove to the Pittsburgh area course after the Memorial Tournament in relatively nearby Columbus to get in some practice rounds. Poulter was one of them, and while there he was cheeky enough to ask Tiger, "How are we getting home?" He knew Tiger had a plane at his disposal, and that he sometimes gave other players who lived in Orlando a ride. But Tiger did that for guys he liked, and he didn't particularly like Poulter. Tiger gave kind of a noncommittal answer and hoped Poulter would take the hint and find an alternative. But at the day's end, there was Poulter at the jetport, acting as if Tiger had said yes. Tiger stretched out on his regular spot, in the two seats in the front right of the plane, and immediately put on his headphones. That left me to talk to Ian, which I didn't mind because I got along with him. As we were conversing, Tiger texted me, "Can you believe how this dick mooched a ride on my plane?" As far as I know, Ian didn't get any more rides.

Most other players never asked. They understood Tiger had to have a killer mind-set to be as good as he was, and going out of his way for other people wasn't part of the equation. So even when he was distant, there was more respect for Tiger than dislike. In his own way, he was being up-front. They didn't know him, but they realized he really couldn't let them.

Self-centeredness went with the territory. Whenever I joined Elin and Tiger for a meal in their home, the moment Tiger finished, he simply got up and left without a word. If you were with him in a restaurant, when he was done—and he habitually ate fast—you were done. Whenever we got takeout food from outside the club, I'd go pick it up, and I always paid.

I always remember a quirky aspect of Tiger's behavior that in retrospect says a lot about how it was with him. When we were watching television after dinner, he'd sometimes go to the refrigerator to get a sugar-free popsicle. But he never offered me one or ever came back with one, and one night I really wanted one of those popsicles. But I found myself sitting kind of frozen, not knowing what to do next. I didn't feel right just going to the refrigerator and taking one, and I kind of started laughing to myself at how hesitant I was to ask Tiger for one. It actually took me a while to summon the courage to blurt out, "Hey, bud, do you think I could have one of those popsicles?" He looked at me as if puzzled that I was asking, and said, "Yeah, sure, go ahead and get one." I did, but even after that, Tiger never offered me a popsicle.

It can sound petty, recalling a slight so ludicrously tiny, but my point is, it was that quality of paying attention only to his own needs that was so central to his ability to win. It allowed Tiger to walk past little-kid autograph seekers who were begging him to stop. I always winced a little when this happened, because I knew in many cases it would be those kids' enduring memory of Tiger. Rather than make a fan for life, he probably spawned a critic. He knew he'd take an image hit for it, especially because Phil Mickelson signed so many, but to Tiger autographs were a time-robber in the best case, and he knew that no matter how many he signed, he was going to leave some people who didn't get one screaming in disappointment. A long time before I began coaching him, he'd made a choice, and he never indicated that he was tortured by it. He was after something bigger than being adored.

He was also a terrible tipper. Tiger once won several hundred thousand dollars playing blackjack in Vegas when I was with him, but gave the dealer and the cocktail waitress only a couple of hundred dollars, when a couple of thousand each would have been more appropriate. Not only did it not seem to occur to him how he could change a life with a significant tip, he didn't consider that casino employees were important reputation makers. These were people who got asked, "Hey, I heard Tiger was in here. How well did he take care of you?" Those answers got around, in particular to other high-rollers and influence makers. Locker-room attendants, maître d's, waiters, valets—these are people whose judgments carry weight. I always wanted to tell Tiger that if he was spending money on a public-relations campaign, the most efficiently spent money would be in tips. Mark O'Meara would get on him about this all the time. Tiger would laugh. He seemed to think it was funny to be cheap.

Sometimes Tiger seemed to suffer pangs of conscience, as if he knew he should try harder with people. He'd try to atone with little flurries of interest or appreciation. In my case, he'd remind me that I'd been the only swing instructor in that old *Golf Digest* article who had prognosticated that he'd be dominating the PGA Tour within a year of turning professional. Or he'd call me Henry. No one else, including my parents and sister, has ever called me that. It always made me feel good. Those gestures might not have seemed like a lot coming from other people, but because of who he is and how he lives his life, it was a lot from him. Almost in spite of myself, I'd feel kind of touched.

Definitely, the closest I felt to Tiger was when we played golf during his practice sessions, especially in our rounds alone. It would just be he and I in his souped-up cart. I'd grown up listening to golf guys talk about their rounds with Hogan or Palmer, but here I was playing with Tiger. Maybe it happened 150 times, which probably makes me the non-tournament player who's played more rounds with the world's greatest player—while he enjoyed that status—than anyone else who has ever lived.

I felt like a witness to history. But more than that, I temporarily felt that warmth you have with a golf buddy, because golf is one of the best games for nurturing a friendship. We didn't talk a lot beyond my commentary on his technique. If he hit a really good one, I'd say, "That was incredible." If I happened to do something that was better than average, he'd never say, "Good shot." He would go with, "Where the fuck did that come from?" or, "How did you do that?" That was Tiger's version of affection.

Tiger was at his most generous in these situations. When I was having trouble with my game, he'd enjoy the role reversal of helping me. He had a very good eye for someone else's swing and was excellent at diagnosis, but what was striking was how much effort he'd put into making sure I got what he was saying. "Hit another one," he'd say after I'd hit a bad one, and then he'd offer some ideas. Then if the next one was better but still not quite there, he'd throw down another ball. He saw the humor in the situation, which might lead to a crack about me needing to bone up on my teaching material, but what I sensed most was that golf was special to Tiger, that a real golfer should always try to do it as well as he could, and that the process of improving was the best part of the game.

Once we got back to his house, things would return to being a little awkward. There were never any substantive life conversations between us, even though I would have welcomed that. I might tell him about my experiences, or even share some problems. He might respond with a general comment like "That's a tough one" or whatever, but he'd never further the discussion with a question or an insightful comment. At first I thought that kind of communication would evolve, but it never did.

Unless Tiger was working out, which I joined him in doing on occasion, mostly we'd sit on the couch watching a lot of TV, especially sports. In his needling way, Tiger would make sure to root against whichever team I was for, especially Dallas teams, such as the Cowboys, Mavericks, or Rangers. His favorite teams were the Los Angeles Lakers and the Oakland Raiders, although he used to root for the NFL's Tampa Bay Buccaneers when Jon Gruden was the coach, because Jon and Tiger had become friendly.

Otherwise he liked to watch documentary-style shows on the Military Channel, the History Channel, the Discovery Channel, Animal Planet, or National Geographic. He liked learning about natural phenomena and especially the behavior of the animal kingdom. We never watched the news or current-events programs. His favorite series was the animated comedy *South Park*. He liked it so much that, in the aftermath of his public scandal, when a Tiger Woods character was lampooned in one of the episodes, Tiger confessed to me that he laughed and actually seemed proud to have made the show.

His most repetitive viewing was a DVD called *Navy SEALs: BUD/S Class 234*. (BUD/S stands for Basic Underwater Demolition/SEALs.) The video followed a group of SEALs candidates through a six-month training course that was so brutal only 30 percent graduated. Tiger knew the whole thing by heart. He'd tell me about Hell Week, when very little sleep was allowed, or how long a person could stay in 50-degree water before the body becomes hypothermic. As I'd watch the documentary with him, I'd realize that some of his sayings, like "Second place is first loser," were borrowed from the SEALs instructors. I was also struck by how the instructors accepted absolutely no excuses for a candidate's not completing a task, no matter how difficult that task was.

Tiger's military fixation really came out in the video game *SOCOM: U.S. Navy SEALs*. (SOCOM stands for Special Operations Command.) To play, Tiger would put on headphones, through which an animated commander would give him orders for the next mission to be carried out. The objective was to keep overcoming increasingly difficult tests. Tiger would get totally immersed, sitting on the edge of the couch, as intense and focused as if he were playing in a major championship. I never played, but after being around him so often while he was playing, I had the urge to try it. But he never offered to show me.

I always wonder if I might have had a closer relationship with Tiger if one incident hadn't happened. I was working for ESPN in 2005, teaching their golf schools and doing some commentary work on their golf telecasts. One Thursday there was a discussion about a tournament the following week, and the producers wanted to cover it only if Tiger was going to play. As was his habit as long as I worked with him, Tiger often didn't commit to playing in a tournament until the deadline, which was the Friday before tournament week. It kept everyone guessing, including TV networks wondering how to allocate resources. In this one instance, I knew that Tiger wasn't going to play, so rather than have the producer make unnecessary arrangements, I thought I'd give him a confidential heads-up. The producer knew not to out me as a source of Tiger's not playing, and ESPN didn't report Tiger's decision not to play until the deadline passed the next day.

The next time I saw Tiger, though, a couple of weeks later, I realized that it had somehow leaked that I'd tipped off the producer. He told me in a flat voice, "Don't tell people where I'm going to play." I said, "OK, sorry; won't happen again." And that was the end of the discussion. But from that moment, I was never again told whether he was entering a tournament until the same day he publicly announced his decision on his website. It made my life harder as far as planning went, but I guess he felt I'd betrayed him, and this was the consequence. In the bigger picture, he probably didn't trust me as much, although I'm not sure. With Tiger, as far as staying in the inner sanctum, you're pretty much one and done.

What I came to realize was that Tiger had to be judged in the context of what he was trying to accomplish, which was to be not just the best golfer in the world, but the best golfer he could be. In his case, the latter was a much higher goal. He was after something unique—something others couldn't realistically aspire to—and part of the price was having some missing pieces as a person. Whenever I was around Tiger off the course, I always felt that so-called normal life was just passing time for him, as if he were storing energy for his real purpose.

That was the explanation I settled on for why Tiger would remain silent for long periods. Steve Williams and I would joke to ourselves about how uncomfortable Tiger's muteness could become. Whenever Steve or I would see Tiger, we would always be the first ones to speak, usually asking Tiger how he was, or how he slept or whatever. Steve told me that before one round he was going to make a point of not being the one to speak first after he met Tiger on the practice tee. Steve has a lot of willpower, but he reported that after about twenty minutes, he finally broke down and said something. And Tiger answered him like everything was normal. "It was getting ridiculous," Steve said. "He was just warming up like I wasn't even there. He is definitely in his own world."

Tiger and I were getting along fine into late 2004, even as he went on his longest winless streak since 1998. On the one hand, he was consistent: From Charlotte through the Tour Championship, he finished in the top four seven times in 12 tournaments. On the other hand, he was disappointing in the major championships that mattered most: He tied for 17th at the U.S. Open, tied for ninth at the British Open, and tied for 24th at the PGA Championship, in the process tying his then-career-worst 0-for-10 streak in the majors.

But Tiger showed commitment to our plan. It had been made easier because up until the Tour Championship, the fact that I was his new swing coach was unconfirmed. Even when I was interviewed about my relationship with Tiger in October, I said that Tiger was just a "friend who I sometimes help with his swing." The interview didn't appear until February 2005, by which time it was clear that, friend or not, Tiger and I had a formal arrangement.

What kept Tiger enthusiastic about our work together was that he was really starting to get into a groove on the practice range and at Isleworth. Although he was mocked for it in the press when he repeatedly said he was "close," he really was.

At the same time, 2004 was the year Vijay Singh dominated the

PGA Tour, winning nine tournaments, including the PGA. He'd supplanted Tiger as number one, and with Phil's victory at the Masters, there was talk that the Tiger Era was over.

Tiger, who wasn't friendly with Vijay but respected him, didn't seem that concerned that he'd been replaced as number one. He knew he was the best, and he was running his own race. He knew that when he began winning again, plenty of recognition and accolades would come with it. I thought he explained our plan well when he told *Golf Digest*, "You can play from the wrong position for a long time with good hands, but eventually it's going to catch up with you. I'd like to play my best more frequently, and that's the whole idea."

He and Elin got married in October. I went to the wedding in Barbados at Sandy Lane, a luxury resort owned by two of Tiger's friends, Irish businessmen Dermot Desmond and J. P. McManus. The best part of the festivities for me was having my longest talk ever with Earl. As a coach I really wanted to get his insights into Tiger. With no offense to me, Earl said he didn't think it was particularly important which swing coach or technique Tiger decided on. He believed he was good enough to adapt to anything and still beat everyone. But Earl did say that it was important for Tiger to have structure, because that was the way he operated best. Earl enjoyed the chance to tell his stories to someone who was interested and would be working with his son. From talking to him, I could see Earl was a natural coach, very bright and intuitive, not only in his ability to impart a golf or life lesson but especially in being able to keep his son interested. I know some top instructors who don't teach their children because they feel that the message gets emotionally complicated when it comes from a father. But Earl somehow knew how to also be Tiger's friend and keep the lessons fun while using his deep love for his son as a strength. It reminded me of something Keith Kleven used to say: "No one cares how much you know until they know how much you care."

After getting back from his honeymoon, Tiger nearly won the

Tour Championship in November but was overtaken in the last round by Retief Goosen, who closed with a 64. It was only the second time in 22 tries that Tiger had lost when holding or sharing the third-round lead. To his critics, it was more evidence that he'd lost something. They could also make a case by citing his ball-striking statistics. Tiger would finish the year 182nd in driving accuracy with an average of 56.1 percent, and he'd notch a career-low 48th in greens in regulation with 66.9 percent.

But then things turned. He went to Japan a couple of weeks later and won the Dunlop Phoenix by eight strokes. Two weeks after that, he won the tournament he hosts, the Target World Challenge at Sherwood Country Club, near Los Angeles. He told me that in his mind, he'd made a breakthrough with the takeaway, in which we were trying to get the wrists cocking up while the forearms rotated. Once that move became natural, the rest of the changes just flowed and freed him mentally.

Just before Christmas, Tiger and Elin joined Mark O'Meara and me and our wives for a ski trip in Park City, Utah. As a precaution, Tiger wore a bulky knee brace like an offensive lineman. The experience was especially fun for him because it was a rare chance to be normal in a public place. No one could recognize him because of all the clothes he was wearing, and no one stopped him, because on a ski slope everyone is always moving. He got bugged a little in the lodge, but he rolled with it, and it didn't ruin his mood. I always felt getting out in public settings was good for Tiger. It seemed to release some of the tension that I thought came from having to live such a controlled existence, and I'd find him noticeably more relaxed in the days after.

Tiger had never skied. He started on the beginner slope and was doing pretty well. He was being careful and concentrating on his form. But Elin, who's an advanced skier, would kind of egg him on to try to keep up with her, which I could see was getting to him. It scared the hell out of me.

Sure enough, after not enough time on the beginner slope, Tiger wanted to graduate to the next level, the green slope. To be safe, he needed some turning skills, because that's the way to control speed and slow down, and he assured everyone he knew how to turn well enough. At the top of the slope, Mark's friend Todd Servick, who was a Salomon ski rep and a near-pro-level skier, coached Tiger a bit, emphasizing that he turn early to keep his speed down. Tiger said, "Don't worry, I'll be fine." Then he took off.

Right away, he went straight down the hill, no turning, and very soon was going too fast. We started yelling for him to turn, but he probably couldn't even hear. There was another, steeper hill about 300 yards ahead of him. If he couldn't stop before getting to that one, his speed would increase to where the only way he'd be able to stop would be to fall or run into a tree. Phil Mickelson, an accomplished skier, had lost control on a difficult slope in the early 1990s and still has the titanium rod in his femur to prove it. As I watched Tiger, I thought I was going to have a heart attack.

Todd went after him, digging as fast as he could. He was really moving, but it didn't look to me that he was going to catch Tiger before he got to the steeper slope. I prepared myself for a disaster and could see the headlines: "Tiger Has Ski Accident During Trip with Haney."

Then out of nowhere, Tiger somehow made a turn and safely stopped.

We all caught up with them, and Tiger was out of breath but clearly stoked. He'd loved the daredevil moment and was especially pleased that it had caused so much panic among his friends. As we all told him to never do that again and even called him an asshole and every other name, he laughed harder than I'd ever heard him laugh before.

Our best days were just ahead.

4

Greatness

Elin is thrilled.

It's about an hour after Tiger has won the 2005 Buick Invitational at Torrey Pines, his first stroke-play victory in nearly 16 months and his first PGA Tour win with me as his coach. His press conference and other post-tournament obligations are over. I'm with him and Elin as they walk back to their suite at The Lodge.

Although Tiger's winning again is a big story, it's also clear that his current and future performance is going to be measured against the legend of his best golf under Butch Harmon. After Tiger's second shot to the 72nd hole, there was plenty of conjecture about his ability to close out a tournament with his new swing. Torrey Pines' eighteenth hole is a reachable-in-two par 5 with a pond that fronts the left side of the green. With a one-stroke lead, Tiger hit a good drive and decided to go for the green with a 2-iron. His intended line was to the right of the pond, but he mis-hit it, and the ball wound up about 20 yards short on the fairway next to the pond. On television, Nick Faldo made a big deal about Tiger being way laid off in his backswing, as if his mechanics were bad.

In his post-round interviews, Tiger readily admitted that he "completely whiffed" the shot but, typically, offered no further explanation. What he didn't say was that he'd intentionally played from a laid-off position all day, basically getting the ball around with a left-to-right fade that he knew wouldn't stray too far into trouble. It was one of those days, which often happens during a swing change, when "correct" felt uncomfortable and tempted a big miss. On the 2-iron, Tiger exaggerated the laid-off position even more to ensure that his ball could not go left no matter how he hit it, the pond being the one place that could cost him the tournament. In essence, Tiger made a "bad" swing to hit a smart shot. His mis-hit, which was not intentional, didn't hurt him. In fact, he chipped up and made birdie to win by three.

All this was something Tiger didn't want to get into, and if asked, I wouldn't have, either. It would only raise questions about why the great Tiger Woods still hadn't mastered his new swing after a year, and by the way, why did he change it again? To me, Tiger had demonstrated that his new swing knowledge allowed him to adjust his mechanics to do the job at hand: winning the tournament. That's the art of competitive golf, and it was important progress. To the outside world, unfamiliar with the concept that golf is a game of controlled misses, it simply appeared that Tiger had lost his superpowers.

Back in the hotel hallway, Tiger isn't acting that enthused about winning. He'd smiled through the trophy presentation and kept it light with the media, but now he's kind of subdued. Maybe he's annoyed that the tone of several questions suggested he's not as good as he used to be. Or perhaps, as I'd be learning soon enough, it's just one of the matter-of-fact ways that Tiger Woods reacts to winning, no matter how long it has been.

I'm pretty happy, but mostly relieved. In the last few weeks, it has become commonly known that I'm Tiger's coach, and I've been getting hammered by much of the golf community for teaching him a swing that isn't as good as what he had with Butch. This win will provide, if not vindication, at least a respite. But outwardly, I'm taking Tiger's lead and acting calm.

Elin, however, is really up. She has witnessed a few of Tiger's victories before, but it's been a while, and this is his first official win since they were married. Because of heavy rain on Saturday, Tiger played 31 holes on Sunday, and Elin had walked the whole way. Now she's both tired and giddy. She kind of leans against Tiger and says, "We have to celebrate. What should we do?" She adds that in her days working as a nanny for Jesper Parnevik, he and his wife, Mia, would throw a party whenever Jesper won.

Tiger slows down and looks at his wife. Gently but firmly, he says, "E, that's not what we do. I'm not Jesper. We're *supposed* to win."

Elin is a little taken aback, suddenly realizing that there are still depths to her husband's intensity and expectations that she hasn't yet seen. She nods acknowledgment, but her smile gets a little smaller. I would notice that in the future Elin would keep her emotions under wraps whenever Tiger won.

I would soon find out that though Tiger might let loose with a fierce uppercut or leg kick when a winning putt dropped on the 72nd hole, he'd become pretty blasé by the time he gathered his stuff in the locker room. After victories, Steve Williams and I developed a little ritual in which we privately congratulated each other in a humorously exaggerated way while we waited for Tiger. And on those occasions when I wasn't at a tournament, I noticed that Tiger would call me on Sunday night to review his round only if he'd won. It was his version of celebration.

But in analyzing the sources of Tiger's greatness as a player, one can see that this sort of reaction makes sense. Tiger never allowed himself to be satisfied, because in his mind satisfaction is the enemy of success. His whole approach was to delay gratification and somehow stay hungry. It's the way of the superachiever: the more celebrations, the less there'll be to celebrate.

On this subject, Tiger was the expert and I was the student. All his winning since junior golf had taught him the way he had to think for the winning to continue. When everybody around him wanted him to look at past glories or look ahead to his assault on Jack Nicklaus's major-championship record, Tiger stubbornly stayed in the present. He ran his career the same way a golfer shoots a low round: one shot at a time. When I worked with him, he never talked about Jack's record: how many more he needed, when he might surpass it, how much he wanted it. He never talked about his total of official victories or catching Sam Snead's all-time PGA Tour record of 82. When he got questions about those things, he'd answer that there was a long way to go and basically try to dismiss the whole subject as quickly and unremarkably as possible. I also noticed that whenever we had discussions that assessed his performances, he never used the word *great*. After a tournament in which he'd been essentially flawless, he might go for a "not bad" or "pretty good." A streak of six straight wins might be called a "nice little run." Great was a level he was planning to reach in the future. Or a word he could use when his career was over. But not while he was still playing.

Studying Tiger in victory, it was tempting to consider him unfeeling. He could certainly give that impression off the course, when he put out the cold stare or left someone hanging in awkward silence. But what about how hot he could flash in reaction to a bad shot? It might have been off-putting to a lot of people, but it was real emotion.

I think one of Tiger's gifts was the ability, when he needed to, to turn off emotion. It was why after a tantrum he could still be serene over the next shot. No doubt he'd learned early on that strong emotions unchecked adversely affect coordination and focus and generally impede winning. His knack for shutting down emotion was a big reason he closed out victories better than anyone else in history, and why he was so incredibly good at making the last putt. It was also why he could win half a dozen tournaments in a row and seem just as focused and collected coming up the 72nd hole in all of them. Meanwhile, it was normal for other players, even regular winners, to admit that a victory mentally exhausted them and would lead to a flat performance the next week. This was especially true with majors. Mark O'Meara was an extremely hard worker and very driven, but when he won his only two majors in 1998, at age 41, he attained a deep satisfaction, and could never again quite summon the kind of will that had gotten him there. That's closer to a normal human reaction. Tiger, who once won four major championships in a row, was beyond abnormal.

The converse of this was Tiger's ability to flash intense anger after a bad shot. He did this a lot and was always criticized, but he was expert at getting rid of all negative emotion by the time he'd arrived at his next shot. He told me that he often got angry on purpose because it allowed him to get rid of frustration, and also served to motivate him and improve his focus. While most players who throw a tantrum produce too much cortisol, the chemical that increases the heart rate, clouds the mind, and tenses the muscles, Tiger was like a yogi who could level his emotions seemingly at will.

To be around Tiger in the immediate aftermath of one of his victories was a little eerie. He'd smile and shake hands, but his eyes would stay blank, never quite fixed on anything. I know it was only golf, but that detached quality brought to mind the term *stone-cold killer*.

To Tiger, winning was business as usual, and he wanted his team to think the same way. So when he didn't congratulate me for a job well done after a victory, I was OK with that. It was consistent with the way he treated everyone in his inner circle.

I understood that any accomplishment was important only as a reference point for future improvement, not as a pleasurable memory to dwell on. Based on the fact that for six years I saw Tiger 110 days a year and exchanged a phone call or text with him 100 days a year, I'd calculate that we had at least 1,200 conversations about his golf game. In all those conversations, there were probably fewer than two dozen times that he thanked me or complimented me on my work. Even after a really productive practice session, it was rare for him to say "Good job today" or "Got a lot out of that, thanks." In contrast, I'd make a point of saying just those sorts of things to him. Usually all it drew was a nod, but that was fine. I came to realize that he'd already put that accomplishment in the past.

I had an intuitive sense of the inner tension he wanted to maintain, probably because I'm wired in a similar way. Because coaching Tiger was the job of a lifetime, while I had it, I never relaxed, never stopped thinking of what my next teaching move would be, never added up his victories. I think Tiger sensed that about me, and it was part of our bond. Sure, sometimes I wished there would be more acknowledgment, but I also believed that deep down he appreciated what I did. And when he did verbalize thanks, it really meant something.

Not that some wins didn't get more of a reaction from Tiger than others. Each of the six times Tiger won a major while I coached him, the smile would stay on his face longer, and I sensed that, momentarily at least, he felt fulfilled. Victories in which he outplayed important rivals, especially head-to-head, also lifted him.

Tiger genuinely enjoyed the extra challenge of a showdown, and he strove to silently send his rivals messages that he believed could have a lasting effect. Early in his career, when Ernie Els was the next-best player, Tiger handed him a string of hard defeats, and he frankly thought it broke Ernie as a serious rival. Tiger was always looking to do that with anyone who challenged him.

So Tiger was more stoked by the two victories that followed Torrey Pines. The first came at Doral, where he beat Phil Mickelson in a duel in the last pairing. It was really an electric atmosphere that Sunday, what I imagined it was like when Hogan was in the last pairing with Snead, or Nicklaus with Palmer. It's actually rare in golf for the best two players to hook up when it means something, and Tiger and Phil had done so less often than other historic rivals.

At the same time, Tiger's overall record was so much better than Phil's that their rivalry didn't really meet that standard. I think Phil got elevated into being Tiger's equal by fans and even some media who wanted—secretly or openly—to see Tiger get beat by good-guy Phil. Some of it was about personality, because Phil was clearly more outgoing with the fans and easier for the media. I suspect Phil might have gone to extra lengths in that area because he knew it made him look good compared to Tiger, and it was why Tiger would smile in agreement anytime one of his player friends or inner circle called Phil a phony.

I believe that a lot of the public obsession about Tiger versus Phil was about race. Racism is part of life, part of America, and definitely alive in the golf culture. I knew that during Tiger's junior golf days, he and Earl had called the unwelcoming glances they'd received at some country clubs "the look," and that since turning pro, Tiger had received hate mail and even death threats that were racially tinged. I have no doubt Tiger felt racial vibes in what he read and heard on and off the course, especially when he was matched up against Phil. He never brought it up, but a few times when I made comments about how skin color might have influenced some of his critics, he stayed silent but gave me a knowing look.

Although he didn't mind if other people believed it, I don't think Tiger hated or even really disliked Phil. But just by natural temperament, Tiger was never going to be most comfortable with Phil's type of personality. Phil is a really verbal, high-energy guy who, for Tiger's taste, is too opinionated, is too much of a know-it-all, and just revs too fast. Tiger is much more at ease around low-key, understated, droll people who can come up with a knowing one-liner—older guys like Jay Haas, Jeff Sluman, and Fred Couples, and younger guys with a sly edge to them like Sean O'Hair. Tiger likes David Feherty, but around Tiger, David tones down the manic stuff while remaining clever. Tiger liked it when there didn't have to be many words, and Phil was just too much work.

But it really didn't matter what Tiger thought of Phil as a person. Because Phil possessed the talent to be a serious competitive threat to Tiger, the two men simply weren't going to be friends. Tiger looked at Phil as a way to further motivate himself to be better—basically as a source of fuel. In 2003, when Phil made the comment that Tiger was playing with "inferior" equipment, I didn't think it was a calculated slam by Phil, as an endorser of Callaway equipment, on Tiger as a Nike endorser. Rather, I think Phil enjoyed noting—correctly—how slow Tiger had been to switch to new technology, like the largest-headed drivers, and how in Phil's view as an early adopter, Tiger was slightly handicapping himself. I'm sure Phil knew the quote was going to get some play, but I think it was him being mischievous more than anything else. But Tiger took that comment as negatively as possible to give himself a competitive jolt. I always thought Tiger was going overboard when he'd privately call Phil lazy or make fun of his body, but it was mostly the spillage from revving himself up. It was interesting that after Michael Jordan was criticized for bringing up petty grudges in his Hall of Fame induction speech, Tiger was asked about it. "I get it," he said. "That's what it takes to be as good as MJ. You are always finding ways to get yourself going." Sometimes they're genuine reasons; sometimes they're manufactured. The bottom line is that to keep beating everybody, fuel is needed.

Tiger never tried to discourage people from believing he and Phil didn't get along. It was that much easier for him to be cold when Phil would try to break down the barrier between them with a friendly word or gesture. Rather than respond in kind, Tiger, it seemed to me, would go out of his way to be even more distant—a kind of competitive bully move that he didn't hesitate to use if he thought it might increase his edge. I can remember a few times when another player would make a conciliatory gesture toward Tiger, like sitting down at the lunch table or stopping to say something nice on the practice tee, and Tiger would respond with the cold shoulder. Sergio Garcia got the treatment after some early success against Tiger, and I think it bothered Sergio to the extent that he never played well in their matchups again. By contrast, Vijay Singh never tried to ingratiate himself with Tiger, and it was part of why Tiger seemed to give him more respect than his other rivals.

Tiger didn't mind that it was awkward with Phil, which made it tricky when Hal Sutton paired them in the 2004 Ryder Cup. Tiger didn't want the pairing because he knew it was going to put him under more of a microscope, and he knew how much criticism a loss would bring. When they did lose, it didn't bother Tiger to see Phil get blamed, with the focus on Phil's sprayed drive on the final hole. But I'm sure he would have rather won the match.

When Tiger and Phil were thrown together in the team atmosphere, I never saw or heard about any real animosity. By all accounts Tiger truly enjoyed the Ping-Pong matches he and Phil had at the Ryder Cup and the Presidents Cup. It was competition, which was Tiger's safe zone as far as personal interaction. I'm sure

Phil tired of Tiger's never giving it up, but he always seemed to take the high road when he talked about Tiger, calling him the best player and thanking him for making everyone richer. And in his own way, Tiger softened a bit. He got a laugh when the Mickelsons sent the Woodses a miniature Ping-Pong table after Charlie was born. And when Phil's wife, Amy, and his mom were diagnosed with cancer in 2009, Tiger and Elin offered support.

Early in Tiger's career on the tour, I don't think Phil worried him much as a player. Tiger had always admired Phil's short game, and I'd see him imitating that dead-arm pitch Phil executes so well. But he thought Phil's full swing was pretty flawed, too handsy and, especially at the more penal major-championship setups, very susceptible to the big miss under pressure. But Phil definitely got better when, with the help of instructor Rick Smith, he tightened up his body action and began favoring a more controlled fade off the tee. Tiger's respect for Phil took a jump when Phil won the 2004 Masters, and it's grown as Phil has won three more majors. Even when Phil blew it with a double bogey on the final hole of the 2006 U.S. Open at Winged Foot, Tiger saw that more as a mechanical breakdown and not some kind of choke job.

Although Phil's head-to-head record against Tiger wasn't very good, he'd gained a lot of confidence from his first Masters victory. Tiger's loss of the number-one ranking and swing transition no doubt gave Phil a sense of opportunity. When they hooked up at Doral on Sunday, Phil's body language signaled he was eager for battle.

Phil started the day with a two-stroke lead, but Tiger caught up, and with an eagle on the par-5 twelfth, took a two-stroke lead. Phil came back to tie with birdies at thirteen and fourteen. At the par-4 sixteenth, both drove poorly, with Phil losing a great opportunity to take the lead by missing a five-footer for par. Then on the seventeenth, Tiger drained a 30-foot dagger for birdie to go ahead. After Phil almost chipped in for birdie on eighteen, Tiger stepped up to his five-footer—far from a gimme even under normal circumstances—and stroked it in with the kind of calm assurance that set him apart. It was indeed a statement win, Tiger's way of telling Phil, "I'm still better than you."

The victory also gave Tiger back the number-one ranking he'd lost to Vijay in 2004. Tiger never mentioned that, but he was pumped about beating Phil. The next time I saw Tiger, I said, "That one meant a little more, huh?" Tiger gave me a stare and said, "Oh, yeah, anytime I can beat that guy." Tiger knew Phil had improved, and he was taking him more seriously than ever.

Tiger also knew that despite the victories, he still had a lot of work to do. We'd pretty much eliminated his bad shots at Isleworth—his sprayed drives to the right had been the most problematic—but they still cropped up in on-site practice rounds and continued to plague him in competition. That's the pattern of swing-change improvement—the fastest gains come where the pressure is lowest.

The driver problem was complicated by Tiger's being ambivalent about his equipment. Late in 2004, he'd finally changed over to a driver that most other players had switched to two years before, one with a 460cc titanium head, the largest allowable under the rules, and up from 380cc. He also went to a longer shaft, up from 43½ inches to 45 inches. Theoretically, the extra size in the head created an internal weighting system that would lead to straighter shots and faster ball speed, while the longer shaft increased clubhead speed. There was no question the combination gave Tiger more distance. In 2005, he'd average a career-high 316.1 yards off the tee, ranking him second in that category. But he also finished near the bottom—191st—in driving accuracy, hitting only 55 percent of the fairways.

Tiger had driven the ball the best of his career in 1999 and 2000 with a 260cc steel head and a 43½-inch steel shaft. Although he'd eventually gone to a 360cc club, he'd resisted going to the largest head even as Mickelson and others had said he was missing the boat. He intuitively felt the new technology didn't help him as it helped others. Every tour player gained distance with the combination of the 460cc drivers and the latest multilayer balls, to the point that more players than ever were reaching par 5s in two. Dominating the par 5s had always been one of Tiger's main advantages, and it was lessened as other players got longer. Unfortunately, though many others retained or even increased their accuracy with the bigger heads, Tiger saw his ball flight become more crooked.

The reasons are complex. First, the big head and new ball were distance-oriented and designed to produce less spin and thus less curve. That made it much more difficult for Tiger to hit his natural draw, a right-to-left shot that carries less backspin than a fade. With the new technology, Tiger found that a draw with his new driver would carry too little spin and "fall out of the air." Indeed, the bigger the heads got on tour, the more players went from favoring a draw off the tee to going with a left-to-right "slider," which had enough spin to retain its carry but didn't lose nearly as much distance as a spin-heavy fade used to with the older drivers and balls. I wanted Tiger to go with that slider to help get him out of his habit of letting the shaft drop behind him on the downswing and coming into the ball on too much of an inside path. But the slider was a shot that Tiger had never grooved, and it went against his "eye" when he looked at the target from the tee. His swing was definitely draw-biased, and with the old equipment, he was used to a ball that would spin back a bit to the left even if it started too far to the right. With the new driver imparting so little spin, a ball that would start right would basically stay right. The result was that Tiger became statistically less accurate.

After he switched to a 460cc driver, when Tiger wanted to hit a draw off the tee, he'd pull out his 3-wood, its 15 degrees of loft producing more spin. I eventually tried to persuade Tiger to increase the loft in his driver from 8.5 degrees to 9.5 degrees, but he didn't want to give up the distance potential of the big-headed driver in certain situations. He finally tried more loft at the 2009 Memorial, and had one of the best driving tournaments of his career. He hit every fairway in the final round, and later told me that was the first time he had ever done that.

Frankly, I thought Nike should have built a driver specifically for Tiger, something with a smaller head that would allow him to curve the ball more easily, even if it cost him a bit of distance. But such a design would have gone against the extra-power theme that sells new clubs in the marketplace. Instead, the reps would bring Tiger the latest models, with some relatively minor customizations. There was no doubt that Tiger would produce impressive readings on the launch monitor when he tested the new clubs. Unfortunately, he'd get seduced by numbers that showed distance gains, especially when he'd hit shots with a higher trajectory and less spin. Tiger knew he had a hard time achieving such a flight consistently in competition, but with each new club he hoped he'd be able to groove the high bomb rather than the low cutter. Except for very short spurts, it never really happened. Bottom line: the ball flight he adopted with me as his coach wasn't ideal in terms of the physics of "laboratory golf," but it was the best way for Tiger to *play* golf and avoid the big miss.

Once everyone switched to a multilayer ball, Tiger still insisted on using a ball that spun more than any other on tour. Stamped with a star, it was not used by anyone else on the Nike staff and it wasn't sold in golf shops. Tiger liked the soft feel and extra stop the ball provided for difficult shots around the green. But that ball was also the shortest on tour, the Nike guys telling me it cost Tiger at least 10 yards in lost distance. If Tiger had used a less spinny ball—and I always thought he tried to play with too much spin around the greens—he could have achieved some distance gains without going to the bigger head and longer shaft in the driver.

Tiger's power wasn't best reflected in his distance off the tee. While Tiger was long, I never considered him "monster" long in the way Hank Kuehne was as a young player or Bubba Watson and Gary Woodland are today. But what Tiger could consistently do that other players couldn't was call on his power to hit special, extremely high-skill shots—getting an extra 25 yards out of a 3-wood from the fairway to reach a long par 5, or sending a long iron over impossibly tall trees when others would have to go under or simply chip out into the fairway. One of the best such shots I ever saw Tiger hit came in the final round of the 2009 WGC Bridgestone Invitational at Firestone. A stroke behind Padraig Harrington on the par-5 sixteenth hole, Tiger drove poorly and had to lay up his second shot 176 yards from an ultra-firm green with a front hole location cut perilously close to the pond. The whole round, players hadn't been able to get sand wedges to stop by the pin, but Tiger powered an 8-iron sky-high that landed behind the hole and spun back to within a foot. It was that kind of shot, not his drives, that other players conceded they simply didn't possess.

In the early years of our work together, improving his driving was just one item on Tiger's checklist for future improvement. Our hope was high, and his work ethic and attitude for learning were exceptional. Tiger never really asked me how long it was going to take before he got comfortable, and it was a question I wanted to avoid because putting a time limit on swing changes is counterproductive. They take the time that they take, and the pressure of a deadline often makes it take longer. So to head off any impatience from Tiger, I used the feel-good moments after Doral to say, "You're doing better all the time. In about two and a half years you're going to have something really good."

He looked at me hard, obviously startled at that time frame. I'm sure he would have guessed something a lot sooner. The fact is, I made up that two-and-a-half-year period. There was a chance he could have mastered everything in a month, but I wanted him to stay engaged with learning. I'd observed that he got his best work done when he knew he had a lot of work to do. It was when he was most determined, least questioning, and most focused. But the moment he perceived that he was just refining—that was when his focus and work rate went down and the experimentation went up. As Butch found out, "maintenance" was the wrong theme. Tiger thrives on the chase.

This is my answer to people who question why Tiger continually changed his swing. Beyond the actual technical improvements, the biggest value of the process is that it kept him interested. As a prodigy, Tiger ran the risk of early burnout, and he needed more stimulation and variety than the average pro, who preferred maintenance to makeovers. Also, with every change, Tiger had gotten better. The improvement might have come at a significant cost of effort and time, but to him it had been worth it.

I also believe Tiger intentionally overstated how much of a change he was undertaking. It helped his mind-set to believe he was doing something major. But the truth is, in many ways I was continuing much of what Butch had given him. Butch and I differed slightly in our conception of the correct swing plane, and I made a big adjustment to Tiger's grip. But mainly my work with Tiger was repackaging what he had worked on with Butch. Tiger's were far from the biggest swing changes ever made by a tour player. But thinking of it all as very dramatic helped him put in a lot of work.

A big swing change had the added benefit to him of lessening outside expectations and giving him an excuse if he happened to play badly. At close quarters, I began to understand just how intense a pressure cooker he lived in and how he devised ways to escape it or turn down the heat. He didn't really talk about it, except for a stray comment like, "With me, nothing is ever good enough." When I'd complain to him about getting slammed by writers and commentators for my teaching, he'd chuckle and say, "Hank, welcome to my world."

Tiger hit a lull after his win at the 2005 Doral. He didn't play great at Bay Hill, beginning with a popped-up 3-wood opening drive that went only 200 yards. He never broke 70 and finished tied for 23rd. He played worse at the Players Championship, tying for 53rd while making four double bogeys. Over my time with

Tiger, the best he ever did in that tournament was eighth in 2009. Although he'd won the tournament in 2001 and the U.S. Amateur there in 1994, the TPC Stadium Course definitely made Tiger uncomfortable. There were at least four tee shots that gave him trouble, the par-4 fourteenth and the eighteenth holes in particular, where the water hazards cut tightly on the left always seemed to produce a big block to the right. Of all the architects, Pete Dye seemed to create the designs that were the hardest for Tiger to negotiate. Pete really knows how tour pros think, and he is very good at punishing those who play away from the big miss.

Tiger left the Players with his game in no shape to win a major championship. But over the next six days at Isleworth, he went into emergency-preparation mode. It was extremely fulfilling for me, because Tiger was always into it before majors, at his most receptive as a student. With me, the only majors where he didn't reach that mind-set were the 2006 U.S. Open right after Earl died and the 2010 Masters. This time, I think he sensed things were coming together, and he stayed on plan.

So much so that I began to mentally label our daylight hours at Isleworth as "Tiger Days." He would begin a typical one by waking at six a.m. and working out until eight. After he showered and ate breakfast, we would meet on the practice tee at nine for 90 minutes of hitting balls. From 10:30 to 11 he would practice putt, then play as many as nine holes on the course until noon. After a one-hour lunch break, we'd meet at one p.m. for an hour of short-game work, followed by another 90 minutes of hitting balls. From 3:30 to 4:45 he'd play nine holes, and then return to the putting green until six p.m. This would be followed by an hour of shoulder exercises before retiring for dinner at seven. If he had a week off from tournament play, he'd start all over the next day.

Tiger respected practice. It was sort of his church, the place he made the sacrifices that would lead to success. He believed in the old-school ways, putting in time, taking a step backward to take two forward, putting his faith in the old Hogan line about "digging it out of the dirt." Even when his mind wandered to places that led to swing experiments, in our first few years together, I never once saw him hit a careless shot in practice.

Watching him in action, I wasn't surprised to learn that Tiger disagreed strongly with the idea that champions are born, not made. "You're a product of your environment," he said, giving credit to his father and mother for providing the conditions that let him fall in love with the game and devote himself to it.

I'm not sure if such focus was an effort. Off the course, Tiger freely admitted that he was easily distracted and restless and needed to constantly be in motion. When I was at the house, he might suddenly go off for a workout at the gym, go for a run, or get on a video game, sometimes excusing himself by saying, "My ADD is kicking in." But he was almost always calm and poised on the course or the practice area. There, he was in his element—and observing his comfort there, I could see that he truly loved hitting a golf ball.

He enjoyed the details. He never hit a shot without knowing exactly how far his target was, so he always had a yardage in mind with every shot he hit. He'd pull out the range finder before hitting at a flag on a practice range. When he switched targets, he'd pull out the gun and figure out the new yardage. He never failed to do this.

Another idiosyncratic trait was the way he'd take small breaks. He'd seldom hit more than 25 balls in a row before stepping away. He might sit down in the cart and just stare out silently for a few minutes. I didn't say anything the first few times, but I finally asked, "What are you doing?" He said, "I'm just thinking about what we just did." Because what we were working on would usually be something that was uncomfortable, he was making sure he understood where he was in the process and where he was going. To me, it was an example of a great performer doing what Geoff Colvin in his book *Talent Is Overrated* calls "deliberate practice." It's the most difficult and highest level of practice because it requires painstaking focus on weaknesses. A lot of players hit a lot of balls but focus only on their strengths. The great improvers are willing to get uncomfortable and make the mental and physical effort to correct a flaw, which often involves difficult "opposite-oriented" remedial learning. But that was Tiger in major-championship preparation mode.

At these times, the dynamic between us was peaceful and attentive. Our voices were soft, and even the occasional laughter was kind of muffled. This learning atmosphere was the way both of us liked it. With Tiger and me, there was not a lot of talking. I didn't want to be a big explainer. I wanted to make a few points, then let him digest them and see if he could find the solution for himself. We might stop if he got a little confused or had a question, but usually things would be pretty wordless until he felt he got it, which was when he might ask, "How's that?" Almost always, my answer would be, "That's it."

One way I helped Tiger impose some structure was by instilling the idea of Nine Shots. It was simply a distillation of the nine ways a ball could be moved based on three curves (straight, starting left/moving right, starting right/moving left) and three trajectories (low, medium, and high), yielding nine combinations. In practice, Tiger wanted to be able to deliberately hit the nine shots with every club, and he'd do so in a structured way. He'd usually start with a sand wedge and work his way through the bag, although, tellingly, the exercise didn't extend to the basically draw-proof driver.

The Ninc Shots did a lot for him. First, it gave him a mental leg up. He knew other players didn't practice that way, and he believed that such an elaborate and demanding practice template gave him an edge. His thought was, "I'm better, so what I do has to be different and better." It matched his self-image and satisfied his ego.

In practical terms, it helped him believe he could hit the proper shot under the gun. And the right shot wasn't just the one that gave him the best chance to get close to the pin. More important, it was the shot that let him most easily play away from trouble either on or around the green. If water guarded the left side of a green and the pin was cut on that side, Tiger could come in with a draw that started well to the right. If there was heavy wind, he could come in low. If the greens were particularly firm, as they were at majors, he could come in high with a lot of spin. He just wanted the fullest toolbox possible.

With the tools at his disposal, he became a more thoughtful shot maker and thus a better course manager. He steadily began eliminating mistakes because he almost always had the right percentage shot for the situation. As a younger player, Tiger might have forced shots at the pin, but as he gained more ways to work the ball, he could start it at the middle of the green and move it toward the pin. It's the shot that allows the most room for error because it reduces the chance of missing the green on the "short side" of the pin, from where a recovery is almost always more difficult. By being able to vary trajectory, he gained better distance control, especially in the wind. Tiger found himself "pin high" more than ever, which is the hallmark of good iron play.

Having more control got Tiger away from trying to blow fields away. When he had fewer shots in his arsenal, he played more aggressively. When he was "on," it could lead to double-digit victories, but more often it led to mistakes that cost him wins. The Nine Shots helped Tiger understand that he was good enough to never really take a chance and still win. It would mean he'd be much less likely to win by 10, but he'd be *more* likely to simply win. It was Tiger becoming more of an expert at "getting the W."

The Nine Shots also helped him understand better than ever the exact causes of different ball flights—such factors as club path, clubface angle, angle of attack, and clubhead speed. It gave him the knowledge to diagnose and fix himself more efficiently on the course. And he really valued having those assurances. To him, being able to make the right corrections during a round was the true measure of a real player.

In essence, the Nine Shots were Tiger's acid test. When he had mastered all of them, he could effortlessly put his swing into "neutral"—perfectly on plane, with no built-in tendency. That wasn't always the case, but it was always his goal, because he understood that the more he moved off neutral, the more shots he wouldn't be able to hit. Some days, he had to accept that neutral wasn't attainable and that the wisest course was to play with what he had. Those would be the days when he gave the pin a wider berth and focused more on avoiding mistakes than on making things happen. He had confidence that he could figure it out before the next round, and that helped him be more patient.

The Nine Shots were also fun. Tiger was a natural worker of the ball; he liked creating shapes and spins. It was something he'd done with his dad, playing "call shot"—Earl requesting a specific shot and Tiger delivering. It was kind of an old-school way of playing, when the less aerodynamically sleek golf ball could be moved around a lot. Such a style was rewarded in the week-to-week modern game because the hole placements on the PGA Tour had gotten so close to the edges of the greens. And the benefits were even more evident in the firmer conditions of the majors. Even when softer conditions didn't really reward shot-making versatility, the style kept Tiger's interest up. But most important, the Nine Shots allowed Tiger to access his artistic abilities in a structured way, and I believe it eventually made him the best iron player of all time.

For the 2005 Masters, the fault that we most wanted to address remained Tiger's tendency to drop his head down and behind the ball on the downswing, especially with the driver. I realized that many great players lowered in their downswing, but I always thought Tiger lowered too much when he struggled. So we worked on staying taller on the backswing, keeping the head from moving or tilting, and staying taller through the ball. One measure of Tiger's motivation and focus was that he wasn't questioning the premise as much as before, though he would question it again. Tiger was trusting me, and it felt good.

At Isleworth the week before the Masters, when we'd go back to his house, we continued to talk golf. One thing I tried to do was interpret statistics in a deeper way than what he might read in a magazine or hear from a television commentator. For example, though Tiger's driving-accuracy percentage (the number of fairways hit divided by the number of attempts) had gone down, I would point out that the increased distance all the players had gained had caused most of their percentages to go down as well, and that his drop in 2005 was negligible compared to the drop in the tour average. I'd say, "Don't let Johnny Miller or the Golf Channel tell you how you're doing. You're doing better, and this proves it." Tiger would smile and say something like, "Man, you're really Mr. Stats," but he'd gained some positive reinforcement.

Because Tiger would tune out lectures, I tried to get my lessons across indirectly. From my first days as Tiger's coach, I had noticed that while he was incredibly good with difficult shots, especially around the green, he was too often ordinary or worse with easy ones, especially straightforward chips. Hoping he would make the connection, I told him about a friend of mine, billiards champion C. J. Wiley. C.J. helps me with my pool game, and one day I complained that "I make all the hard ones but miss all the easy ones." He responded, "Hank, that's because there are no easy shots. There are just shots." Tiger liked that story, and shortly after, when he won in Dubai in early 2006, he called me. "I got all the easy ones up and in," he said, pausing slightly, "because there are no easy ones." He wanted me to know the lesson had taken, and his short game became tidier once it did.

Long conversations were rare, but golf was one topic Tiger would warm up to more than any other. In the end, he was a golfer. We'd watch tournaments and analyze swings, usually commenting on particular moves that he liked. For example, the way Vijay stayed tall and kept his body moving through the ball, or Steve Elkington's way of keeping the club on plane, or Hunter Mahan's turn away from the ball. Even guys with supposedly bad swings—he'd pick out the good thing they did, the thing that made them good enough to play the tour. I remember once we were watching Allen Doyle in a Champions Tour event. Doyle's style was unorthodox, but he hit the ball straight and won a lot of tournaments. Tiger said, "That club really stays low after impact a long time."

Ben Hogan was probably the only player whose whole swing Tiger admired. He watched videos of Hogan closely. He could relate to Hogan's athleticism, but he especially focused on how Hogan kept the club on plane even with a really aggressive lower-body move. That was an action Tiger had a hard time with, his lower body supposedly "outracing" his upper body, while Hogan, who as a younger player had fought a hook because he got the club across the line and too flat on the downswing, had solved the problem. I also found it beyond coincidence that Hogan's path to eliminating the big miss was similar to Tiger's. Both men weakened their grips well into their professional careers. And just as Tiger learned to count on our "saw across" shot as a reliable way to get his driver in play, Hogan devoted a lot of his practice time to hitting intentional cuts and slices with a long iron in a remedial effort to groove the power fade that became the cornerstone of his greatest golf.

But Tiger wasn't in awe of Hogan. In fact, when we talked about it, he noted how Hogan in a *Shell's Wonderful World of Golf* match seemed to hit a lot of low, punchy shots into the soft greens—shots that wouldn't stop quickly enough on the firmer and faster surfaces of today. I also thought it was telling how Tiger publicly referred to Hogan as "Ben." There was none of the "Mr. Hogan" deference that many modern players showed. Same as he did with "Jack," "Arnold," "Byron," and "Sam." Some people thought Tiger wasn't being respectful enough, but I thought he was just being honest. He knew he'd earned his way into that club.

It was a very good week at Isleworth preparing for the 2005

Masters, probably our most productive to that point. At our last practice session on Saturday before leaving for Augusta the next morning, he told me, "This is the best I've ever hit the ball in my life." Once we got there, I thought his biggest challenge would be not getting too keyed-up. He hadn't won a major since the 2002 U.S. Open, and the scrutiny was going to be higher than ever. As much as he wished otherwise, whatever pass he'd gotten for his swing changes was over, and his Hank Haney swing would be on trial.

On Thursday, because of rain that threatened chances of the tournament's ending on time, Tiger started on the tenth tee and was one over par when he reached the par-5 thirteenth. He had a downhill 70-foot putt for eagle that he hit too hard and watched roll into Rae's Creek, leading to another bogey. After making the turn, he bogeyed the first hole, where his second shot hit the pin and ricocheted into a downhill lie in the bunker. He followed that bogey with a drop-kicked 3-wood off the second tee that barely got off the ground. When play was stopped, he was two over for 12 holes.

Tiger wasn't happy when he left the course. On the way to the parking lot, Elin asked me if I was coming to dinner at the house they'd rented. When I said I didn't think so, she surprised me by saying she thought I should come because Tiger was down and it would help if I talked to him. It was a rare case of Elin independently imposing her judgment on Tiger's behalf, and naturally I accepted the invitation.

When I got to the house, Tiger was discouraged, but I emphasized the positives about his round, and his mood improved. We then worked on his swing in the living room, which had suitably high ceilings. As a teacher, I like to manually guide my students into positions so that they can know what correct and incorrect feel like. Although I almost never did this with Tiger on a tournament practice range because of all the cameras and comments it would have drawn, we did it all the time at Isleworth, and we did it in private in Augusta. Once Tiger knew the right feelings, I encouraged him to ingrain them with practice swings. In my time with him, one of the ways he was different as a player was in the number of practice or "rehearsal" swings he'd take before hitting a shot. From those swings I'd often learn more about his comfort level on the course, or his understanding of what he was doing, than from his actual shots.

He felt good about his swing when he resumed his round on Friday morning, and he finished with a 74 after making an annoying bogey on his second-to-last hole, the par-5 eighth. But things were turning. He got in only nine holes of his second round before more lightning came, but he played well and shot three under. On Saturday morning, he shot another 33 to post a second-round 66, then after a break went out for his third round. He was able to get in another nine, and as darkness fell, he closed with three birdies to shoot 31. For the day, he made 12 birdies in 27 holes, and with another 27 holes to play, he was four behind Chris DiMarco.

On the eve of the final day, we went back to the living room to continue work on staying taller, but also to work on another move. I wanted him to get the club on a wider arc coming down by creating more separation between his arms and shoulders. It was an anti-stuck move, and I knew with the pressure of the final round, he might need an extra safeguard against his always-lurking habit. Before I went to bed, I sent him a text: "All you have to do is what you're doing. There is no one here who can beat you. Even if it takes you extra holes, this is your tournament."

On Sunday, Tiger came out and had a great warm-up. His first shot of the day was going to be a 6-iron off a side hill lie on the tenth hole. The practice range at Augusta is flat, but the short-game area isn't, so when Tiger went over to work on his short game, he found a spot where he could exactly re-create the lie that he was going to have on the tenth fairway, and he hit one 6-iron from that lie. Tiger always would make his last ball warming up the exact shot that he was going to play on the first shot of the day, and that day was no exception. I remember thinking how smart that was. Sure enough he went out to the tenth hole and hit his 6-iron to two feet and birdied the hole. He followed with birdies at the eleventh, twelfth, and thirteenth holes. The amazing run of seven birdies in a row gave him the outright lead. Even though he three-putted the fourteenth hole and bogeyed the fifteenth—his third bogey on a par 5 for the week—he shot 65. At the end of the round, his lead over DiMarco was three.

At the time, Tiger had held or shared the 54-hole lead in a major eight times and never lost, and he'd lost only twice from that position in 34 official events total. When he began the fourth round with birdies on the first two holes to stretch the lead to four, he looked to be in full closer mode, but it turned out to be a very nervy round. DiMarco was really dogged, hitting a bunch of short irons and wedge shots close and making big putts to keep hanging around. Tiger opened the door a bit with a three-putt on the fifth hole from 25 feet. He led by only one on the sixteenth tee when, after DiMarco put his tee shot inside of 15 feet, Tiger badly pulled an 8-iron into the hollow left of the green. Such a wide miss with a short iron was a sign that his swing was becoming uncomfortable.

Of course, he holed perhaps the most dramatic chip shot in history to actually expand his lead, but he still felt uncertain about his swing when he got up on the par-4 seventeenth. It was a hole that went from being an easy driving hole for him on the old Augusta to a difficult one in the redesign. He used to be able to bail to the right with impunity, but that shot would be punished after tall trees were planted where his misses used to go. Now, reverting to his fault under pressure, he hit a big push into the trees. He couldn't get to the green and failed to save his par. With his lead back down to one, he pulled his drive on the eighteenth but still faced only a fairly straightforward 8-iron. But he pushed it into the bunker—a shocking miss for Tiger under the circumstances—and again failed to get up and down.

It was hard to process, but Tiger had bogeyed the last two holes of a major to give up a two-stroke lead, proving his swing wasn't quite there yet. I was shaken. If Tiger was, he didn't show it. But he was now in a sudden-death playoff with DiMarco, and if he lost, I knew it would be open season on the Haney swing change.

But at that moment, Tiger somehow transformed. When he'd missed shots on the last three holes, it had been with the lead. In sudden death, he truly couldn't afford a miss, and so he didn't hit one. I could tell from his practice swings as he gathered himself on the eighteenth tee for the first hole of the playoff that his mind was on what we'd worked on. Then he delivered with a perfect 3-wood and striped an 8-iron right over the pin. They weren't safe swings, like those he'd made at Torrey Pines. Remarkably, they were his orthodox "good" swings. As I liked to say, when Tiger had wiggle room, he'd wiggle. But with no wiggle room, he was a rock.

It was what the great ones do. When Michael Jordan's team was up by five with two minutes to go, he might miss a 15-foot jump shot. But down by one in the last 20 seconds, it seemed that he rarely did. But the best analogy for tournament golf, especially the way Tiger played it, is tennis. There are regular points and big points: break points, long rallies, tiebreakers. A tennis player can lose points early in a match and not be hurt, just as a golfer can miss a fairway and not lose a stroke. But every golf course presents a player with big shots: a tight drive on a long par 4, a long second over water to a par 5, an eight-foot par save late in a round. The great ones raise themselves for the big points. I don't think it was an accident that Tiger really liked watching tennis, particularly the way Roger Federer went about winning. Faced with ultra-big shots in the playoff, Tiger delivered.

It will probably always be a mystery where the clutch component of Tiger's personality comes from, but it struck me that for a pretty straight kid who had grown up following the rules, he liked doing daredevil stuff. It was apparent in his scuba and free diving, his bungee jumping, and his military training. Even his beginning forays into skiing were characterized by thrill seeking. He liked the edge of the cliff. That's a great asset in competitive golf, where the mental precipice can be dizzying. Sport psychologists always urge their guys to "embrace" the pressure. It's easier said than done, but Tiger really did.

Of course, after seeing a student make two near-perfect swings when he absolutely has to, it's tempting for a coach to think, *Why the heck can't he do that all the time?* With Tiger, I realized that getting past all the fear and discomfort takes a lot of energy. Even someone with Tiger's makeup can dig that deep only so often. Like a tennis player, Tiger conserved his mental energy for the big points. It was probably why he got more nervous at the beginning of a round than at the end. My guess is that, at the beginning, he didn't access his mental reserves, and it made him more vulnerable on the first tee. But at the end of a round, when Tiger went to the well, he always seemed to find what he was looking for. In sudden death, he went there one more time on the downhill 15-footer for the winning birdie, and he drilled it.

The Masters victory was a turning point in Tiger's trust in his new mechanics. Blowing it could have really set him back and perhaps ended our partnership. Instead, he felt vindicated enough to take a shot at his critics. "I made a big, giant leap with my ball-striking since Augusta," he said. "For all the people who slammed me for making the changes, now you understand why I did it."

At the ceremonial dinner for the winner in the Augusta National clubhouse that night, I sat at the table with Tiger's mother, Tida. Over the years I had only polite and always brief interchanges with Tida, and Tiger didn't talk about her much. But I had sensed from observing her that Tiger's killer instinct came from his mother even more than it did from Earl. When Tida was the parent driving little Tiger to junior tournaments and following him on every hole, she helped instill in him a "no mercy" attitude in competition, and it had stuck. Tida was a tough lady who had a powerful stoic presence in public, though she could exhibit a playful sense of humor among friends, especially when it came to aiming zingers at Tiger's rivals such as Phil and Sergio. On this ceremonial occasion she was calm and dignified, as if Tiger had simply done what he always did and was supposed to do—win. To me, Tida's influence did nothing but add to Tiger's greatness as a golfer.

Despite Tiger's breakthrough at Augusta, his swing remained a work in progress. A few weeks later, at the Byron Nelson, Tiger missed the cut, ending a streak of 142 consecutive cuts made that had begun in 1998, one of the greatest records in sports. At the Nelson, Tiger battled his takeaway. He had a lifelong tendency to take it back too low and inside. He would sometimes overcompensate and get the shaft too upright about halfway back. From there he would react by getting the shaft too flat on the downswing and getting stuck.

We continued to work on getting a slightly upward wrist-cocking to start the swing and began to install more forearm rotation on the backswing. This gave him a better, more down-the-line path going back, and the result was a more compact, rounded-off look at the top, with the club pointing the slightest bit left. At Isleworth the week before the 2005 U.S. Open at Pinehurst, I could really see his new swing taking shape. It was flatter than it had been in the past but also longer. My feeling was that though Butch had shortened Tiger's backswing to keep it from looking as though it was across the line, the adjustments we'd made allowed Tiger to be on plane no matter how far he took the club back.

Tiger had his way of vetting moves before taking them into competition. When I suggested something, he'd try it. Usually there would be some resistance, as there was to his grip change, and then varying degrees of acceptance. Tiger would hit shots trying the new move or position, often not saying anything until after he'd hit a dozen or more. Sometimes he'd reject something with no explanation. Other times he'd qualify a rejection by saying, "You know, this is a good idea, I get it, but right now there's no way I can go with that under the gun." This was the case with the low-flying driver stinger that I really had hopes might be the solution to some of his driving problem. It was rare that he took something straight into competition, as he did his grip change. Often he'd go with a modified version of what we were working on, so it wouldn't feel too uncomfortable under pressure. Sometimes Tiger would actually sabotage a swing-change idea by making intentionally bad shots. It was a way of calling me off—or even calling himself off—something that might be intriguing but that he didn't want to feel conflicted about. Especially at a tournament site, Tiger always wanted to leave a practice session settled on what to leave in and what to leave out, and what he was going to go with the next day.

When he did commit to learning a new move, one of the things that he had a knack for was finding what I called his feel parameters. In other words, he'd identify the move he was thinking about—let's say, more forearm rotation—and then tell me before he hit a shot that he was going to hit it in a way that felt extreme. I'd then monitor if it was too much, still not enough, or just right. When he learned what the right position felt like, he was capable of taking it into competition. The tricky thing with this is that a feel that produces the right result will eventually, and sometimes very quickly, lead to overdoing the move. This is why teachers often say "feel is not real." Tiger had an uncanny ability to keep adjusting his feels in a way that kept producing the move he wanted. Going to Pinehurst, he had a good handle on the right amount of forearm rotation, and it made his ball striking very consistent.

The unique design of Pinehurst No. 2 makes it very difficult to keep approach shots on the putting surface, but Tiger hit the ball superbly all four days and led in greens in regulation, hitting 54 of 72, 18 more than the field average. He also led in driving distance with a 326-yard average. He missed a few drives to the right, but not nearly as many as at the Nelson and not by a lot. After a lot of talk about the so-called Big Five who had emerged after 2002 when Tiger stopped playing as well—a group made up of Vijay, Tiger, Phil, Ernie Els, and Retief Goosen—Tiger was beginning to reassert his superiority.

Tiger lost the Open at Pinehurst because of putting. Officially, he had four three-putts, but there were at least as many times when he putted from off the edge and took three to get down. He took 128 putts, the second-worst total in the entire field. On Sunday he got off to a shaky start with two bogeys but then put on a charge that was undone with two crucial short misses late: an eight-footer for par on the sixteenth after a mediocre chip, and a three-putt from 20 feet on the seventeenth when he thought he had to have a birdie. He lost by two strokes to Michael Campbell, who had the week of his life.

"I just didn't make enough putts," Tiger said. But he was alluding to not converting midrange putts for birdies. I felt strongly that second-guessing those midrange opportunities was the wrong way to evaluate the week. I used the freshness of the wound to hammer home my message. "Tiger," I said, "you don't have to make putts. Nobody makes a lot outside fifteen feet. Your analysis is wrong. Just don't three-putt. If you don't three-putt, they can't beat you. Charging birdie putts is fine if you're trying to win by five. But all you have to do is win by one."

What was maddening was that most of Tiger's three-putts came when he charged low-percentage birdie chances in the 18- to 30-foot range. Usually the aggression would occur after he hadn't converted a few good iron shots, leading to impatience that would result in a missed six-foot comebacker and a bogey. When he was just trying to two-putt from a greater distance, he was one of the best lag putters ever. It was one of the big reasons he was so good at holding leads. When all Tiger needed was solid pars, he knew he didn't have to try to hit the ball close to the flag.

He was confident he could two-putt from distance, not a given for many players under pressure. I believe one of the reasons Phil Mickelson has been prone to making mistakes with a lead is that he doesn't trust himself to make four- and five-foot par putts, so he takes chances from the fairway to get his approaches into an easier two-putt range. It wasn't written about, but I think Tom Watson hit an 8-iron rather than a 9-iron to a back pin on the 72nd hole at the 2009 British Open at Turnberry because he knew that, though the 9-iron would never go long like the 8-iron, it was more likely to leave him a long putt from the front of the green that would be nerve-wracking to get down in two. Conversely, when Jack Nicklaus won the 1986 Masters, he took going over the green out of play on the 72nd by hitting a 5-iron that left him an uphill 50-footer, which he lagged to within a foot. Behind him, Greg Norman faced the same situation but tried to stuff a 4-iron that went long right and led to a killing bogey.

Both Steve and I walked away from Pinehurst feeling it was a major that Tiger threw away. To be honest, now that Tiger was getting comfortable with our plan, I began feeling that way after most of the tournaments he didn't win. Some of it, I'm sure, was bias and emotional involvement, but looking at all the factors, I can honestly conclude that Tiger was simply that good. He did so many things better than anyone else—whether it was generating power, being precise from the fairway, scrambling, putting, or clutch finishing—that I didn't see anyone with enough game to beat him over 72 holes. In about a year, he'd get to the point where all he had to do was play his regular game and he'd win. He wasn't quite there in 2005, but he was trending.

At his next tournament, the Western Open at Cog Hill, Tiger was in a developmental sweet spot. The swing was still in discovery mode, but in the fun late stages where progress starts coming fast. And a very big major, the British Open at St. Andrews, was coming up.

On the Cog Hill range and putting green, Tiger put in the most productive week of work that we ever had at a tournament site. I especially recall our session following his opening 73 on Thursday morning when, after he emerged from lunch, we practiced a solid six hours until dark.

He was a bit upset at what he'd shot but channeled that into incredible determination. That's Tiger's ideal attitude: quiet aggravation and a goal. For me it was perfect because I love to grind. That's the way I've always been, and it's probably my greatest asset as a teacher of good players. I've actually never had a student outwork me. There were times when Mark almost did, and a few times when Tiger got close. I just have a lot of patience for work, and the more I recognized that as a key to my success, the more my capacity increased. When I was the golf coach at SMU, I convinced our guys to stay on the practice range until every other player in the tournament had left. It might be dark, but we'd be the last team there, no matter what. It increased our mental toughness, became a point of pride, and eventually led to more victories.

I believe in Thomas Edison's dictum "Genius is one percent inspiration and 99 percent perspiration." To me, the essence of Tiger Woods lay in a photo I saw of him with Butch, taken on the practice tee in the gathering dark after the third round of the 2000 PGA Championship at Valhalla. That was the time I was envious of Butch Harmon as a teacher. Not just because Tiger was so talented, but because Butch had a student with that much talent who was willing to put in so much effort. At Cog Hill, Tiger reenacted that scene, and my conscious thought as it was happening was *This is incredible. This is as good as it gets.*

The main thing we were working on was getting Tiger to stand tall on the downswing and allow his head to turn toward the target in the manner of Annika Sörenstam and David Duval. It was a classic "opposite" correction for his habit of lowering his body and tilting his head back through impact. Though it was a big change, it was the right one, and Tiger took to it well and got immediate results. He also put in a couple of hours on the putting green. We didn't leave until after eight p.m. with dusk falling. After that session, Tiger knew he was on the road of earned success.

At Cog Hill, Tiger drove the ball beautifully. Although he didn't win, finishing second to Jim Furyk, he was obviously excited afterward. We went straight to Isleworth, where he continued in his ideal-student mode, working hard and listening. He was very consciously peaking, which is more difficult to do in golf than other sports. But it's an art Tiger had begun to master as a boy preparing to win his age group every year at the Junior World.

Now Tiger again was in major-championship mode, his target the Old Course at St. Andrews. The week before majors, I noticed that Tiger wouldn't hit the ball as well on Monday or Tuesday, almost as if he was holding back. He might even get worse on Tuesday. But he'd almost never take a step backward after Wednesday. On Thursday, Friday, and especially Saturday, his ball striking would build to a climax.

Those moments, usually with just the two of us alone on the practice tee across from his home, were for me the pinnacle of golf skill. He would literally not miss a shot, lob wedge through the driver. People really have no idea how good professional athletes in any sport can be when they are in a groove without the pressure and irregularities of competition. I've been told that when former Boston Celtics great Larry Bird was shooting one ball after another in practice, he could make 300 free throws in a row and 95 out of 100 three-pointers. Tiger would get into the same kind of flow, and as I watched him, I had no doubt I was witnessing the greatest ball striking in history.

I know every era can boast its example. Jack Nicklaus says the greatest display of ball control he ever saw was by Byron Nelson at a clinic before the 1954 U.S. Junior Amateur. Years later Byron confirmed that he remembered that clinic because he had indeed never missed a shot. There are a thousand similar stories about Hogan or Moe Norman or Johnny Miller. I got to see a lot of Lee Trevino practicing, as well as Nick Faldo and Nick Price in their primes, and they were amazing.

But here's the difference: In terms of power, those guys were all middleweights compared to Tiger, who's a heavyweight. I would argue that no one who has hit the ball as hard and as far as Tiger has ever hit it so well. Jack was a heavyweight who certainly had tremendous control and probably hit more greens than anyone, but almost none of his contemporaries consider him the best ball striker of his time. I'm also pretty positive he didn't have as many shots as Tiger. When Tiger would get lost in hitting the Nine Shots on those Saturday afternoons at Isleworth, I felt honored just to watch.

Sometimes Tiger would raise himself into that zone when he wanted to impress another player. It might happen at Isleworth when a fellow pro whom he didn't see very often or maybe even didn't like very much would stop to watch him hit balls. After briefly acknowledging the player, Tiger would shift into another gear. It was interesting to observe the player's reaction. Sometimes a shot would draw an audible "Whoa!" but even when nothing was said, I could see that the player was leaving with a mixture of awe and discouragement. When we were alone again, I'd say to Tiger, "Sending a little message there, huh?" He'd just smile. The other guys Tiger liked to step it up for were television commentators who stopped by the practice tee at a tournament, particularly Miller or Faldo, both of whom had been critical of his swing changes. Tiger would know when they were watching, and if they walked in close, he'd say hello but then get back to work. But I know he'd bear down to show them they were wrong. Miller was particularly complimentary of Tiger's Nine Shots, saying that he used to do the same thing and would try to go 9-for-9. "I didn't do it that often," Miller said. I know Tiger was thinking, *I do it all the time,* but he didn't say anything.

Not long after that encounter, Miller approached me to say he thought he'd been a little too hard on Tiger on the air and that he was going to give him more credit. When I saw Tiger, I told him what Johnny had said and added, "I thought that was pretty nice of him." Tiger looked straight at me and said, "I wouldn't trust that guy for two seconds."

When we got to St. Andrews, Tiger was in a great mood. He had positive memories of the Old Course from winning the tournament by eight strokes in 2000, but beyond that, he loved that he was in the place where golf began. He has always called St. Andrews his favorite course and "the coolest place on earth."

He was very confident in his ball striking and hit just enough balls to keep his edge. What was different was the amount of time he devoted to his putting. The hardest Tiger ever practiced his putting at a tournament site while I was his coach was at St. Andrews in 2005. The Old Course's greens are the largest in the world, and distance control is crucial. They're also on the slow side, and Tiger has often said he's best on fast greens. But at St. Andrews his speed was perfect all week. He was flawless in the must-make zone between four and eight feet, the length that is especially tricky at St. Andrews because so many putts look straight but almost always have a subtle movement. He three-putted only once, getting a par after driving the twelfth green on Saturday. At the end of the week I told him, "Tiger, the moral of this story is, you putt better when you practice." I was basically calling him out about paying the price with the putter. I wasn't surprised that his response was silence.

St. Andrews was where Tiger finally got off to a good start in a major, shooting 66 on Thursday. It was his lowest first round in a major since 2000, and the lowest opener in a major that he'd ever shoot with me as his coach. It was the main reason his five-stroke victory was the easiest of the six majors he won while I was his coach. He seemed to breeze around the wide fairways of the Old

Course, free to hit his driver without a lot of fear. He averaged 342 yards off the tee to lead the field and also took the fewest putts, with 120. That combination on that course made him unbeatable.

On Friday, while Tiger was shooting a 67, Jack Nicklaus played his final hole in the British Open, making that great birdie on the eighteenth. It was a good omen. Every time Jack retired from playing in a major—the U.S. Open and PGA in 2000, the Masters in 2005, and now the British Open—Tiger won the championship. In 2000, they'd been paired together in Jack's last round at the PGA, when Jack also had birdied his final hole.

They had a good relationship but a complicated one. Tiger always said all the right things about Jack, once saying that they understood each other without ever having to say anything. Tiger wasn't too big on giving someone a lot of credit or hero worshipping, but when it came to Jack, he'd pay respect. One day we were noting Jack's tremendous consistency in majors, and Tiger said, "How about those nineteen seconds." When I first tried to convince Tiger to stop trying to blow fields away because he'd win more often if he was satisfied with winning by one or two, he didn't really listen. But when he read that Nicklaus said the same thing, it got his attention and changed him into a more strategic golfer.

Jack has always been very complimentary of Tiger, often saying he had no doubt Tiger would break his major-championship record. Jack was his captain at the Presidents Cup in 2005, and I remember him affectionately patting Tiger on the cheek after a match. But as Tiger got closer to his record, I noted a competitive edge in Jack's comments. Before the 2010 season, when the U.S. and British Opens were being held at Pebble Beach and St. Andrews, Jack said it was going to be a big year for Tiger if he was going to pass him, because Tiger "owned" those two courses, and if he didn't win there, it was going to make things more difficult. That was a statement intended to apply pressure. I know Tiger noticed, because he reads and watches everything in golf, but he never mentioned it. Doing so would have been admitting it bothered him. But for all of Jack's graciousness, Tiger understood that the Golden Bear—understandably—wanted him to come up short. Since then, my sense is that Tiger has looked upon Jack more as a rival than a friend.

On Sunday at St. Andrews in 2005, Tiger woke up with a two-stroke lead, and his warm-up on the practice range was freakishly good. He'd comment later that it was one of the best of his life. He hit the 50-yard sign four times in a row, the 100-yard sign three times in a row, and the 150-yard sign on his first shot. In the midst of it, I made him laugh when I said, "It's always a good sign when you're hitting shit." I jokingly told Steve that on shots around 100 yards he should remind Tiger to aim right or left of the pin. Sure enough, on the third hole Tiger's wedge hit the pin and bounced off the green. Tiger played a really controlled last round, and as he walked up the last fairway, he made a point of searching for me and holding eye contact. That was his thank-you, and it felt very good.

After finishing tied for second at the Buick Open, Tiger came to the PGA Championship at Baltusrol looking for his third major of the year. But he opened with a loose five-over-par 75 in which he had 35 putts, including two three-putts. It left him with too much to do, and three rounds in the 60s weren't enough. He finished tied for fourth, two shots behind Phil, who won his second major championship.

Tiger didn't acknowledge his first-round trouble, but I thought it was becoming an issue. I think the problem was that he began playing not to lose. He knew that, especially in majors, at the end of the tournament, players start to fall back, owing to the pressure and difficulty, so he was more focused on avoiding doing anything that would take him out of contention. He knew he was the best closer, but he started to perhaps over-rely on that skill. The result was that he'd play defensively on Thursdays, when, as the cliché goes, a good round won't win you the tournament but a bad round will lose it. He ended up playing so tight that he'd stop making birdies, so that a couple of bogeys would result in an over-par score. It was particularly true at Augusta, where he never broke 70 in the opening round until 2010. Steve often made the comment, "We'll be fine if we can just get past the first round."

At Baltusrol, I made a bad call on the practice range before the final round. Tiger was trailing the lead by six, really in need of a low one, and during his warm-up, I saw that he was getting a little too upright in the middle of his backswing again. A teacher's constant dilemma is when to say something about a fault. Bringing it up can introduce doubt or get a player obsessed with making the correction. But staying silent might allow the problem to ruin the round. At what variance does the bad tendency warrant a comment? In this case, I thought Tiger's mental plate was already pretty full. I wanted him to go out and play freely, and I decided saying something could mess that up.

After a 68 in which he hadn't hit the ball that well, I told Tiger what I'd seen on the range and said, "I probably should have said something to you." He didn't say anything right then. But the next time we got together, a couple of weeks later, he said, "I need to talk to you. At Baltusrol, you told me you saw something and didn't say anything. You can't do that. If you see something, I want to know." He didn't say I cost him the tournament, but in my mind, to this day, I think maybe I did. I made a mistake at Baltusrol.

Tiger ended the 2005 PGA Tour season with six wins, four seconds, and 13 top tens in 21 events. He was back on top, and the critics were temporarily muffled. Still, my predominant thought was that it was a year Tiger could have won the Grand Slam pretty easily with a little better putting at Pinehurst and Baltusrol.

During the holidays, Tiger and Elin stayed at my home in Park City for another ski vacation. He was a lot more sure of himself than the first time and was obsessed with improving. He kept saying, "Watch me, I've got to work on my turns." He was still in learning mode, his happy place.

On Tiger's 30th birthday, on December 30, Elin's gift to him was a border collie they named Taz. Tiger is a true dog person, and he really liked that Taz was smart, focused, and task-oriented. He didn't mind that Taz wasn't very cuddly. They were a good match.

Before playing in 2006, Tiger took a 24-day break from touching a club, the longest, he said, that he'd ever taken. It helped him feel refreshed, but he also spent time with his father, who was in the last stages of his battle with cancer. Tiger kept all that private when we got together before his first tournament of the year—at Torrey Pines, where he was the defending champion. He'd go on to win in a playoff, win his next start in Dubai, and then again at Doral. He'd put a 5-wood in the bag—he called it his "old-man club"—to replace the 2-iron, and he was using it to hit the low stinger off the tee. It was also a good club for second shots into par 5s, because Tiger could hit it higher and stop it faster than he could a 2-iron. But he also hit it under the heavy South Florida wind at Doral, which added up to a net gain in versatility.

Tiger really threw himself into his Masters preparation. For the first time, Earl wasn't going to be able to attend, and Tiger's preparation was determined and intense because he wanted to give his father one last thrill. But the extra emotional burden was less than ideal.

At Augusta, Tiger simply tried too hard. His state of mind showed up most in his putting—he had six three-putts, three of them in the last round. The final one came on the seventeenth when he jammed a last-gasp 12-footer for a birdie well past and missed coming back. "As good as I hit it, that's as bad as I putted," Tiger said, his rounds of 72-71-71-70 leaving him in a tie for third, three strokes back.

Phil won his second Masters in three years, and even on a

course that had been lengthened and redesigned, it was becoming clear that his left-handedness combined with the newest driver technology was giving him an advantage at Augusta. The course still favored a right-to-left ball flight off the tee because of several holes that doglegged left. Whereas right-handed players were having a harder time curving the ball that way with the big-headed drivers, Phil could go with the power fade that was the easiest shot to repeat with the new technology and cut off a lot of distance on some crucial holes, particularly the par-5 thirteenth.

As he left for California to see Earl, Tiger was subdued. While he was out West, he left an image for posterity. Two weeks after the Masters, he went to a Las Vegas sound studio to film a commercial for Nike. The cinematographer Janusz Kaminski, who won an Academy Award for *Schindler's List,* used a super-high-speed camera and shot Tiger hitting a driver. The angle was face-on, and Tiger wore black. As captured in the commercial, Tiger's swing took a full 53 seconds, from takeaway to follow-through, the entire sequence accompanied by a cello solo. Tiger later told me that he'd made about 25 slow swings for the cameras to make sure he executed all the changes we'd worked on just right, and gave final approval to the one that was chosen. What I loved about it was how quiet his head was, how tall he stayed on his downswing, and how free and unencumbered he was as he released his upper body and arms. It was the swing I envisioned him making with the driver, which really hadn't come out in competition. Of course, I'm biased, but I think that commercial is a record of the greatest swing in history. I'm proud to hold that swing up as what I was after.

Earl died on May 3, 2006. I attended the funeral in Southern California and was struck by how composed Tiger was in his eulogy and later at a gathering at the Tiger Woods Learning Center. I wondered how his father's death would affect him. I hadn't had much contact with Earl, and Tiger very rarely talked about him in my presence while he was alive. But everything about Tiger's story in golf went back to his father. It was he who set Tiger off on his journey, first acting as a leader and then as an always available guide. Now Tiger would be on his own.

He didn't seem any different when I next saw him at Isleworth a week before the U.S. Open at Winged Foot. Tiger had skipped the Memorial Tournament in the wake of Earl's death, but he definitely didn't want to miss a major championship. By now I realized that he loved the stage of the biggest events, that he considered them his showcase as a champion. He never put it in those terms, of course. When he'd called me to say that he was going to play at Winged Foot and I asked if he was sure he was ready to go, his answer was matter-of-fact. "Gotta get back sometime. Might as well be now."

Tiger worked hard in his preparation at Isleworth, but for some reason, something went out of him once we got to Winged Foot. He kind of rushed through his sessions, and his focus was lacking. Once play began, every part of his game was at least a little off, and he shot 76-76 to miss the cut by five shots. Not that it was on his mind, but it meant he'd only tied Jack Nicklaus's record of 39 straight cuts made in major championships.

In retrospect, it was clear that Tiger came back too soon, though he never admitted he had. But even taking into account the emotional upheaval, Tiger's performance bothered me. A microcosm of the week occurred on the very first hole. During our practice rounds, I'd urged Tiger to practice his long chip shots because Winged Foot presented a lot of those and they required an extra degree of touch. Tiger had kept saying he would but never did. Sure enough, he was faced with a 50-foot chip right out of the gate, and predictably, he hit a poor one that led to a bogey.

That incident stuck in my mind and led me to send Tiger a long e-mail in which I made some pointed comments that—considering Tiger's predictable nonresponsiveness—would have been awkward saying face-to-face. I began gently, alluding to the short time since Earl's death as the main reason for his poor play, and referring to myself as the Bear, which was what Tiger would sometimes laughingly call me during our more grueling practice sessions in the Florida heat and humidity. But once I got rolling, I decided to get in some shots I thought were necessary.

We'd managed only one full practice round at Winged Foot, so I expressed regret that Tiger had waited until Monday of tournament week to leave Isleworth, particularly because in New York he could have stayed on his boat, which had been docked in a harbor near the course. "I should have made a suggestion that we go up early," I wrote, adding, "not that you would have listened."

I was miffed that Tiger suddenly decided he was going to emulate Ben Hogan and not employ practice swings during competition. I felt strongly that, particularly because he was still mastering the techniques we'd worked on, practice swings were an important tool in his preshot preparation. He'd tried forgoing practice swings at the 2005 Byron Nelson, which was the last time he'd missed a cut.

> I know it is a pain in the ass to work as hard as you do taking a bunch of practice swings, but on the course it is one of the only things that you can do in an effort to get a feel for what you are doing. (Instead), you came with your Ben Hogan routine that came out of nowhere.

That led to my venting about Tiger's habit of going off plan, and I included this zinger:

> Your track record for ball striking when you are flying the plane alone and I am hanging onto the wings isn't real strong since I have been on board.

I also chided him for getting annoyed about people taking pictures of him in the practice rounds:

> Either make it your mission to talk to the commissioner and get the cameras off the courses in the practice rounds, or make it your goal not to let it bother you. Anything other than those two options is not helping you at all . . . it is pure craziness to let something like cameras going off distract you so much. That act is a total waste of time and energy.

Finally, I challenged his work ethic, which I knew would hit him where he lived:

> When we practice and prepare, we need to kick it up a couple of notches. I feel we are getting outworked and that is not a good feeling for the Bear. Not my style and definitely not yours.

By the end of the e-mail, I'd softened, but I made one last plea for Tiger to become a more active student during our sessions:

> This is all for now, but I never stop thinking about this shit. I wake up every day thinking about it and I go to sleep every night thinking about it. I have a lot to share but one thing (I've learned) is that to really teach someone the student needs to ask for help. . . . I always have ideas that I think will help you but I am not fond of talking just for the sake of talking. Talking doesn't teach anyone anything, listening does and someone will only listen when they want to.

I concluded the e-mail, "Your friend and greatest fan who will always be there to help, Hank aka the Bear."

Tiger did not answer the e-mail or even acknowledge that he received it. However, a couple of weeks later when I was back at Isleworth, Elin told me, "Hank, Tiger really liked your e-mail. He read it twice."

It might have been a backhanded acknowledgment, but Tiger's

practice spark was back when we went to the Western Open, where our sessions at Cog Hill were nearly as good as they'd been a year before. Tiger again finished second and went into his preparation for the 2006 British Open at Hoylake with a lot of momentum.

The biggest challenge in playing the links courses in the British Isles, which all lie on firm, open ground near a coastline, is controlling the ball in heavy wind, mostly by being able to hit it low. Before Hoylake we worked on getting Tiger's release more "condensed" into a shorter follow-through. It was a different finish from what he'd use on an American course, where carrying the ball in the air is important, achieved with a fuller "throwing" release. But the more compact swing was always a good antidote for Tiger's tendencies, and usually led to his striking the ball really well.

Nobody knew much about Hoylake because it hadn't hosted the British Open since 1967. We'd heard the layout was kind of tight and quirky and might not be ideal for Tiger's game. The spring had been dry, so the course was going to be really firm and fast. Such conditions had become a comfort zone for Tiger because he knew he wouldn't have to hit many drivers.

What we found when we got to Liverpool was that, in an unexpected way, Hoylake suited Tiger as well or even better than St. Andrews. The course's main defense was its deep, steep-faced fairway bunkers. They were basically like water hazards because it was almost impossible to advance the ball more than 100 yards from one of them. The bunkers were about 290 yards out, and in his first practice round, Tiger hit a driver off the first tee and put it in the right fairway bunker. He immediately took another ball and hit a 2-iron that rolled out about 15 yards short of the bunker. That shot set the pattern for the week. Tiger tried the driver on a couple more holes in the practice rounds, but once the championship started he used it only once, on the sixteenth hole of the first round.

Tiger's 2-iron stinger was the perfect shot at Hoylake. Because he was swinging well, he was hitting it very straight, and in fact would lead the championship in fairways hit with 48 out of 56. He could hit it hard without fear of reaching the bunkers except when he was downwind, when he might drop down to a 3- or 4-iron. He had an advantage on the field because his straightest driving club was the one he could hit the lowest, which just enhanced his accuracy. Because the fairways were so fast, he could get the 2-iron out farther than other players. They either hadn't mastered the technique for hitting a 2-iron in such a way or didn't have the power to hit it as far. Those players were forced to hit hybrids and fairway woods, which were harder to keep low in the wind and so more difficult to hit straight.

Regularly hitting his approaches from the fairway, Tiger was a true virtuoso at Hoylake. Although he was often left with shots of 200 yards or more, his swing was on such a good plane that it didn't matter much whether he was hitting a 7-iron or a 4-iron, and Tiger would end the week second in greens in regulation with 58. On the long par 4s and par 3s, Tiger aimed at the middle of the relatively small greens, leaving himself a bunch of 30-foot putts. He made a few, but more important, he was able to string together a lot of low-stress pars. He knew the birdies would come on the three par 5s and the shorter par 4s. If he'd hit a driver or 3-wood and left himself some shorter approaches, it might have led to three or four more birdies, but it would have surely produced some bogeys or bigger numbers.

To me, Tiger's performance stands as the best iron play ever. No one had ever hit such good approaches so consistently from so far away. Particularly memorable was a holed 4-iron from 212 yards on the par-4 fourteenth hole on Friday. Hoylake was the perfect place to display the Nine Shots, and Tiger put on a clinic.

Still, it was a grind. When Tiger three-putted three times in eight holes on the back nine on Saturday, once from four feet, I was afraid he might lose it mentally. But he stayed composed and birdied the eighteenth hole to take a one-stroke lead into the last round. He was paired with Sergio, who he knew would be nervous and uncomfortable, and Tiger started out well. Chris DiMarco again turned out to be his main challenger. But when Chris birdied the thirteenth to get within one, Tiger ran off three birdies to take command and finish strong.

When he broke down in tears after holing his final putt, I was surprised. I hadn't seen that kind of emotion coming, and probably nobody did. But a few hours later, in his jet on the way home, Tiger was the most excited I ever saw him after winning a major. He poured champagne in the trophy and passed it around for everyone to drink. He was so happy that for the first and only time I asked him to sign something for me. I handed him one of the Hoylake yardage books and a championship program. He signed both "Tiger Woods." I thanked him, but I'd been kind of hoping he'd write something personal and include my name. When I got home, I donated the signed items to a charity auction.

The British Open victory really put Tiger in a great frame of mind competitively. Two weeks later he went to Firestone and won. Then at the PGA Championship at Medinah outside Chicago, he played three solid rounds to get himself in the last group on Sunday, tied with Luke Donald. With a birdie on the first hole, Tiger got a magical feeling with his putter, and he holed three more long ones on the front nine to take command. He shot a closing 68 to win by five.

The victory made Tiger the first player in history to win multiple professional majors in consecutive years. It was also the third of what would be seven consecutive wins in official tournaments.

His next event, the Deutsche Bank in Boston in early September, was the one tournament Tiger played in 2006 that, because of some family matters, I didn't attend. After he shot 67 in the third round to trail Vijay Singh by three shots, Tiger called me in Dallas. He said, "I hit it so bad. As good as Vijay is playing, I can't beat him if I hit it that way tomorrow." He described the flight of his shots and asked me what he should work on before the final round, in which he'd be paired with Vijay.

I hadn't watched any of his play on television for that day, which was also a first for me when I was home. I told him I'd call him back and watched the recorded telecasts of the first three rounds, studying all the shots by Tiger that were shown.

When I called Tiger back, I told him to get in front of the mirror in his hotel room and practice his backswing for 30 minutes, working on starting his takeaway straighter back and keeping his eyes level. Then to practice his downswing for 30 minutes, getting the club more in front of him and feeling like he was adding loft as he came down. "Do that, bud, and you'll be good to go tomorrow," I said.

Tiger called me back the next morning, a few hours before his starting time. He said he'd worked two hours in front of the mirror before going to bed. Then, when he awoke at two a.m. to go to the bathroom, he looked in the mirror and started working on his swing again. He said he spent another 90 minutes working on the same stuff before going back to bed. Then after rising in the morning, he did another hour of mirror work, a total of four and a half hours of studying positions and movements since I'd passed along my suggestions. In the final round, Tiger went out and shot 29 on the front nine and passed Vijay. He ended up shooting 63 to win by three. He called me back and said, "That was a nice win."

Tiger's last official victory of the year came at the American Express World Golf Championship, at a course called The Grove outside London. It was the best I ever saw Tiger play. A week before, Tiger had played just OK in the Ryder Cup as the U.S. team lost in Ireland, but he was on in every phase of the game at The Grove. Tiger used a driver regularly all week, and missed only 11 fairways. He eagled the par-5 eighteenth in each of the first three rounds, and birdied it the last day. He shot 23-under 63-64-67-67-261 to win by eight. As for his shot-making quality, it was the closest I ever saw Tiger come to the level he'd attain on the practice range at

Isleworth. He was even hitting the stinger with the driver, a shot he'd never before put into play, but the shot I most wanted him to master. After the tournament, Steve said, "Finally, we saw how he can play."

For good measure, Tiger ended the year by winning the Target World Challenge, which he hosted at Sherwood Country Club. It was unofficial, but it put a ribbon on the year. He went skiing again, in the off-season, then came back and won his first official tournament of 2007, at Torrey Pines. It would give him seven consecutive official victories, the closest any player has come to Byron Nelson's epic record of 11 straight set in 1945.

As I studied Tiger's greatness, I realized he'd morphed into a slightly different player than he'd been in 1999 and 2000. With a younger body, he'd been a longer hitter relative to the field and a better driver. Based on the way he completely ran the table in the majors, I'd say he was also a better putter. Those are two of the most important areas in the game, and the key to Tiger's most dominating performances from that period.

But I would argue that in every other area of the game, he was better in 2005 and 2006. Better with the irons, with more distance control and more shots. More precise with his wedge play from 120 yards and in, and steadier around the green and out of sand. He was a smarter strategist and a superior manager of his mistakes. His weapons weren't as gaudy, but he had more of them.

It wasn't a comparison Tiger liked to make, but in the flush of victory at the PGA at Medinah he answered "Yes" when asked if he thought he was a better player than he'd been in 2000—and he explained why. "Understanding how to get myself around the golf course, how to control things, all the different shots I've learned since then," he said. "Yes, I feel that things are pretty darn good right now."

All I knew for sure was that Tiger was better at the end of 2006 than he was at the beginning of 2004, when I began coaching him. He'd restored his edge over the competition. It's an incredibly hard thing to establish in pro golf. Everyone really is so close and, with more good players from all over the world and advances in equipment technology, constantly getting closer. Having an edge is the definition of a dominant player, and when you really look at history, there have been only a handful who sustained one. In my book, only Vardon, Jones, Nelson, Hogan, Nicklaus, and Woods had an edge based on varying degrees of power, precision, putting, and nerve. The fact that Jack and Tiger kept their edge for the longest time is why they're the greatest ever to play.

The more I was exposed to Tiger, the more I began to think he was an incredible mixture of extremes, all of which added up to an ability that was so remarkable he was probably better at his sport than any other athlete was or had been at theirs. Which led me to what I began to think of as the Package.

The Package was the sum of all of Tiger's qualities and characteristics, the good and the bad. Working from the starting point that Tiger was better and different from any other player, it followed that those differences were things that made him better. It meant that tampering with the Package was perilous. To put it another way: Messing with Tiger was like fiddling with a solved Rubik's Cube.

Though he never articulated it, I know Tiger believed in the idea of the Package. It went along with the sense of destiny his father had passed to him—that he was put on this earth to do something extraordinary with his special qualities, to "let the legend grow." But those qualities, foremost among them an extraordinary ability to focus and stay calm under stress, also included selfishness, obsessiveness, stubbornness, coldness, ruthlessness, pettiness, and cheapness. When they were all at work in the competitive arena, they helped him win. And winning gave him permission to remain a flawed and in some ways immature person.

I was one of Tiger's many enablers. As a person who grew up with sports and loved sports and was always trying to figure out how to succeed in sports, there was part of me that was in awe of Tiger. Better than anyone else who ever lived, he could do that thing that other great athletes from Michael Jordan on down thought was harder than anything else in sports—close out a golf tournament. And my admiration for what that took kept me from ever really challenging Tiger to be a better human being—though, honestly, I never saw anyone else step up to the challenge, either.

Maybe Earl had, and maybe that was the thing Tiger would miss most. It was telling that when Tiger was asked to assess 2006, he called it his worst year, because of his father's death. That comment might have been a bit calculated, the thing he knew other people would be impressed to hear. But even as he was playing better than ever, perhaps he could sense something essential beginning to wear down.

5

Distraction

As Tiger stands over his short putt in the bright Tucson sunlight at the 2007 WGC-Accenture Match Play to end his third-round match against Nick O'Hern, everyone watching is thinking the same thing: *He never misses these.*

The three variables—a simple four-footer, a big moment, and Tiger Woods—add up to a guaranteed result. Tiger will simply access his superpowers under pressure, pop in what for him is a gimme, and move on to the quarterfinals.

Except that the ball misses the hole on the right, not even lipping out. Time seems to stop as the collective thought becomes, *Did that just happen?*

On the next hole, Tiger fails to get up and down from a bunker, and watches as O'Hern, a journeyman from Australia, makes a 12-footer for par to win the match. Tiger takes off his hat and shakes O'Hern's hand. He is out of the tournament. There will be no eighth consecutive victory.

No one could remember Tiger ever missing a short putt on the final hole to win a tournament or a match. Some recalled a missed five-footer for par on the 71st hole at the 1999 U.S. Open at Pinehurst, but even if he'd made that one, he still would have finished a stroke behind Payne Stewart. I'd seen him miss plenty of short putts, a lot of them very important. But in the time I'd coached him, and even before, it was the first time I'd ever seen him fail on a "close-out" putt from short range. Part of Tiger's aura with the other players was his ability to "make the last putt." He seemingly always had, and now he hadn't.

I was interested to see how Tiger was going to talk about the miss to the media. There were a few ways he could go. The tried and true was to say he'd made a good stroke but misread the line. I didn't expect him to concede that he'd hit a poor putt, or admit that thoughts of his winning streak came into his head. Either of those would be messing with his confidence and unleashing the monster of questions, speculation, and analysis.

In my view, a tour pro not telling the truth in such circumstances isn't really lying. Rather, he's being pragmatic. The goal is to protect the ego and scrub the memory of any negativity as quickly as possible. Every famous player, from Jack Nicklaus on down, has made sketchy excuses that don't acknowledge the possibility of nerves or bad thinking.

So Tiger, in going for something a little more elaborate, both didn't and *did* surprise me. He said his ball had hit the remnants of a ball mark and been thrown off line.

This meant that Tiger had somehow neglected to repair the indentation—which he was allowed to fix—before hitting the putt. His explanation was that, somehow, he'd forgotten to do so. "I was so enthralled with the line, I didn't see the ball mark," he told the media. "I knew if I hit it left-center, the match would be over. It's my fault for not paying attention to detail." He also made it sound as if Byron Nelson's record of 11 straight victories—one of the greatest records in all of professional sports—hadn't mattered that much, saying, "It's not the streak. I'm disappointed I didn't pay attention to detail, something so simple."

I didn't believe it. Especially when it came to big putts, I'd always known Tiger to be thoroughly meticulous with his read and the housekeeping around the hole. Other than a loose impediment like a pebble or a leaf, the remnant of a ball mark big enough to misdirect a putt would be the most noticeable of fixable obstructions. It was hard to fathom Tiger's not attending to it.

Also, replays of the putt didn't indicate it had bounced or veered off. It looked as if Tiger had simply started the putt too far to the right. Certainly Tiger had the record to get the benefit of the doubt, but most insiders came away from the miss believing Tiger had been less than straight.

I took it as a humanizing moment. Part of me had expected Tiger to slough it off. After all, he'd made so many, one miss wasn't going to ruin his reputation, and even mechanical putting machines sometimes miss from relatively short range. Then again, a golfer can never be casual in seeking perfection. To approach it, Tiger had to have zero tolerance.

I realized that, without intending to do so, Tiger had maneuvered himself onto the slipperiest of slopes. Missing the first one means the next one will be easier to miss. Focusing on constant improvement was Tiger's mental shield against the game's wounds. But the wounds are inevitable, and they take their toll.

Tiger and I never talked about this process after a loss or even after a victory. He was very good at leaving the past in the past and simply moving forward. But the 2007 season was when I first began to think that Tiger was closer to the end of his greatness than he was to the beginning. In hindsight, I think Tiger did, too.

Not that it was evident in his record. Tiger won seven tournaments, including a major championship, out of 16. As he'd been in 2006, he was first in greens hit in regulation, first in scoring average, first in all-around, first in par breakers. He was hitting fewer and fewer poor shots. His course management was superb. And while it wasn't really reflected in the statistics, I thought his driver was slowly getting better.

In the midst of his winning streak at the start of the year, Tiger let his guard down just long enough to say the Grand Slam was "easily within reason." He'd end the year with another streak of five in a row and seven of eight, the non-win being a second. And at the end, he was blowing fields away. Tiger was only 31, yet Nicklaus contemporaries like Gary Player and Lee Trevino were conceding that Jack had never been so dominant.

But there were subtle changes below the surface. Tiger's work habits started to slip. There were more distractions. Even as I thought he continued to get better, I could feel the ceiling closing in. I was beginning to think that, except for the driver, there wasn't much more room for improvement. He hadn't putted as well as when he was younger, and I knew there was a good chance that wouldn't change.

And there was the specter of injury. Back in 2004, Tiger had told me that he had only 20 percent of his ACL remaining in his left knee. Was the knee a ticking bomb?

Psychologically, Tiger was entering a difficult time. At the top of the bell curve of a career, expectation is greater than ever, but by definition decline overtakes improvement. Certainly Tiger wasn't going to concede reaching the top of the curve, but even *he* had to know he was very close, and it was going to take all he had to keep pushing against the forces of time. And it didn't help that the standard he'd established meant criticism—of his swing, of his putting, of his attitude—whenever he didn't win. No other player in history had ever faced such high expectations. Sometimes, in his attitude or his work habits, the weight of it would all show, and he'd say, "Nothing is ever good enough."

For me, the job got harder. There was more urgency and less fun. Tiger was more irritable and impatient. The process of improvement had been his emphasis when we first began our work, but he began to be much more concerned about results, or in his words, "getting the W." He never mentioned Nicklaus's record, but it started to weigh more heavily at every major. And Tiger's actions indicated he believed he had less time to do it than everyone else thought.

In retrospect, 2007 was when Tiger began to lose the joy of playing and began to look at his career as something he wanted to get over with sooner rather than later. And the most obvious sign was his growing obsession with the military.

It had gone far beyond video games and into the real world. That its roots were in his connection to Earl, who'd achieved the rank of Lieutenant Colonel in the Army Special Forces and served in Vietnam, had been clear for a few years. Right after the 2004 Masters, only a month after we'd begun working together, Tiger went to Fort Bragg, North Carolina, to do four days of Army special-operations training. With Earl in attendance, Tiger did two tandem parachute jumps, engaged in hand-to-hand combat exercises, went on four-mile runs wearing combat boots, and did drills in a wind tunnel. Tiger loved it, but Keith Kleven went a little crazy worrying about the further damage Tiger might be doing to his left knee.

Tiger's military activities now began to take the form of two- or three-day sessions at naval and marine outposts involving exercises with Navy SEALs teams, and would increase dramatically. Less than two weeks after Earl's funeral and three weeks before the 2006 U.S. Open at Winged Foot, he'd gone to installations near San Diego for a three-day session in parachuting. In my long e-mail to Tiger after that tournament, here is what I said:

> With the US Open 18 days away, do you think it was a good idea to go on a Navy SEALs mission? You need to get that whole SEALs thing out of your system and stick to playing Navy SEAL on the video games. I can tell by the way you are talking and acting that you still want to become a Navy SEAL. Man, are you crazy? You have history to make in golf and people to influence and help. Focus on your destiny, and that isn't flushing bad guys out of buildings in Iraq, just play the video games some more. That Navy SEAL stuff is serious business, they use real bullets.

I took a dismissive tone in that e-mail because I really thought the military stuff was a phase that Tiger would soon realize was ridiculous. I was trying to shake him back to his senses regarding this G.I. Joe fantasy. But a year later, I realized I'd underestimated. When we were at his house and he was watching the Military Channel or the BUD/S (Basic Underwater Demolition/SEALs) DVD, an exercise or training mission would catch his eye and he'd make a comment like, "That would be cool," or "I'd really like to do that." He was telling me that this SEAL thing was more than fun and games to him. One morning I was in the kitchen when he came back from a long run around Isleworth, and I noticed he was wearing Army boots. Tiger admitted that he'd worn the heavy shoes before on the same route. "I beat my best time," he said.

The military became central to his life, and in 2007 Tiger probably went on half a dozen SEALs trips. When the new season began, one of Tiger's first public acts was to visit a "special warfare" SEALs unit on the Tuesday of Torrey Pines. According to news reports, he told the assembled group at a facility in Coronado, outside San Diego, "If I hadn't been in golf, I would have been here with you guys. When I was younger, I always dreamed of being a Navy SEAL." The first PGA Tour event where he was named host—the 2007 AT&T National—took place outside Washington, D.C., over the July 4 weekend and allowed active military personnel into the gates free.

I was beginning to realize that his sentiment ran deep, and that as incredible as it seemed, Tiger was seriously considering actually becoming a Navy SEAL. I didn't know how he'd go about it, but when he talked about it, it was clear that he had a plan. After finding out that the Navy SEAL age limit is 28, I asked Tiger about his being too old to join. "It's not a problem," he said. "They're making a special age exception for me."

I thought, *Wow. Here is Tiger Woods, the greatest athlete on the planet, maybe the greatest athlete ever, right in the middle of his prime, basically ready to leave it all behind for a military life.* It was Pat Tillman times 100. The only thing that probably rivals it in sports history is Michael Jordan leaving basketball to play minor league baseball. Although Tiger ultimately didn't enlist, the lengths to which he went to make a SEALs career a real possibility still stun me.

Tiger formed close connections with some ex-SEALs. One was someone whom Tiger would eventually hire as his family and personal bodyguard. The guy had accompanied Tiger on the Torrey Pines visit, and he seemed to be a kind of liaison who was smoothing Tiger's path toward the military.

He was a muscular guy around 40 with a short haircut and an intense expression. While he was working for Tiger, with duties that included giving Tiger and Elin lessons in self-defense, he'd sometimes stay at the house in Isleworth. In fact, my first meeting with him took place when I got to Isleworth past midnight after a late flight from Dallas. I didn't have a key to Tiger's house, but Tiger would leave the door unlocked whenever I came in late. This time, I opened it quietly, only to find the guy peering at me through the darkness with one of those scary Navy SEALs looks. I assumed he wasn't expecting me, so I just said, "Hi, I'm Hank." The guy was staying in the bedroom I normally used, so after an awkward introduction he helped me choose another one.

I talked to the guy only a couple more times, and never in depth. He didn't volunteer much, and I didn't probe. Steve Williams had been around him more, and he told me he didn't like his influence on Tiger. He thought the self-defense stuff and other working out with Tiger that the guy was doing could get Tiger hurt. He also thought the guy was weird. Steve said the guy told him that Earl was speaking to him on a regular basis and giving him instructions on how to help Tiger. Steve said he played dumb and asked him, "You mean Earl, Tiger's father, who died last year?" Steve said the guy answered, "Yeah."

Tiger's SEALs exercises were scheduled on the calendars of his inner circle, but everyone knew not to talk about them to anyone. Unlike Tiger's first trip to Fort Bragg, in 2004, or his PR-oriented visit to the SEALs around the time of Torrey Pines, the other SEALs visits were kept quiet by the Navy. It was understood that if the extent of Tiger's military activities got out, it would start a media frenzy.

I was never totally clear on the exact nature of Tiger's sojourns. All I'm sure about is that it was more than some kind of risk-free fantasy camp. Tiger didn't tell me a lot, but from what he did tell me and what Corey Carroll, who joined him on several trips, confirmed, he was participating in a program that approximated the training for a Navy SEAL candidate. The purpose was a sort of "dry run" to determine whether he could physically and mentally handle the demands, and if so, whether he wanted to go forward with actually becoming a Navy SEAL.

To my knowledge, he did training in parachuting, self-defense, urban-warfare simulations, and shooting. I never heard of Tiger doing any training in the water with the SEALs, but he was already a pretty accomplished diver. He had his scuba certification and had also done a lot of free diving to depths of more than 100 feet. He claimed to be able to hold his breath a long time—up to four minutes. Supposedly, he used a technique called "lung packing," in which lung capacity is increased through "swallowing" air after inhaling to capacity.

When I asked Tiger how his trips had gone, he might confirm having completed a training session in a specific discipline by making a comment like, "Yeah, I knocked that out," as if he was passing progressive steps. When he shared some things about the experience, it was clear from phrases like "total rush" and "intense" that it was all a thrill.

Tiger said that a three-day trip that was focused on parachuting might include as many as ten jumps a day. He'd jump solo or in tandem. Corey told me that Tiger once hurt his shoulder in a tandem jump when he smashed into his partner in midair.

Tiger came back almost boastful from his firearms training, saying that he'd excelled in long-range marksmanship. He talked all about the different guns and how to allow for wind and the flight of the bullet, almost as if he were describing a golf shot.

Self-defense stuff was a favorite topic. He'd gotten more into it as fatherhood approached, telling me that he really wanted to be able to protect his family and his home if anything ever happened. After his training, he explained about the different martial arts that are incorporated into the SEALs style of hand-to-hand combat. Once, in his living room in Isleworth, he had me stand up so he could demonstrate some moves. He got me in one position with his arm around my neck where I couldn't really move. "From here," he said, "I could kill you in about two seconds." I kind of laughed and said, "Please don't." But hearing those words from Tiger was creepy.

Maybe the most dangerous-sounding exercise that Tiger engaged in with the SEALs involved what was called a Kill House, an urban-warfare simulator full of rooms, doors, and even pop-up targets used to train for rescues, captures, and other team operations.

Tiger told me he actually got shot with a rubber bullet in a Kill House exercise. He said he failed to look around a corner before moving into an open area and was shot in the thigh. "I screwed up," he said. "In a real mission I probably would have gotten some of my squad killed." Then he proudly showed me a bruise the size of a baseball. I said, "That had to really hurt." He answered with a smile: "It still hurts."

Though I stayed pretty calm on the outside, my inner reaction was shock. I'd ask myself if these conversations were really happening. And there were times when I couldn't contain my exasperation. "Tiger," I'd say. "Man, what are you doing? Are you out of your mind? What about Nicklaus's record? Don't you care about that?" He looked at me and said, "No. I'm satisfied with what I've done in my career." End of discussion. He knew how we all felt, but he wasn't going to debate it.

There is a strong likelihood that a Kill House is where Tiger did serious damage to his career. In early 2011, about a year after I stopped coaching Tiger, I was in Minneapolis doing an outing when a woman approached me and said her husband was a Navy SEAL stationed in California when Tiger would come in. She said that one day in 2007 her husband called and told her, "Tiger was in here today, doing an exercise at the Kill House. He got in the wrong place and got kicked pretty hard in the leg, and I think he hurt his knee pretty bad."

I had filed that astounding story away under the category "Unsolved Tiger Woods Mysteries." But recently I was communicating with Corey when he told me that Tiger once confessed to him that the complete tear of his ACL had actually occurred in a Kill House exercise in which he had lost his balance and been kicked in the knee.

My immediate thought upon hearing Corey's account, which so closely paralleled that of the woman in Minneapolis, was that it was true. And if so, it meant that if Tiger never catches Jack Nicklaus, it will very likely have as much to do with the time and physical capacity he lost as a result of his bizarre Navy SEALs adventure as anything else.

The recklessness of Tiger's military adventures made me wonder whether he had self-destructive urges when it came to his golf. Joining the SEALs would have been, if not the end, at least a major interruption of his career. And yet he definitely had some kind of plan that made me believe he might really do it. Steve and Keith thought the same thing. But when I told Mark Steinberg that this was a serious possibility, he couldn't seem to process it. "He's not going to do that," he said. "There is no way. He can't. He's got obligations. He's got to pay for that sixty-million-dollar house," referring to the beachfront property near Palm Beach where Tiger and Elin were building a new house.

Tiger never went into the motivation for his military obsession. I got a better understanding after talking to one of my good friends, Ken Hitchcock, who at the time was the coach of the Columbus Blue Jackets in the National Hockey League. Ken has been around a lot of elite athletes and was always interested in Tiger. When I told Ken about Tiger's military fixation, he said very confidently that it related to Earl being an ex-soldier. "It happens a lot with our players," he said. "Their fathers die, and they have the urge to go back to their hometowns and do what their dads did: work in a coal mine, fix cars, whatever. It usually lasts about six months." Ken pointed out that baseball had been Michael Jordan's father's favorite sport.

It made sense. Tiger had very seldom brought up Earl while he was alive, but since his death the previous May, he'd started speaking about his father a lot more. Sometimes he'd talk about his dad's military career and how Earl taught Tiger to always complete the mission. Or he'd repeat Earl's golf lessons, saying wistful things on the practice range. Once, on the range at Isleworth, Tiger was struggling with a new move I wanted him to try, and he said, "My dad always said I was a slow learner."

Tiger also started allowing another distraction to interfere with his practice. His cell phone was going off a lot more, and whereas before, he either turned it off or simply ignored it, now he was taking time to answer it or check out the texts. He always used a flip phone, which allowed more privacy as far as the number or message being readily visible. Of course, the whole world would eventually see and hear some of the messages, but at the time, I never suspected that he was texting women.

History would show this was a time when Tiger's affairs were going pretty strong, and they couldn't have done much for his peace of mind. As he said at the Masters in 2010, "When you live a life where you're lying all the time, life is not fun."

In early 2007, Tiger had to deal with a thorny problem. According to sources in a December 2009 story in the *Wall Street Journal,* the *National Enquirer* obtained photos of Tiger having an encounter with a woman in a parking lot near his home, sometime in the late winter or early spring of 2007. This led to an alleged deal in which American Media, the owners of the tabloid, agreed not to publish the photos in exchange for Tiger's doing a cover story for the American Media magazine *Men's Fitness.* The interview for the fitness magazine, which centered on Tiger's workout but also talked about fatherhood and his marriage, was done in May, and Tiger appeared on the cover of the August issue. When it came out, I wondered why Tiger went public about his workout, which he'd always kept so private. I was hoping that it was to give some credit to Keith, but that wasn't the case. He'd been forced to do it. Although neither Tiger nor Mark ever said anything to me about this crisis, in hindsight, Tiger had to have been quite stressed, contemplating the possibility of his world somehow falling apart.

Amid all this chaos, Tiger—incredibly—kept performing at an extremely high level. After winning at Doral, he went into the 2007 Masters with victories in eight of his last 10 official events. The media was again writing about him as if he was without peer, declaring that he'd conquered his latest swing changes, but most of all, that his biggest advantage was mental. Fellow players Stewart Cink, for example, said, "I think we should cut him open and find out what's inside."

However, at the Masters, Tiger seemed particularly stressed. In my experience, Tiger was always more tense at majors. It was the reason he'd often get sick before the tournament, coming down with a cold, flu, or headache. At Augusta, he had the additional problem of dealing with heavy spring pollen that made his allergies act up.

But Tiger was more noticeably impatient in 2007. The week before, on the practice tee at Isleworth, he seemed to challenge me more often. It was on the range that I always felt the most pressure teaching Tiger, because it was where I had to prove I knew what I was talking about. If Tiger hit a shot that flew a certain way and then immediately asked, "OK, what was the cause of that?" I had to have a good answer. Usually, I had about 30 seconds to explain what happened and how to correct it before he hit the next one. And then if the fix didn't make sense to him or the next shot wasn't a good one, I knew that he was going to file that away.

The stakes were high, because depending on when it occurred, a bad shot on the range could ruin a whole practice session and be a confidence killer. And when Tiger left a session, he had to feel sure that he knew the cause of a swing issue, and more important, what he was going to do to address it in his next session or round.

Tiger came to Augusta hitting the ball pretty well, but I still felt put on the spot. In the practice rounds, Tiger hadn't been happy with his putting, but on Wednesday evening when we met on the practice tee he told me he was really excited about how he had just rolled the ball on the putting green. I asked him what he changed, and he said that Mark O'Meara had watched him hit some putts and suggested that he put more weight on his left foot at address. Tiger said it worked and that he was making everything. I didn't really know what more weight on his left foot was going to do, but a lot of putting is mental, so I figured that if Tiger thought it would help it probably would. As it turned out, though, his mind was eased only temporarily.

On the morning of the first round, Tiger went to the putting green for a quick session before going to the range. He didn't like me hovering around him when he was putting, so I'd stand off to the side of the green with Steve Williams and wait. But Tiger was missing some short putts, and he kind of waved me in. "It doesn't feel good," he said. When I wondered about the fix of more weight on the left foot, he tersely said, "That's not working." Because I thought I detected a very small inside-to-out loop in his backswing, I suggested he try to do the opposite with a slight outside-to-in loop. He tried it for a few minutes, but as he left to go to the range, he told me quietly but in a hard tone, "You better fucking figure something out before we get back here."

I was used to Tiger being sullen, but he'd never snapped at me before. I was kind of stunned, but just figured, *Man, he is really nervous.* It was so out of character that I actually found it kind of funny. After Tiger had warmed up on the range, we came back to the putting green, where I offered the same advice I'd given him 45 minutes before, which he accepted without comment.

It was a Masters in which the course was very difficult because of wind and firmness. Since 2002, Augusta National had been lengthened and redesigned twice, and it was pretty obvious that the changes hadn't helped Tiger. The extra length didn't hurt him, but the narrowed landing areas for the tee shots did. In the old design, three of the par-5 holes—the second, thirteenth, and fifteenth—had allowed Tiger to smash the ball off the tee without much fear and position himself for easy birdies. Now those holes required a much more accurate drive. Whether the club's leadership realized it or not, the changes more fully exposed Tiger's weakness with the driver.

In round one, he sprayed his drives on the final two holes and closed with two bogeys to shoot 73. In the second round, he hit shots into Rae's Creek on the twelfth and thirteenth holes and shot 74. On Saturday, he again bogeyed the final two holes to shoot 72. Still, the course was playing so hard that when Tiger teed off on Sunday, he was only a stroke out of the lead.

Tiger started strong and actually went into a tie for the lead on the fourth hole. But then he hit some poor shots, making bogeys on the sixth and the tenth. He eagled the thirteenth with a great 5-iron to three feet. But he didn't make a birdie the rest of the way. He shot 72 and finished tied for second, two behind Zach Johnson, who'd closed with a 69. Tiger students noticed that he finally didn't win a major after taking a Sunday lead. Once again, three-putts had been his undoing.

Whenever Tiger didn't win at Augusta, I'd just leave after the final round without saying good-bye. He wouldn't be in the mood to go over his performance, so I'd go back to Dallas and wait for him to call or text me. When we got together in person a couple of weeks later at Isleworth, we discussed the Masters. I didn't want the way he'd snapped at me to linger in any kind of negative way, so I chose a light moment to say, "By the way, that was nice before the first round—your saying you were going with the weight on the left leg and then telling me I'd better fuckin' figure something out." Tiger only laughed, his way of saying he was sorry.

He won his next tournament, at Quail Hollow in Charlotte. The victory was notable for the comments of the runner-up, Rory Sabbatini, who said this of Tiger: "I've seen Tiger where there is not a facet of his game that you're not amazed by. But I think, Sunday, he struggled out there. He had to battle for that win. And I think that made me realize . . . he's as beatable as ever. I've seen him when he figures it out. It's scary. I don't want to see that anymore. I like the new Tiger."

Tiger would use those words for motivation later, but in the short term, like everything said about Tiger, it caused a stir. Despite his finishing first at Quail Hollow, because he hadn't won at the Masters, the comments got some traction. And when Tiger played mediocre golf at the Players, tying for 37th, and had an ordinary performance at the Memorial, tying for 15th, where he'd won three times before, there was more talk that he wasn't what he had been, and that his new swing wasn't as good as his old one.

Maybe Tiger was right. Whatever he did was never going to be enough.

I started to notice that he seemed more consumed with his workouts. Lifting sessions were a major part of how he filled out his off-season time, and when Tiger showed up at Torrey Pines for the start of the 2007 season, his upper body and biceps looked bigger and more defined than ever. The tighter fit of Nike's latest styles enhanced the effect, especially because Tiger also wore a size medium shirt, which for a buff guy weighing 185 pounds is pretty snug. Tiger told me he actually got up to over 190 pounds for a short time.

I thought that, for a golfer, Tiger was inordinately interested in muscle-building. He had a lot of muscle magazines in his house, and he'd read the articles. No doubt he was well built and looked great in clothes. But my view was that it didn't help his golf. To me the best golf body is lean and flexible. The only place big upper-body muscles arguably help is in the rough, but even that is marginal. I'd never seen anyone get appreciably longer off the tee by developing bigger muscles in the weight room. I'd also seen a lot of guys get injured lifting weights and really damage their games, the most prominent being David Duval.

I'd questioned Tiger on the effects of his working out so heavily in my long e-mail the previous year, writing,

> You seem like you're determined to get too big before you realize that you are too big, and then you will do something about it. That is your pattern. Realize it and don't let it happen. You are already the fittest guy on the planet. Isn't that enough?

But I didn't keep pressing him on the subject, mostly because I didn't think he'd listen. Anyway, I could tell that the lifting was important to Tiger. I reminded myself that it was another thing that was different about him, which probably meant it was another reason he was better. And there were definitely some positives to be gained. I know that Tiger believed the mental discipline required in hard training made his mind tougher in competition, that by paying the price in the gym he earned success on the course. And it also made sense that all that physical exertion and concentration relieved stress.

But I wasn't alone in being skeptical about Tiger getting bigger. Steve Williams thought Tiger was getting close to muscle-bound and that it was affecting his touch in the short game and in putting. Keith Kleven always held to the view that Tiger was naturally slender and small-boned, more like a racehorse than a Clydesdale, and didn't have the frame to carry too much weight without risking injury. Keith would have liked Tiger to drop 10 pounds and especially stay away from lifting heavy weight with low reps. My advice to Keith was to keep changing Tiger's workout in a way that would achieve the objectives they were after, but that was still different enough that Tiger wouldn't get bored or try to experiment or increase the load. This was what I tried to do with golf practice to keep him eager. For Tiger, as Butch found out and Keith was finding out, *maintenance* was the poison word. But I think being in Las Vegas made it difficult for Keith to monitor Tiger, and there was no guarantee he'd listen anyway.

Keith really got worried when Tiger started incorporating a lot of military training into his workouts. Keith believed the exercises Tiger saw on the Navy SEALs DVDs were overly hard on the joints, especially the pull-ups that are such a big part of military workouts. Corey Carroll told me that Tiger did a lot of pull-ups whenever he worked out with Navy SEALs, and Corey believed that Tiger had strained his shoulder more than once. Most trainers want their golfers to have loose shoulder joints unencumbered by a lot of muscle, and they're careful to avoid strain on the rotator cuff.

But Tiger was adamant that all his injuries came from golf, never from his workouts or military stuff. In the *Men's Fitness* article, he maintained that he always lifted light with high reps and had never injured himself. "I've never, ever hurt myself lifting," he told the magazine. "I hear people say, 'I hurt this,' or 'I hurt that,' I don't even know what that feels like. I've been sore, but I've always been able to function and do whatever I wanted to. A lot of people have had injuries or been so sore they can't do anything. I've never experienced that. Some people let their ego get in the way. You have to listen to your inner self. Your body knows what it can and can't handle."

In the time I coached him, I never saw Tiger get hurt from playing golf. He might wince after hitting a practice shot, sit there and make a face until the pain subsided. But he'd never say why the pain was there, and he'd start hitting again without a problem. Except for a short period after his surgery in April 2008, when he was getting ready to play in the U.S. Open at Torrey Pines, and after his major surgery following that event, I never saw his swing speed go down, never saw flexibility restricted, never saw his ability to hit shots physically impaired in a noticeable way.

On the other hand, I witnessed at least one occasion when Tiger ended a fitness workout limping. One afternoon in the summer of 2007, I was coaching him through a practice session on the range at Isleworth when he took a break and went home. When he did this, sometimes I'd move over to watch Corey hit balls, or even hit some myself, until Tiger came out again to finish the session. About five p.m., Tiger came back in a workout outfit wearing a weighted vest. He then ran the length of the practice tee, about 60 yards, in a full sprint. He then walked back and did it again, until he had completed 10 wind sprints and was drenched in sweat.

After about the fifth wind sprint, I noticed Tiger was limping as he walked back. I couldn't help myself and said, "Tiger, you're limping. C'mon, what are you doing?" He said, "No, I'm fine. This helps me build up [body] speed." He said he got the idea for the workout from his friend Vencie Glenn, a former defensive back for the San Diego Chargers, who sometimes visited Tiger in Orlando. The source of this advice was ironic, because in the past I'd heard Tiger make comments about how NFL guys broke down their bodies not just with the hitting in the games but also through the intensity of their workouts, and here he was doing something an NFL guy did.

It seemed that the harder the workout was, the more enthusiastic Tiger would get about its possibilities. But Keith and I both believed that such an approach would inevitably have a bad end.

By this time I had begun to doubt that Tiger's knee complaints were brought on by golf. He would soon tell *Golf Digest* that the original injury to his left knee was caused by skateboarding spills when he was a kid. If that was true, then it seemed likely that his habit of hyperextending his left knee at impact, a move he blamed on Butch, hadn't had much to do with his problem. If I had known that to be the case, I wouldn't have tried to immediately eliminate the straightening move altogether, because it was an action that Tiger was used to and it had helped him fade the ball and keep it in play. Instead, I would have tried to gradually install some knee flex at impact—for purely technical rather than injury-prevention reasons—which I think would have made Tiger's transition to my teaching less drastic and lessened our early struggles.

Of course, Tiger still could have worsened his knee with heavy workouts or Navy SEALs activities. But Tiger preferred that people see his injuries related to his sport, so that he could wear them as an athletic badge of honor. To him, injuries were a way of being accepted into the fraternity of superstars who played more physical sports than golf. For example, a couple of times when I knew he'd just gotten off the phone with Derek Jeter, I'd asked what they had talked about. Both times Tiger said the conversation was about injuries they were each dealing with. Once in the clubhouse at Isleworth, Shaquille O'Neal came by the lunch table and exchanged pleasantries with Tiger. When Tiger asked him how he was doing, Shaq said, "Trying to get through this thing with my knee," and Tiger had nodded knowingly.

Until Tiger came along, professional golfers were never really considered athletes in the same sense as football, baseball, and basketball players. For a long time, a popular debate was, "Are golfers athletes?" It didn't seem to matter that, growing up, a lot of them had been very good in other sports. The stereotype was that golfers were mostly out-of-shape white guys. It really wasn't until Tiger that the whole perspective on golfers changed. Earl Woods had a lot to do with it when he called Tiger the first "golfer who is a true athlete." That was actually a ridiculous statement, but it caught on. I believe the biggest reason it did was because of Tiger's black heritage. Though other sports had a preponderance of black athletes, golf remained almost exclusively white. Yet here was Tiger, about the only black man in the sport, and the best player by a lot. To the casual eye, it wasn't a coincidence, and there were always narrow-minded sports fans out there who believed a black athlete "got by" on physical talent rather than work ethic or smarts. Golf stereotypes were bad enough, but racial stereotypes took even longer to die.

At the same time, Tiger took a lot of pride in changing the way pro golfers are perceived. He liked being one of Nike's so-called golf athletes. He liked being considered buff. He liked using terms from other sports, like "reps," "game speed," "taking it deep," or "getting good looks," and applying them to golf. And he liked the impression that his swing was so violently athletic that it put him on constant guard against injury.

It got to the point where Steve Williams and Mark Steinberg would just roll their eyes when Tiger had another injury complaint. I'd be concerned, because if he *was* hurt, I didn't want to make it worse by having him hitting shots or making certain swing moves. But Steve would tell me, "Don't worry about it. It's always something."

I thought Tiger was more susceptible to the whole injury drama because of his self-image. It occurred to me that he never forgot being the skinny kid who was an outsider. Even though he was a golfing prodigy, he was never the popular jock or the big man on campus. He was the nerdy kid with glasses and braces, the golfer who wore uncool clothes. When Tiger first got to Stanford, Notah Begay called him Urkel, after the hopelessly geeky character on *Family Matters.*

In that context, it's not surprising that Tiger overcompensated by putting big muscles on his narrow frame. In the *Men's Fitness* story, Tiger said that he'd really wanted to put on weight in his early 20s but hadn't been able to. It wasn't until his mid-20s that he was able to "lay down muscle." He said, "It was exciting. I'd never experienced that before." As Mark Calcavecchia, who is friendly with Tiger, once said, "He wants us all to think he's Superman."

Eventually, the two people most in charge of his body thought he overdid it. Keith Kleven always wanted Tiger to be leaner. After performing ACL surgery on Tiger in 2008, Dr. Thomas Rosenberg would recommend that he get down to 165 pounds. Tiger told me that and said, "No way."

He was a long hitter, and he enjoyed that image. When the great majority of players switched to hybrids, Tiger continued to carry a 2-iron—the most macho club in the bag. He insisted on using the "spinniest" ball, contending he needed it to be aggressive around the green. I didn't agree, and one day when I challenged him by asking, "Why do you need this ball?" he said, "Chicks dig the spin." We laughed, but I began to think that there was something to it.

When Tiger would eventually get out of control with women, he knew that racking up "conquests" played big in the jock culture. In the end, having once been a bit nerdy, Tiger had too much to prove, not just to others but to himself. A friend of mine has called what happened to Tiger a "geek tragedy."

Tiger had always been such a detail-oriented person, and yet I began to think that his preoccupations were causing him to become careless. One example occurred before the 2007 U.S. Open at Oakmont. About a month before the championship, mutual friend Tom Barton arranged for Tiger to play a practice round at the course with one of its most prominent members, Stan Druckenmiller. Stan is one of the richest men in America and one of the most charitable. In 2006, he gave $25 million to the Harlem Children's Zone, which helps disadvantaged kids and their families. He's a huge golf fan. To ensure that Oakmont got the U.S. Open, he wrote a check in the neighborhood of $800,000 to build a spectator bridge across the Pennsylvania Turnpike.

Stan was an admirer of Tiger and had long wanted to play with him. He's also a single-digit handicapper who knows Oakmont's famous greens inside out and might have been able to offer some suggestions that could help Tiger with his preparation. But where Stan could *really* help Tiger was with his foundation. Before we played, I told Tiger all about Stan.

We had a great day. Tiger and Stan, who is very personable, got along very well. After the round ended, Tom, who understands the world of charitable donations, told me, "OK, here's how this thing can work. Tiger should play with Stan one more time in the future, and at that time he should ask him to be on his board. Stan would love to do that, and he'd be very good at it. And if that happened, there's no doubt that Stan would open the doors to a lot of money getting donated to Tiger's foundation."

The foundation was important to Tiger. He put on two annual events, his Tiger Jam in Las Vegas and his Block Party in Anaheim, California. Tiger told me the Block Party netted about $400,000 a year. When I told Tiger about the opportunity with Stan, he nodded. But to my knowledge he never played with Stan again or asked him to join his board.

Tiger played solidly at Oakmont, a course where ball-striking matters. Elin was back in Orlando in the last days of her pregnancy, with the birth expected early the following week. The baby would come earlier than expected. Tiger never said anything to me about

Elin experiencing any problems, but he did seem distracted. In the tournament he got off to a slow start of 71 and 74 that put him five behind. And on Saturday, he hit the first seventeen greens but missed the eighteenth to finish with a deflating bogey for a 69 that should have been 65. Still, he was only two behind the leader, Aaron Baddeley, whom he'd be paired with in the final round.

After Baddeley made a triple bogey on the first hole, which Tiger parred, Tiger was in a tie for the lead with Stephen Ames. But on the par-4 third hole, Tiger went over the green with his approach. He faced a difficult shot, because if he didn't hit it hard enough, it would roll back to his feet. Instead, he did the opposite, blading the chip across the green into heavy rough, and took three more to get down for double bogey. It was a big miss.

He fought back at the fourth, but it was his last birdie of the day. He trailed by one when he got to the seventeenth hole, a drivable par 4. He put his 3-wood into the right greenside bunker, leaving a 25-yard bunker shot. Tiger appeared to have a good lie, but his ball shot out too far and without much spin, forcing him to chip and one-putt for his par. At Oakmont, Tiger got up and down from greenside sand only three times out of ten. If he had been able to achieve just an average conversion rate of 50 percent, it would have given him a one-stroke victory.

In that final round, Tiger hit a good drive on the eighteenth, but it kicked right and rolled off the edge of the fairway. From the rough, he couldn't get enough spin on the ball to keep it by the pin, and his wedge shot didn't stop until it was 25 feet past the hole. To tie Angel Cabrera, Tiger was left with the kind of double-breaking putt that makes Oakmont's greens so difficult. He looked it over from every angle, and trickled the downhiller toward the hole. It hung to the right and never came back, stopping a foot away.

It was the second major championship in a row where Tiger had a piece of the lead on Sunday but failed to win—the first two times that had happened to him. Even more than he had at the Masters, Tiger felt he'd let this one get away.

"Man, is he hot," Steve said as we waited for Tiger to clean out his locker. On the ride to the airport, Tiger barely spoke. Before we boarded Tiger's plane to Orlando, Steve said, "It's going to take a while to get over this one."

By the time we landed in Orlando at about eleven p.m., Tiger was in a better mood but hadn't said anything about Elin's condition. We said good-bye, and I went to stay in a hotel because I had an early flight out. I later learned that Tiger went straight to the hospital and that Elin had given birth within an hour of his arrival. The next morning, a couple of minutes before the press release went out, he called me in Dallas and told me about his new daughter, Sam. It was a short conversation, but he sounded genuinely happy. Whenever I've seen Tiger with Sam, and later with his son, Charlie, he's been a doting father.

The U.S. Open made two straight majors in which poor putting had cost Tiger the W. He seemed to be trying to remember his father's lessons about putting by saying them to me more often—mostly Earl's favorite, "Putt to the picture"—but it was as if Tiger felt he was missing the one person he could trust on the subject to check on him.

He was so consistent and so correct in his form that, for the most part, I left his putting alone. He occasionally lapsed into a tendency to aim too far to the left with his shoulder alignment, but that was about it as far as flaws went. Still, he often doubted his putting and always blamed his mechanics. I'd arranged to have installed in Tiger's house a SAM Puttlab—a computer that graphically traced the putting stroke as well as measured 28 different putting parameters. It was a device on which hundreds of tour pros had been measured, and Tiger had achieved the most consistently solid impact. My suggestion to Tiger was to record his good stroke and use the machine as a reference point when he got a little bit off. We recorded his stroke when he first got the SAM, but as far as I know, he never used the computer again, despite my urging.

But I didn't do a lot of worrying about Tiger's putting. In 2011,

PGA Tour statistics would retroactively show that in the new and revealing "strokes saved putting" category, throughout my time coaching Tiger he was consistently one of the three best putters on the tour. To me, it was about his eliminating the occasional unforced error—the silly three-putt from a relatively short distance. It all came down to Tiger doing the necessary work on the greens. When Tiger practiced his putting, he putted well.

The trouble was that as Tiger's devotion to the weight room was going up, his golf work ethic was diminishing. It wasn't a big drop-off, but I noticed it. He wasn't as focused, and he wasn't giving the extra effort he used to give before major championships. Even Steve seemed to be getting a bit complacent. Rather than urging Tiger to hit balls after rounds, he was preaching more rest.

Steve privately told me that he didn't see the point in Tiger's putting more time in on the practice range. Tiger always hit the ball well on the range, Steve said, so what was the point? But implied in this view was that Tiger was having a harder time taking his range game to the course, something I was beginning to notice as well.

I agreed that there was more than just a waning of physical effort involved. There was a big psychological component as well. In my mind, its root was the enormous pressure on Tiger to perform, and the wearing effect that had on his ability to be truly great. Tiger showed some self-awareness in continuing to bring up "Ranger Rick," his nickname for himself as a player who hit the ball beautifully on the practice range but not in competition. Usually the comment came across as a bid for a laugh, but I saw in it an acknowledgment that he was feeling the pressure of being Tiger Woods.

So began a vicious cycle. Because it was discouraging and confidence-killing to see great practice not followed up on the course, Tiger began to become reluctant to be at his best in practice. Rather than hit it great and be disappointed later, he found that hitting it just OK in practice would make hitting it just OK on the course easier to take mentally. But this didn't confront Tiger's performance issue, and it also led to less practice altogether, which hurt his performance even more.

Tiger was so good that even with his practice drop-off he could still win with less than his best stuff. But that was harder to do at majors, where the conditions were most demanding. If I had to point to one reason Tiger won only two majors with me in our last three years, versus the four he won in the two years prior, it was work ethic.

The British Open at Carnoustie was a good example of Tiger's not being "there" enough to really focus and do the work. For the second major in a row, his sand play was shoddy, as he got up and down only twice in eight tries. Like putting, it was an area of the game in which Tiger excelled when he practiced hard, but quickly lost its sharpness when he didn't.

Tiger was in a bad mood all week. He was going for three claret jugs in a row, but it was not with a sense of joy. He was more resistant to me in practice, at one point dismissing a point I tried to make about his putting by saying, "My dad never said anything about that." Tiger also complained about pain in his right shoulder. When I asked him to describe its intensity on a scale of 10, he said, with total seriousness, "Nine-point-nine." And the tone of his complaints implied that the golf swing we were working on had caused the injury. I already knew about all the pull-ups he'd been doing, but I just let him vent.

A couple of weeks later, I'd ask Tiger about the shoulder, and he said he'd undergone an MRI that had found the "labrum was torn off the bone" along with rotator-cuff damage. From talking to Keith, I knew that was exaggerated, but I played along and asked, "Wow, that sounds really bad. I guess you're going to need surgery, huh?" He said that he'd be all right with some rehab and rest. I thought, *Labrum torn off the bone—yeah, right.*

At Carnoustie, Tiger opened with a pretty solid 69, but the course was playing soft and the scores were low. In the second round, his opening tee shot with a 2-iron had Ranger Rick written all over it. After striping that club on the range, Tiger hit an awful, low hook that shot way left and bounced out-of-bounds. He made double bogey, shot 74, and fell seven shots back. He could make up only a couple of shots on the leaders over the weekend with scores of 69 and 70, and finished tied for 12th.

I didn't think Tiger had the right game plan at Carnoustie. As he had the year before at Hoylake, Tiger chose to go mostly with a 2-iron off the tee. But Carnoustie is a bigger course than Hoylake, with wider landing areas and fairways that weren't running nearly as fast. It led a lot of players to hit driver off the tee, which meant Tiger was giving away a lot more yardage than he had at Hoylake. From where he was playing most of his approaches, it was hard to hit the ball close.

Tiger was smart enough to know that with his strategy he had to play almost perfect golf to win, and he simply didn't. I thought he should have gone with more drivers and 3-woods, but I was never asked. Tiger made his own game plans. He'd consult strategy with Steve and occasionally with me, but other than occasional over-aggression on the greens that could lead to three-putts, I always considered him a superb course manager who didn't need much help in that department. Carnoustie was the exception.

I think Tiger was influenced in his decision by the way he'd played at Hoylake, and also by so many commentators saying that the Hoylake victory proved that all he had to do to win was be in the fairway. I thought that was simplistic thinking. To me, he needed the driver more often at Carnoustie, but his lingering driving issues kept him from pulling the trigger on that club.

I met with Steve after the final round and found him depressed about Tiger's attitude. "We've just walked eighteen holes, and he spoke to me twice," he said. "The first time was on fifteen, where he goes, 'I think this chip might go right.' Then in the fairway on seventeen he says, 'It's getting colder out here, isn't it?' Like we'd been chatting all day. I don't know what his problem is, but he was horrible to me all week."

After Carnoustie, Tiger went home and kind of hunkered down. Several months later, he'd reveal that this was the period when he tore his ACL taking a bad step while running on a golf course. He never got any more specific than that about the injury and had never told me he hurt his knee. Short of getting an MRI, there was no way he could have known if the ACL was fully torn. But assuming it was, his subsequent vagueness, along with Corey's later account, makes me doubt Tiger's public version of how the injury occurred.

By this time, Mark Steinberg had acknowledged that Tiger's military obsession had to be confronted. Mark always hosted a dinner at his home near Cleveland the week of the WGC Bridgestone Invitational at Firestone in Akron, and he told me that it was where "I'm going to have a talk with Tiger." On Tuesday night, Tiger, Steve, and I met at Mark's home, and after dinner, he and Tiger went into Mark's downstairs office, where they spent about an hour.

I don't know what Mark told him, but afterward, Tiger was different. To my knowledge, he at least cut down on the military trips. It was a moment that proved to me that Mark had a good feel for how to reach Tiger, and on this occasion the message had gotten through.

As it turned out, Tiger went on to win the Bridgestone at Firestone. In the last round, he was paired with Rory Sabbatini, who had made the "he's as beatable as ever" comments after Tiger's April victory in Charlotte. Tiger accessed his A-game, shooting a 65 to Rory's 74, and won by eight. It was Tiger's favorite scenario, a silent beat-down of a cocky foe. "Everyone knows how Rory is," Tiger told the media. "I just go out there and let my clubs do the talking."

I'd left the tournament on Thursday because my wife at the

time, Jerilynn, was having health problems. It was a difficult situation that required my presence for an extended period of time. I wouldn't see Tiger again until December.

It was during this period that Tiger most demonstrated friendship toward me. We spoke on the phone nearly every day about his golf, but the conversation would also veer into the personal, and he was quite supportive. He'd inquire about Jerilynn's progress and ask me how I was holding up. He'd often say, "Don't worry about me, you've got more important things to deal with. Do what you gotta do."

Tiger's surprising empathy, and my temporary absence from tournaments, led me to imagine how our relationship might ideally evolve. I hoped for a situation where Tiger wouldn't feel he needed to see me in person as much, and certainly not as much at tournaments. I envisioned some long sessions at Isleworth to start the year to lay down a foundation and a plan, and perhaps a few others before and during the majors. The rest of the time we could check in by phone. I foresaw a modern-day version of what Jack Nicklaus had with his lifelong teacher, Jack Grout, who used to visit Nicklaus at the start of the year, then basically leave him alone unless Jack asked for help. The more self-sufficiency a player can manage, the better. A coach hovering all the time can be a crutch. I never felt I became that for Tiger, but as his knowledge of the plan became more sophisticated, I actually wanted him to need me less.

But in the meantime, Tiger started playing tremendously. He won the PGA at Southern Hills in Tulsa, a tight, classically designed course that I'd played many times in college. He used mostly 3-woods and 5-woods off the tee to find the wide part of the many doglegs, and when he had to, he got the driver in play as well. In the second round, Tiger shot a 63 that would have been a major-championship-record 62 if his 15-footer for birdie on the eighteenth hole hadn't gone all the way around the cup without falling.

Tiger and I were having productive phone conversations daily.

Before the final round, Tiger told me he felt in control. We went over the usual few swing keys, but I could tell it was one of those weeks when he didn't have many doubts.

Still, it wasn't easy on Sunday. After getting his lead up to six, he made some mistakes. When he bogeyed the fourteenth, he was up by only one. But that's when Tiger tapped the extra energy he saves for such occasions. He birdied the fifteenth, and then on the very long and difficult sixteenth, which required a driver to set up a reasonable approach, he made the "good swing" I always wanted him to trust and piped one down the middle. It was a proud moment for both of us, and Tiger showed his satisfaction with his trademark flourish, giving the club a hard twirl on the recoil of his follow-through.

He won by two, earning his 13th major championship and his fifth in the last 12. I would sense more relief from Tiger in the aftermath. He knew he was entering the home stretch toward Nicklaus's record, and the pressure was making the whole deal harder. No matter how well he played otherwise, a year without a major victory would be a disappointment, and he'd had to wait until the last one of the season to turn the year into a success.

The win at the PGA also relaxed me a little. My absence had already spawned rumors that Tiger and I were splitting, and if he hadn't won at Southern Hills, they would have grown louder. Because Tiger and I were communicating regularly, I wasn't threatened that Tiger had won without my being there. Still, the speculation got intense enough that Tiger finally decided it required a rare response. In late October, he wrote on his website:

> *Contrary to rumors, I have not split with Hank Haney, my friend and swing coach. He's spent more time at home helping his wife deal with health issues, which is the way it should be. Besides, I've become much better at correcting my swing flaws, and that's ultimately where you want to get to with a coach-pupil relationship. Hank is still going to be my coach; that's not changing.*

Tiger won four of his last five tournaments of 2007, finishing second in the other. He played as if on automatic. It wasn't perfect golf, though there were streaks of brilliance. Mainly it was beautifully managed play, the kind that avoids mistakes and produces one clean round after another. Above all, it was winning golf. In a way, the best thing I could say about it was that it didn't surprise me. He was that good, and I knew that what he was doing was well within his comfort zone.

After his victory at the Tour Championship in September, Tiger played only two more events, the Presidents Cup and his tournament at Sherwood, which he won again. He later said that he used the extra time to build up more leg muscle to protect his left knee, but that was the first I heard about anything like that. In fact, neither Tiger nor anyone in his inner circle gave me any indication his left knee was bothering him beyond the discomfort he'd periodically complained about for years. After Christmas, he even went on one more skiing trip, this time to Colorado with Elin and members of her family.

When he came back in 2008, Tiger picked up where he'd left off, winning his first three events. His latest streak of official victories ended at five when he finished fifth at Doral. Throughout, there was still nothing out of the ordinary that I could tell about Tiger's left knee. I was still working off what he'd told me in 2004, that he had only 20 percent of his ACL. I didn't know if he had any less, and certainly was unaware of the ACL's being completely torn. Tiger would occasionally grimace after a shot, but he'd been doing that since I'd begun working with him. He always went back to hitting without any apparent compensation.

Before Augusta, we spent our normal week at Isleworth. He'd gotten a good handle on his swing issues, including the head-dropping problem, and he was going with his "good swing" more often. I'd made some notes to myself, and one was: "Best I have ever seen him going into a major."

The first indications of Tiger having a serious physical problem came at the Masters. He'd said early in the week that his knee hurt, and when I inquired later, he said, "Nothing that some drugs can't take care of. I'm fine." I later learned from Keith Kleven that Tiger had taken Vicodin during the tournament, the first time to my knowledge Tiger had used that prescription drug during competition. Tiger again putted poorly at Augusta, his 120 putts eight more than winner Trevor Immelman, and Keith said strong painkillers can affect feel and touch. It was why Tiger resisted taking the same drugs two months later at the U.S. Open.

It was another frustrating Masters for Tiger. In the first round, he made an eagle on the fifteenth hole, but it was offset by his two-chip bogey on the par-5 thirteenth, his first bogey on a par 5 since the previous August. Until he made a 60-foot bomb on the eleventh on Sunday, his longest birdie putt of the week was a 12-footer on Saturday. However, he also missed from inside eight feet five times on Sunday.

In the final round, Tiger trailed by three when he came to the par-5 fifteenth hole looking for an eagle. He drove into the second cut right of the fairway. Steve told him a normal 5-iron would be enough. Tiger hit it solidly, but the ball landed on the front of the green and rolled back into the water. It was a rare mental error at a big moment, because Tiger knew that if he was going to miss on that hole, it had to be long. He saved par, but he'd needed at least a birdie. He finished three strokes behind Immelman, tied for second.

I didn't talk to Tiger until two days later, when he informed me that he was going to have arthroscopic surgery on his left knee. "Yeah, I'm going to have it cleaned out," he said. He still made no mention of a torn ACL. My sense of the surgery was that it was intended to be exploratory, to cut away and trim some worn cartilage and to assess the general state of the knee going forward. However, once Dr. Rosenberg went in, he found more damage than expected.

I was shocked to learn of the blown-out ACL. And also

saddened. Tiger was coming off a period when everything we'd worked on was solidifying and the wins were coming in bunches. He seemed to be over the distractions of 2007, and had reenergized his work ethic. He hadn't won at Augusta, but even in a loose performance he'd come excruciatingly close. He was right on the verge of achieving a level both of us had been waiting for, and now, heading into a U.S. Open on a course where Tiger had won more tournaments going back to junior golf than anywhere else, it seemed that all that momentum would be lost.

Golf historians may eventually argue that Tiger would never be quite as good again. Perhaps, but that didn't prevent him from achieving his greatest victory.

6

Highest Mountain

It's Sunday, May 18, 2008, a month after the knee operation, and I'm sitting at the dinner table with Tiger and Elin at their home in Isleworth. It's quieter than usual, as Elin has recently instituted a "no television" rule during dinner. Tiger has gone along with the prohibition, but if the intent of the change was to stimulate more conversation, it's not working tonight.

Tiger rises to get something to drink in the kitchen. About halfway there, he suddenly stops and grimaces, then bends over slightly with his eyes still closed. He holds this position for a full 20 seconds. It's the same pose that in a few weeks will become familiar to the millions who will watch the U.S. Open.

I look at Elin, who seems as surprised as I am. This isn't good.

I ask Tiger if he is all right. "I just landed on my foot wrong," he says. "I'm fine." But the strain in his voice belies the explanation. I don't want to go negative, but it just comes out. "Tiger, you can't even walk. How are you going to be able to play?"

I'd arrived in Orlando that day to initiate Tiger's reentry into competition, his target the Memorial Tournament in less than two weeks. That would be followed by the U.S. Open at Torrey Pines, the first round of which was June 12. It was the first day I'd seen Tiger since Sunday of the Masters. We'd spoken on the phone, and he'd indicated that his recovery was going well. But as soon as we got on the golf course, it was clear that he was having problems. He was hitting the ball poorly, but more tellingly, moving slowly with a halting gait. Somehow, he'd lost a lot.

His latest surgery had turned out to be a mixed bag. Although he never specified the reason for the procedure publicly, Tiger had wanted to alleviate pain that had been increasing from the effects of loose cartilage in his left knee joint. Dr. Thomas Rosenberg had cleaned out the cartilage, but he also discovered that Tiger's left anterior cruciate ligament (ACL)—the thick ligament that connects the thigh bone and the shin bone through the front of the knee joint—was fully torn. It meant that Tiger was without the normal ability to limit side-to-side motion or to keep the leg from straightening too much.

Rosenberg was the same doctor who'd found Tiger's left ACL to be badly deteriorated in 2002, when he operated on him to remove cysts from his knee. But while Rosenberg was well aware that Tiger would have ongoing knee issues, I was told that he was still surprised to find it fully torn. Tiger had played so well in late 2007 and early 2008, winning nine of 12 tournaments, with two seconds and a fifth, that Rosenberg had expected Tiger to still have a functioning ACL. Once Rosenberg was inside the knee, he considered repairing the ACL on the spot. He didn't because Tiger was unconscious and couldn't give his consent. A reconstruction at that time also would have meant that Tiger would have missed the remaining three majors of 2008. There was also the question of whether the new ligament would come from a cadaver or be grafted from the hamstring of the opposite leg, which is the way Tiger would eventually go.

After Rosenberg trimmed away the loose cartilage and left the ACL alone, the plan going forward was for Tiger to rest and rehabilitate for a few weeks, then return to competition and continue to manage the torn ACL through the year's three remaining majors. He would then undergo major reconstructive surgery and, if all went well, be ready to resume his assault on Jack Nicklaus's record at the 2009 Masters.

Unfortunately, there was an aspect of the plan that Tiger didn't consider.

What had allowed him to get by with a torn ACL were the exceptionally strong muscles surrounding his knee, which he'd strengthened with years of lower-body training. The muscles had acted as an imperfect but workable substitute for the ACL, providing enough stability to the knee joint that Tiger wasn't severely hampered as a golfer, though he would have been in a sport that required running, jumping, or contact.

However, the minor surgery changed things. Immediate atrophy after even minor invasive surgery is normal, and the muscles supporting Tiger's knee lost their strength as swelling, stiffness, and soreness set in. That caused the joint to become much less stable, to the point that the tips of the tibia, fibula, and femur began to touch where they met at the knee. Ideally, Tiger would have taken more time for his legs to regain their strength and again provide a stable cushion for the joint, but because he was determined to play at the U.S. Open, he began to train and practice while the atrophy was wreaking havoc.

If the U.S. Open hadn't been at Torrey Pines, he might not have rushed things. But the course on the cliffs of La Jolla was the site of more Tiger victories than any other. He'd begun accumulating titles there as a junior golfer, and after turning professional he'd won the PGA Tour event at Torrey Pines six times. Since I'd been his coach, Tiger had been victorious at the course each of the four times he'd played there. Torrey Pines' big dimensions suited Tiger. He knew the greens, and he could access winning memories. Torrey Pines had never before held the U.S. Open, and Tiger had been looking forward to the occasion and the opportunity for years.

When he began hitting balls again in mid-May, the jolt to his knee was more jarring than it had been when his surrounding muscles were strong. Despite hitting only a predesignated and reduced number of practice balls each day, and riding a cart as he played the course, the healing process was slow. Two weeks before the Memorial, on the eighteenth hole of a round at Isleworth, Tiger said he hit a 5-iron approach from a downhill lie and felt a crack below his left knee. I arrived two days later, and Tiger clearly wasn't in good shape. After seeing the state of Tiger's golf game and the way he doubled over in the kitchen, I didn't see how he'd be able to be ready for the Open, let alone the Memorial.

The next day, Tiger was worse. On the practice tee, he could hit only four or five balls without needing to sit down in the cart, and he was reduced to using his club as a cane to cover the few yards back to the seat. Certainly, Tiger had verbally exaggerated injuries in the past, but this was about action more than words. He wasn't complaining, he was just limping. Clearly discouraged, he informed me at lunch that he was pulling out of the Memorial. All his efforts would be focused on playing at Torrey Pines.

I returned home and came back to Orlando on Friday, May 30, after Tiger had undergone an MRI on his knee. The next day, Dr. Rosenberg came in from Utah to evaluate the results and consult with Tiger. He and an associate sat down in the middle of an L-shaped couch in the family room, Tiger and I on opposite ends.

Rosenberg opened his laptop on the coffee table and showed us the images, pointing to two small, dark lines at the top of the lower bone connecting to Tiger's knee. He said the lines represented stress fractures of the left tibia. As he was conveying the bad news, I could see Tiger taking on a blank look that didn't register any acknowledgment of the fractures. It was as if he were trying to will them away. With Tiger silent, I asked about how such stress fractures are normally treated. Rosenberg said the remedy was four to six weeks on crutches, followed by four more weeks of rehab. Doing the math, I calculated that that length of time would have Tiger still convalescing beyond the British Open and leave too little time to get ready for the PGA Championship in August. My thought was that our season was over, and there was now no point in waiting to fix the ACL.

Finally, Tiger spoke. "I'm playing in the U.S. Open," he said. "And I'm going to win it." His tone was so serious that Rosenberg didn't argue. "Tiger, you can try to play," he said. "There's not too much more damage you can do at this point. It's just a matter of how much pain you can take."

Tiger answered with a phrase that he'd repeat several times in the next month: "It's just pain." Then he started putting his golf shoes on. "C'mon, Hank," he said. "Let's go practice." Realizing that a decision had been made, Rosenberg urged Tiger not to hit full shots for a couple of days in order to let the pain from the stress fractures calm down. He also gave him an elaborate and bulky leg brace that injured football players commonly wear. Tiger put it on, and we rode out in a cart to the practice green, where he chipped and putted for about 45 minutes. The next day, he did the same thing.

On Monday, June 2, Tiger again began hitting balls, keeping the count below 50. It became very clear that the leg brace impaired his ability to transfer his weight from his right to his left side on the downswing. This caused his body rotation to stop, which in turn caused his hands to turn over prematurely in the hitting area. As a result, he was hooking the heck out of the ball. To counteract the brace, I further increased the anti-hook measures that I'd already installed, getting him to point the club farther to the left of the target at the top of his swing, and encouraging him to feel as if he was opening the clubface as he started down. I also reemphasized the importance of avoiding any cocking or tilting of his head on the backswing, urging him to keep his eyes level.

The brace was a major obstacle. That night I spoke to Mark Steinberg. I told him Tiger was giving it his best, but that in the end, I didn't think he was going to be able to play. Still, Tiger was expressing no doubt, and I realized that I'd never seen him exhibit so much quiet determination. On Tuesday, the day before we were scheduled to leave for California, I decided that if Tiger was going to pull this off, his attitude would have to be one designed to save, rather than expend, energy. "You're going to have to be the most patient you've ever been," I said. "Because of your leg, you're going to miss more shots, and you can't get all upset every time that happens. You're going to have to accept mistakes and move on." I was surprised how responsive he was to the message. "Yeah, you're right," he said. It was so different from the usual noncommittal blank stare. Something different was going on.

Early on Wednesday, Tiger and I flew in his plane from Orlando, arriving at the Carlsbad airport, about 30 miles north of San Diego, before noon. We made the short drive to Torrey Pines, and with no media or fans allowed on the course, Tiger played nine holes in a cart and wearing the brace. The level of his golf wasn't close to being good enough to contend in the U.S. Open. After the round, Tiger and I drove north about 50 miles. He was going to stay at his home on Newport Coast. I'd stayed there with him before, and thought I'd be doing so again. But in a switch, he told me on the drive up that I'd be in a nearby hotel that Tiger's office had already booked for me. I didn't think anything of it at the time, especially because it was a nice hotel.

The next day we played nine holes at Shady Canyon Golf Club

in Irvine with the cart and the brace. On Friday we went to Big Canyon Country Club in Newport Beach, where Tiger had been given playing privileges when he was a junior. He was still having trouble swinging with the brace but played a little more respectably. But on Saturday morning, he was terrible again. He sprayed shots over fences and into hazards, losing six balls in nine holes. He actually ran out of balls after hooking his second shot into the water on the ninth hole. But instead of expressing disgust, he kept his reaction amazingly light. "Wow, ran out of balls," he said after searching his golf bag. "Not good. Got a little work to do."

At lunch, Tiger took off his knee brace with a sense of finality, saying, "I can't play with this thing." As he was evaluating possibilities, I suggested that Tiger try walking nine holes that afternoon, something he hadn't done since his operation. "To be ready to play, you're going to have to start walking sooner or later," I said. "Let's see if you can." We agreed.

As we began the round with me driving the cart and Tiger walking alone down the fairway, I figured there was a good chance that without the brace, and having to stay continuously on his feet, Tiger would soon accept that his dream of playing the Open at Torrey was over. But free of the device, not only did he move pretty well, with just the slightest limp, but his swing was much freer and more rhythmic. He shot even par for the nine holes and hit a lot of good shots. His pain was manageable. It was a huge step forward, and Tiger got a charge out of it.

It was clear he was enjoying the challenge. Far from getting upset at poor shots, he was making a conscious effort to stay calm, accept the situation, and remain positive. It made me think of how much Tiger loved watching the video of the Navy SEALs' "Hell Week," when recruits are forced to endure being cold, hungry, wet, and sleep-deprived for five days and five nights or drop out of the program. It seemed to me that Tiger was framing his ordeal coming into the U.S. Open as his own Hell Week, reveling in accomplishing the mission. Also helping his perspective was that for one of the few times in his career, he wasn't facing crazy expectations. Because he was injured, the pressure to win was largely off, and he basically had a free run. It all gave him the perfect attitude—highly motivated but with little to lose.

On Sunday we drove back down Interstate 5 to Torrey Pines, where Tiger checked into a second-floor suite at the Lodge, adjacent to the course. Steve was waiting, and the three of us went to the par-5 ninth hole, which was the closest to the hotel, to start a practice round. Tiger promptly hooked his first drive over a boundary fence on the left, out-of-bounds. He turned to Steve, who hadn't seen him play since the Masters, and said in a deadpan voice, "Oh, yeah, I've got a new miss." Steve and I laughed at Tiger's gallows humor, and the mood remained positive.

After his bad first tee shot, Tiger played nine pretty good holes. One thing I noticed was that he was driving the ball farther than normal. His leg pain wasn't slowing down his clubhead speed. And without the strength and stability in his lower body to "hold off" the clubhead from releasing, Tiger with his driver was hitting a lot of draws, which produce more run and overall distance than more controlled fades. For the week of competition, Tiger averaged 321 yards off the tee, second longest in the entire field.

It's ironic because despite all that Tiger had to deal with to play at Torrey, the week was actually one of the easiest I ever had as Tiger's coach. His more patient attitude, the fact that he could hit so few practice balls, and the lessened pressure on Tiger to perform all reduced both my workload and my stress. I also stayed at a hotel about a mile away, which kept me apart from the intense effort in the evenings to rehab Tiger's leg. As much as I was part of helping Tiger at Torrey, I was also able to relax and observe his achievement from an enjoyable distance.

Tiger's most important helper for the championship was Keith Kleven. For all his expertise and discipline, Keith is a soft, sensitive guy, kindhearted and very devoted to Tiger. Tiger appreciated Keith's work and always felt that a visit to his clinic in Las Vegas was time well spent. Of course, Tiger didn't always show it, and when Keith felt a cold shoulder, his reaction was to worry about what he'd done wrong, to the point that he'd sometimes blurt out to Tiger, "Are you mad at me?" Tiger didn't have the time or the inclination to soothe Keith, which just made Keith more nervous.

Certainly Keith had been in some high-stress situations in his career, especially training boxers for big fights, but nothing like Torrey. He was more responsible for Tiger's performance than he'd ever been, and it was a lot to ask of a guy in his 60s. "It was probably the toughest week I've ever had in any sport, and the most relieved I've ever felt about anything when it was finally over," Keith would tell *Golf Digest*.

At Torrey Pines, Keith spent more time with Tiger than Steve did. He would get up early to supervise Tiger's morning workout, which was intended to retain his leg strength, and follow that with long sessions of manual manipulation and icing designed to get the swelling out of the knee and block the pain. After Tiger played his round, he'd come back to his room nearly spent from the increasing pain, and Keith would work on him again in multiple sessions between dinner and midnight. "I broke it, you fix it" was Tiger's refrain with Keith, as if he were a machine. But Keith knew that with each fix Tiger's condition was deteriorating. The trauma from the stress fractures was getting worse, causing swelling and stiffness, so that Keith's skills were in a race against the quickly diminishing strength and rapidly escalating pain in Tiger's leg. It wasn't a race he was confident he would win.

"That knee's getting weaker every day," Keith told me early in the week. "It's getting harder to get that swelling out. He's hurting more and more. I don't know."

"Keith, you're doing great," I told him, trying to give him a boost. "Just keep doing what you're doing."

Complicating the matter was that Tiger wouldn't take any strong painkillers, as he had at the Masters. Keith told me that to avoid his putting touch being affected, Tiger was taking only Motrin or Advil at Torrey Pines. Somehow, though, what Keith was doing was working, because, in his practice rounds at least, Tiger was limping less. While all the other players knew that Tiger was coming back from surgery, none knew about his ACL or that he had stress fractures and was fighting pain. They seemed to figure that Tiger's nine-hole practice rounds were a precautionary measure and that he wasn't significantly impaired.

Because he was hitting so few practice balls and was skipping any post-round sessions, Tiger wanted me to discuss with him in depth what he needed to do in his swing, so each evening we talked on the phone for about 20 minutes. We reviewed basics and specifics, in particular combating his new tendency to hook because of his less dynamic lower body. I could tell the next morning how well he'd been listening by the way he'd very deliberately execute what we'd talked about. And all week he hit the ball superbly in his warm-ups. He hardly missed a shot, working quietly, calmly, and methodically through the bag, his concentration at its highest. At Torrey Pines, more than anywhere else, Tiger was the model student.

In the more than a week that Tiger was at Torrey Pines, I never once saw him limp or wince in pain on the practice tee. This would lead some people to surmise that Tiger was being overly dramatic or even faking by grimacing on the course. But I think his lack of pain early in the day was a tribute to Keith's work. As the hours went by, and Tiger's leg began to tire, the discomfort would increase. Mostly it was blunted by adrenaline, but at certain moments or with certain shots, pain flashed through Tiger's system and left him in the same pose I'd first seen in his kitchen.

Besides pain, Tiger's biggest problem at Torrey Pines was his opening tee shot. The first hole was a tough uphill par 4 of 448 yards, but it didn't have an out-of-bounds or any hazards. Yet in four rounds, Tiger hit three awful 3-woods from its tee, leading unbelievably to three double bogeys. Apart from the psychological blow of beginning the day so poorly, producing three double bogeys over 72 holes is usually enough to preclude a victory.

Because Tiger had hit the ball so well in his warm-ups, I knew the issue wasn't his injury or his swing mechanics. It went back to a growing difficulty he was having with the opening shot of the day—in plain terms, first-tee jitters. When he violently hooked his first tee shot 40 yards left of the fairway on Thursday and made a double, my thought walking to the second tee was, *Well, this could be a short week.*

But Tiger steadied and battled back. Steve told me later that all week, especially when things got tough on the course, Tiger would repeat a refrain that became an all-purpose saying between them. "Stevie, I don't give a shit what you say, I'm going to win this tournament." He said it early in the round on Thursday, and they'd laughed and Tiger had played better. Though he had another double bogey on the fourteenth hole, in the first round in which he'd walked 18 holes since the Masters, Tiger shot a respectable 72.

It wasn't what he wanted, but he didn't show any disappointment when he came off the course. When he saw me, he was direct. "My knee is killing me," he said. "We're not practicing. I've got to go have Keith work on me. I'll talk to you tonight."

Tiger started his second round on the back nine, and promptly bogeyed the tenth hole. He was three over for the championship when he made the turn, but birdied the first hole and came home with a five-under-par 30 for a 68 that put him among the leaders. Even though he knew bad shots lurked because of the instability in his leg, he was finding a way to get around the course. That's when I thought, *He's really going to do this.*

Maybe I would have felt differently if I'd been in Tiger's suite late at night as Keith desperately tried to revitalize that leg. Steve told me that at one point, with Tiger clearly in pain, Mark Steinberg yelled, "Keith, you've got to do something!" nearly bringing

Keith to tears. The next morning, Tiger laughed as he re-created the scene. "I had to be the referee," he said. "Here I am with my leg falling apart, and I've got to be the calm one. I'm going to make it. But I don't know if Keith is going to make it." The retelling brought some needed levity to an otherwise grim situation. It also brought more drama to the special achievement Tiger was trying to pull off, which further fed his motivation.

Tiger began his third round on Saturday with a pushed 3-wood into deep rough and another double bogey on the first hole. But he stayed in a good place mentally and rebounded on the back nine by making monster eagle putts on the par-5 thirteenth and the eighteenth, and pitching in from the rough for a miracle birdie on the seventeenth. His 70 gave him a one-stroke lead over second-place Lee Westwood. Even though he was making many of the mistakes that lose tournaments, he was also producing the miracles that win them.

On Sunday, Tiger was paired with Westwood and primed to put together a patented closing round in a major. But incredibly, he again hooked his opening 3-wood into the trees and made another double bogey. He also bogeyed the second hole to fall three strokes behind. Walking along, I started to think that it was a bridge too far.

But his resilience at Torrey was amazing. He played one under the rest of the way. I again thought he'd blown it when he pulled his second shot on thirteen into a hazard and made a bogey 6 on a birdie hole. He also bogeyed the fifteenth. But he was the only one of the contenders to make a birdie on the eighteenth, and it was an all-timer.

He needed it to tie Rocco Mediate, who'd already finished. Tiger pulled his drive slightly into a fairway bunker. Having to play short of the pond in front of the green, he pushed his second into the rough, about 100 yards from the hole. From there, Steve made a courageous call under the greatest pressure, convincing Tiger to hit a 60-degree wedge rather than the 56-degree wedge he'd wanted to use. Tiger was originally going to try to land the ball short of the green and have it bounce toward the hole, but Steve felt the slope in front of the putting surface would kick the ball too far left. He made a case for Tiger taking the higher-lofted club and hitting it an extra 20 yards by swinging hard, in the process creating enough spin to fly the ball all the way to the pin and stop it. Tiger pulled the shot off, leaving himself a 12-footer for birdie.

There will always be mystery as to what makes Tiger Woods so amazing under pressure. I still don't exactly know, and I wonder if he does. But what was revealed in his thought process before that putt was not a hard "this ball can only go in" mind-set, but rather a healthy, almost Zen, fatalism. Some of it might have had to do with Torrey Pines greens, which are notoriously bumpy, especially late in the day in the final round of a tournament. But I found it amazing that for a person who was so bent on having control, Tiger instinctively knew when he had a better chance of success by surrendering.

"You can't control the bounces," Tiger said he later told himself. "All you can control is making a pure stroke. Go ahead and release the blade, and just make a pure stroke. If it bounces off line, so be it, you lose the U.S. Open. If it goes in, that's even better." When that putt went in, because of all that Tiger had sacrificed to get to that moment and all that winning a major meant to him, it immediately went down as one of the most clutch putts in history.

Because so many people were following Tiger on Sunday, it got almost impossible to see, so on the front nine I went into the Buick corporate tent and watched the rest of the round on a big-screen television while sitting at a table. As Tiger stood over his putt on the last green, I leaned back on my stool and saw a penny on the floor. I thought about what my mom always said, "Find a penny, pick it up, and all day long you'll have good luck." I bent over and picked it up, and he made that putt. The next day, during the 18-hole playoff, I would keep that penny in my pocket.

Sunday night, Tiger seemed more worried than elated. He'd mentally geared up for his leg to survive 72 holes, but now he had to go at least 18 more, and it meant digging even deeper than he'd anticipated. He knew Rocco was going to be steady, but his biggest concern was himself. He was focused and responsive during our swing discussion, which was brief as we emphasized the anti-hook keys that had proved most reliable during the week. Keith worked longer than ever in his evening and morning sessions before the playoff, and Tiger came out ready. He warmed up well, and managed to put his 3-wood into the fairway on the first hole and make a par. He led by three after nine holes. But he made two bogeys early in the back nine, and when Rocco rallied with a couple of birdies, Tiger suddenly trailed by one with three to play. As I walked along the fairway, somehow I wasn't worried about how devastating a loss would be. I just kept telling myself, *He's Tiger Woods. He'll figure something out.*

He still trailed by one on the eighteenth. Taking every precaution we talked about against a hook, he faded his drive into the fairway and, after Rocco laid up, faded his 5-wood onto the green. Tiger still had to get down in two from 50 feet, and he ran the first putt four feet past but made the slider for the tying birdie. One hole later, making a par to Rocco's bogey, he'd done it.

For a long moment, it didn't seem real that it was over and Tiger had actually won. I waited until after the trophy presentation on the eighteenth green to congratulate him. Words seemed inadequate, and all I could manage was, "Great job, bud. Incredible win. The most amazing win there has ever been." There was too much commotion for Tiger to be reflective, and he quickly answered, "Thanks for your help."

After his press conference, Tiger called me from his plane. In the most appreciative tone I'd ever heard from him, he said, "Hank, man, we really did some great work this week." That meant a lot.

Still coaching, I wanted to leave him with the thought that what he accomplished at Torrey Pines could provide him with the key to his future improvement. In his determination and in his patience, he'd demonstrated a level of mental strength that I thought was historic, as great or greater than Ben Hogan's comeback victory at the 1950 U.S. Open at Merion after nearly dying in a car crash. "Think about it, bud," I said. "See, when you are like this, how good you can play?"

He didn't answer. Instead, he told me the year was over. "I'm shutting it down," he said. "I'm going to get my leg fixed."

A week later, on June 24, Dr. Rosenberg performed ACL reconstructive surgery in Utah. A couple of days before the surgery, Tiger had called me to ask for a list of things I thought he should be working on in his swing. I didn't send it, telling him there would be plenty of time, but I liked the way he was thinking.

Still, looking back on Tiger's victory, I began to wonder about the cost. Because of his decision to have surgery to repair cartilage damage after the Masters, Tiger lost the chance to compete in two majors at a time when, despite a torn ACL, he was playing at very close to his peak. If he'd delayed his cleanout surgery until after the PGA Championship, he would have played in all four of the 2008 majors instead of two. And while he surely would have been in more pain at Torrey Pines than at the Masters, it's doubtful it would have approached the level that he eventually had to endure. Based on what he accomplished at Torrey Pines with a physically compromised game, I now think there was a reasonable chance that Tiger without surgery could have won all of the last three majors of 2008.

There's no telling what kind of long-term damage Tiger did to his knee joint by playing with the stress fractures, but it's arguable that the recurring leg problems he's had since Torrey Pines would be fewer without the trauma of that week.

The biggest cost may have been psychological. Tiger knew he was climbing the biggest mountain of his career at Torrey Pines, and it inspired him to an incredible achievement. Afterward, Tiger had finally congratulated himself. But what if the satisfaction he'd gained took the edge off his hunger? What if it meant he wouldn't be able to find a higher mountain that he wanted to climb?

Perhaps he'll be able to imagine such a mountain if and when he gets to the verge of Nicklaus's major-championship record. But even Tiger's reserves aren't unlimited. History might prove that he was never again able to dig as deep as he did at Torrey Pines.

I saw Tiger only once while he was recovering, when I was in Orlando on some business and stopped by briefly to say hello. He was stuck in a knee brace with his leg elevated on the couch, he'd complain in occasional text messages of a lot of pain and boredom, but he'd also say that he was looking forward to getting back. Once the world had been informed about the extent of his injury and the recovery before him, I'm sure he wanted to shock everyone again by coming back better than ever.

Finally, in mid-October, Tiger got clearance to begin swinging a golf club again. Dr. Rosenberg recommended that he begin with easy sand-wedge pitch shots, and progress by going to the next longest club each week. I thought following that program would take Tiger too long to get to the longer clubs. Instead, I set up a plan based on a fixed clubhead speed for all of the clubs. Tiger began swinging at 35 mph, which produced about a 40-yard pitch shot, while the driver traveled about 80 yards without getting off the ground. After the first month, Tiger was able to swing at 65 mph while hitting an increased number of balls, the driver traveling about 150 yards. Finally, by early February, he was swinging at full speed and getting his ball count up to nearly normal, while once again producing drivers in excess of 300 yards.

The exercise had a lot of benefits. Because he was swinging so slowly, Tiger avoided favoring the injury and getting into bad habits. The slow swing with the longer clubs also made him more conscious of correct technique and really ingrained the moves we were working on, just as had occurred when Tiger had filmed the Nike commercial in slow motion, but to a much greater extent. As far as he knew, he was the only player who'd ever used such a program to come back. It was different and special, and he always thought that gave him an edge.

Tiger wasn't quite as diligent in working on his short game, which was disappointing to me because it would have been the most productive use of his time while his leg wasn't yet at full strength. Tiger's short game was one of the game's best, but there was still room for improvement, and he knew it. I worried that not taking that on was a sign that his drive was beginning to wane in the same way it had early in 2007.

I wasn't in Orlando a lot during this period, but I tried to be there enough to keep Tiger on track. After President Obama was elected in November, Tiger was invited to be a guest speaker at his inauguration, joining a dozen or so other prominent Americans. He didn't say anything about the invitation to me, and I didn't know about it until I saw him on television before a podium in front of the Lincoln Memorial. The next time I saw him, I complimented him on the honor and his speech and asked, "What was the president like?"

"He's a nice guy," Tiger said, and didn't elaborate. He'd been quoted as saying his father would have been moved to tears at seeing an African American elected president, and that as a multiracial person he, too, was gratified. But Tiger never said whether he'd voted for Obama, and his speech was only about his appreciation for the military, making no reference to the new president. As I heard his speech, I imagined that he'd made sure it couldn't be construed as a political endorsement.

Tiger was impressed by very few people. Outside of sports figures, I can't recall him ever talking about a person he particularly admired. Earl had made a big deal about Tiger feeling a kinship with Nelson Mandela when the two met in South Africa, but I never heard Tiger mention Mandela. If Tiger liked a movie, he'd never single out one of the actors for a great performance. He wasn't a wannabe musician like a lot of athletes, and from what I saw, he didn't pal around with those who performed at his Tiger Jam charity concert in Las Vegas, like Jon Bon Jovi or Glen Frey. Tiger was more likely to be friendly with artists who played in pro-ams or showed up at tour events, like singer Darius Rucker, who sang at Tiger's wedding, or comedian Kevin James. Tiger once took me to watch Kevin perform in Orlando. We went backstage afterward and had a nice chat with him, but I never heard Tiger say anything that indicated a curiosity about the comedian's craft.

Among athletes, Tiger had great respect for Michael Jordan, though they spent less time together when I was Tiger's coach than they had earlier in his career. Among contemporaries, Tiger had the most admiration for Roger Federer and Lance Armstrong. Tiger and Federer had been brought together by Nike and had become friends. Tiger didn't know Armstrong well and didn't cycle, but he was impressed by the way Lance had come back from cancer and how mentally tough he had to be to keep winning the Tour de France. In the case of both Federer and Armstrong, what Tiger most related to was their dominance in an individual sport.

But from what I saw, Tiger still didn't let any of these figures close, even when they reached out. My sense was that Tiger would be more likely to engage someone he admired if he thought he could learn something from him or her. Once at Isleworth another tour player, Grant Waite, approached Tiger on the range and introduced him to motocross champion James Stewart. Tiger didn't know who he was, but after Grant gave him a rundown on how James was one of the best in the world at his sport, Tiger showed some interest and started asking James how he trained. Tiger listened and then asked what he ate before competition. James said, "Oh, nothing special. A Coke and a Snickers." That answer told Tiger that James wasn't in his league as a serious athlete, and he quickly ended the conversation and went back to hitting balls.

During his rehab, Tiger seemed more committed to his new training regimen than he was to his golf. Because Keith was in Las Vegas and Tiger needed to work out near his house, he hired a new trainer, a chiropractor and physical therapist named Mark Lindsay, who was renowned for his postoperative work with elite athletes such as Alex Rodriguez and sprinter Donovan Bailey. Mark specialized in the same kind of soft-tissue manipulation that Keith is expert in.

Lindsay also brought in Bill Knowles, a strength coach from Vermont who was known for helping skiers recover from ACL surgery. According to Corey, at Tiger's urging Bill's workouts included Olympic-style lifts like the clean and press, designed to develop explosive power. Keith had avoided giving Tiger these kinds of exercises because they invited injury and because they opened the door to other strength training routines from football and similar power sports that Tiger was only too eager to try.

I knew the programs were helping Tiger's recovery, and the medical checkups he was getting confirmed he was ahead of schedule, but I worried that Tiger might revert to his pattern of overdoing. He tended to believe that if three sets were prescribed, six would be twice as good. I warned Bill that he was basically giving Tiger a new toy, and that he might get carried away. Sure enough, right around New Year's Day, Tiger hurt his right Achilles tendon—doing Olympic-style lifts, according to Corey. Tiger would later say that he hurt the Achilles running sprints while testing new shoes for Nike. Shortly after, I received an e-mail from Bill Knowles telling me that I'd been right, and that he was curtailing Tiger's Olympic-style lifting.

Getting the right Achilles treated was the reason Dr. Anthony Galea was called in. Mark Lindsay had worked with Galea in Toronto, and Lindsay believed in Galea's specialty—platelet-rich plasma therapy, or "blood spinning." The procedure involved extracting a patient's blood and putting it into a centrifuge, separating the platelet-rich plasma, and injecting it back into the problem area, promoting faster healing. Galea came to Tiger's house the first time right around the Super Bowl in Tampa, where he'd been administering blood-spinning therapy to Pittsburgh Steelers receiver Hines Ward. I watched Galea treat Tiger and winced as he inserted a long needle into his Achilles tendon. The next day Tiger said his Achilles was less sore, and Galea would come back to Tiger's house four more times in February and March to repeat the procedure—both on the Achilles and on an area below the left knee, where Tiger had persistent pain.

Later, Galea's visits to Tiger became controversial after the Canadian doctor was charged with unlawful distribution of HGH. But as I'd eventually tell the Golf Channel's Jim Gray, I never saw any evidence of Tiger receiving any treatment other than blood spinning, which is legal. For the record, I feel very strongly that Tiger has never taken any kind of banned performance-enhancing drug.

By this time, Tiger was able to hit balls full out. There was a difference in his action—his knee was definitely more stable through impact. While I'd never really noticed Tiger's knee wobble when he hit the ball, even in the run-up to Torrey Pines, the before-and-after contrast showed that the joint had previously been compromised, even if it hadn't slowed the force of his swing. It gave me hope that, to use Tiger's words, "finally with a left leg to hit against," the best swings of his life were ahead.

Although history won't record 2009 as a great year for Tiger, I thought it was the year he made more good swings than ever before. It told in his consistency, as he won seven of 19 tournaments with sixteen top-ten finishes worldwide. It also was reflected in his improved driving, as Tiger finished 12th in the Total Driving statistic—which combines average driving distance with driving accuracy—by far the best he'd ever done with me as his coach. Coming off his knee surgery, he had a better body to execute proper mechanics, and even though he didn't win a major championship, I could see real progress.

Tiger began his comeback slowly by losing to Tim Clark in the second round of the WGC-Accenture Match Play Championship, but his swing was much improved at Doral, and he finished tied for ninth. He won at Bay Hill with a great birdie on the 72nd hole, and looked primed to play well at the Masters.

He didn't quite have it, and finished tied for sixth. I thought that once he got to Augusta, he showed less focus in his practice. He didn't spend enough time on the putting green, and it told in the tournament, where he took 122 putts to finish 45th in the field, a statistical position that makes winning nearly impossible. I pointed out to Tiger that in the previous 32 PGA Tour events, the winner had finished in the top 15 in putting for the week 28 times and never worse than 33rd. I thought his stroke looked slightly off and that he just needed to devote more time to the practice green.

Tiger was also more moody than usual at Augusta, and he became more difficult as the week went on. After he bogeyed the eighteenth hole on Friday to fall seven shots behind the leaders, he came to the practice range angry. He immediately pulled out his driver, the club with which he never begins practice sessions, and between extra-hard swings vented his frustrations to me for five minutes.

He made up no ground on a third-round 70, and on Sunday he met me on the practice tee in a negative frame of mind. He'd later say it was "one of the worst warm-up sessions I've ever had." He was paired with Phil Mickelson, who got off to a flying start. Tiger kept up with an eagle on the eighth hole, and when he birdied 16, it put him within two of the lead. But he pulled his drive on the seventeenth and made a bogey, then pushed his drive on the eighteenth to make another, his third bogey in four days on that hole. It was startling to see Tiger finish so poorly at the Masters, especially because in the 54 times he'd played the eighteenth hole before the 2009 tournament, he'd bogeyed it only three times.

Tiger was seething when he left the course, and told the media, "I fought my swing all day and just kind of Band-Aided it around and almost won the tournament with a Band-Aid swing." Without mentioning my name, Tiger had taken a shot at me and made me a target for blame.

It was discouraging, and I wrote him a long e-mail after the Masters that recapped his performance and offered some thoughts going forward. I thought the most important issue at Augusta had been his attitude. I wanted him to realize that as much as his great attitude at Torrey Pines had helped him, his poor attitude at Augusta had hurt him.

"No one in the world, not me or anyone else, can even come close to knowing the pressure that you are under as Tiger Woods and I don't pretend to," I wrote, trying to show some sensitivity. But I added, "What I know is that having a positive attitude and patience is a big key to making any bad situation better. You didn't make any friends or fans with the way you acted at the Masters. You just looked stressed and pissed the whole time you were there."

I also tried to ease into another delicate issue. "Your greatness is undeniable. The records you will set will never be broken. You are probably the greatest athlete in the history of the world. But your Isleworth and practice tee game is better by a long shot than your tournament game. It is obvious that you have an issue with taking your game from the driving range to the course."

Finally, without mentioning his quotes after the last round, I wanted Tiger to know that he'd hurt me with both his demeanor and his words at the Masters, and that going forward it was up to him to tell me how much I could help him. "At the tournaments it is sometimes a difficult situation because you just don't seem to want much input at all and then when I do say something it doesn't seem like you like what I have to say," I wrote. "Anyway, I am the most loyal person in the world. I love helping you and I have worked my ass off for you. You just let me know when you want me to help you and I will be there."

As anticipated, Tiger's form at the Masters had led to some rumors that I was about to be fired. At his next tournament, in Charlotte, he didn't exactly come to my rescue when the question was put to him, saying only, "That's complete speculation."

Tiger's outlook changed at the Memorial Tournament in early June, where he won by a stroke with birdies on the last two holes. It was a notable week because Tiger had finally acceded to suggestions from me and others to try a driver with more loft, going up a degree from 8.5 to nearly 10 and having one of the best driving tournaments of his career. Muirfield Village's fairways are generous, but Tiger was impressive in hitting 49 of 56 fairways, his best statistical week for driving accuracy since 1998. With his mood improved, he was more open with the media and blamed himself for his relatively slow progress since coming back by admitting that in his first few tournaments he'd been inhibited by a fear that his newly repaired ACL might still be susceptible to reinjury. He also took some heat off me by saying, "Hank's been absolutely phenomenal for my game and helped me through a lot."

Those words improved our partnership, and we worked well together at the U.S. Open at Bethpage, where Tiger hit the ball beautifully but missed 20 putts inside 15 feet and would finish four strokes behind the winner, Lucas Glover. I had to miss the British Open because I was finalizing my divorce, and I felt bad when Tiger missed only his second cut at a major as a professional.

At the next major, the PGA Championship at Hazeltine near Minneapolis, Tiger again was very good tee to green and mediocre with the putter. Still, his ball control earned him a four-stroke lead after 36 holes and a two-stroke lead after 54 holes. Because Tiger hadn't lost when holding the lead alone after three rounds since the first time he'd faced the situation as a pro in 1996 at Quad Cities, his victory was all but conceded.

But Tiger's poor putting cost him in the last round, as he missed seven putts under 10 feet, the first one a six-footer on the first hole for a birdie. That set the tone for the day. I contend that Tiger's biggest opponent at Hazeltine was the law of averages. He was simply due for things to not go his way on the final day of a major, balancing out what had gone so right at Torrey Pines. Besides his own mistakes, he saw Y. E. Yang make the kind of winning shots that he was used to pulling off, especially Yang's chip in for eagle on the fourteenth hole. Tiger could have tied on the 71st hole with a par, but after he hit a solid 7-iron over the flag and into the rough, he made a mediocre chip, and missed the kind of eight-footer he customarily buried in such situations. He came to the 72nd a stroke behind, but Yang, continuing the magic, stiffed a hybrid approach from 210 yards to close it out.

Tiger knew that he'd let one get away, but he wasn't as upset as I'd seen him after some other losses at majors. He'd been proud of his 14–0 run of winning majors after holding or sharing the third-round lead, but he never expected it to last forever. He was well aware of how many close calls Jack Nicklaus had suffered in major championships, and with only six second-place finishes in majors compared to Jack's 19, Tiger knew he was due for at least a few frustrating runner-up placings.

As was becoming his habit, Tiger played at an extremely high level the last part of the year, finishing either first or second in six of his last seven official tournaments. Without a major, it didn't seem to matter much, and I could see his outlook souring as he received the latest evidence that for him, the expectations would always be impossible to fulfill. In September, he threw his driver in anger at the Deutsche Bank event near Boston, and in his last appearance of the year, a victory at the Australian Masters in November, he whipped it down so hard after a poor tee shot that it bounced into the gallery. Tiger was lucky nobody was hurt, but I thought what was most telling was the way he barely looked at the person who handed the club back to him, as if it was other people's role to clean up his messes. I didn't go to Australia, but watching it on television, I thought, *This is a troubled guy.*

I and everyone else would soon find out the reason, and Tiger's life issue would reduce the strides he was making in his game to irrelevancy. As his coach, I found that sad, because I still considered it a noble undertaking to help the most gifted golfer ever fulfill his awesome potential.

By the end of 2009, I believed that even though Tiger's putting had started to cost him major championships, he could easily solve the problem by rededicating himself to that crucial part of the game. I didn't see any evidence that he was losing his stroke or his nerve, only that he wasn't putting in the time necessary to be exceptional on the greens.

For me the ultimate challenge was Tiger's driving, which for the myriad reasons I've discussed had been his biggest weakness since I'd become his coach. But I was proud that he'd made slow but steady progress in the last few years, and before things fell apart I was looking at 2010 as the year he'd make the breakthrough that would truly put his golf on a level never before seen.

What Tiger had long been missing—and perhaps never really had—was the kind of automatic go-to shot with the driver that could be relied on no matter how he was playing. The great drivers of the ball—in particular Byron Nelson, Ben Hogan, and Lee Trevino—all had such a shot, and it had lent an ease to their games that was a joy to watch and, more important, a joy to possess. I thought that, for the sake of his own longevity, Tiger needed something similar because his driver had forced him to work awfully hard during his rounds, and I thought the strain was starting to tell.

What I'd set my mind on installing in 2009 was a driver "stinger" to go along with his cut shot as a go-to shot. I knew in my bones Tiger could master the shot because he already did it well with the 5-wood and 3-wood. It would be a low-flying shot with little curve that he'd find was easy to keep on line, and though it might cost him 15 yards or so in distance, the ball would go far enough. Tiger already had the technique down and could perform the driver stinger on the range, but I hadn't been able to get him to trust it on the course. He never gave a reason, but it seemed as if the pressure he felt to perform had gotten so great that it had turned him conservative when it came to risking a new shot in competition. There was also the fact that the big miss was for him more possible with the driver than any other club.

But he also understood that the whole point of the stinger driver was to make the big miss go away. I could feel that he was getting closer to trusting the shot, because he'd often break it out in a practice round or on the range, often unannounced. He knew how much I loved the shot and wanted him to use it, and he'd enjoy hitting it and silently sharing with me an admiration of its flight. He might then give me a sly look, or even keep his head down but say, "Like that one, huh?" In 2009, he was tantalizing me with that routine more and more, and it was heartening. I'd seize the opportunity to implore him, saying stuff like, "Tiger, that's the ultimate shot. No one else has that shot. No one else is good enough to hit it. Put that in your bag and you jump ahead of everyone even more. That shot gives you the whole package."

It should have happened.

7

Quitting

"Hank, I want to give you a heads-up."

The voice on my cell phone belongs to Mark Steinberg. He's just returned from Australia, where a few days before, Tiger had won the 2009 Australian Masters in Melbourne. I'm on my way to China, where I'm working on establishing a junior golf academy at Misson Hills Golf Club.

Mark's tone is brisk and businesslike. "There's going to be a story coming out about Tiger and this girl," he says. "It's not true. Everything is going to be fine. But if anybody asks you about it, don't say anything."

I assure him I won't. Mark is clearly in a hurry and says good-bye. The conversation has lasted about 30 seconds.

A little more than a week later, I was still in China when I received another call, this one at about two a.m. It was from a reporter calling from America, who asked if I'd heard about Tiger's car crash in Orlando. I said no, and after hanging up got on the Internet and began reading about Tiger hitting the fire hydrant.

I called Mark, who was back in the United States. My concern was about Tiger being injured, but Mark said, "He's going to be fine." He sounded even more hurried than in his earlier call, so I said good-bye and hung up.

By the time I returned home to Dallas several days later, Tiger's whole world had changed. The story Mark had been talking about, in the *National Enquirer,* had been the first of a series of reports that made it pretty clear Tiger had been having multiple extramarital affairs.

My first reaction was shock. I began coaching Tiger a few months before he married Elin in October 2004, and I'd known them as a couple since 2002. During that time, on the road or in Orlando, I never saw Tiger flirting or acting inappropriately with another woman, or even heard rumors that he was seeing others.

He had, very occasionally, commented on how attractive a woman in our presence might be, but that was the extent of Tiger being a "player" from my view.

I'd noticed that while he and E had been playful in the early years of their relationship—competing against each other in tennis, Ping-Pong, skiing, or running—there was some distance between them as the years went on, a certain coolness. But a lot of marriages are like that. I hadn't jumped to any conclusions.

I have no doubt that many people will have a hard time believing I knew nothing about Tiger's women. Almost automatically, they'll consider me, at best, an enabler. So be it. Probably nothing I can say will change their minds. In the aftermath of Tiger's scandal, I didn't issue a public denial because I knew such a statement would also have gotten me labeled a liar. But after the shock, there was recognition. Whether working with me on his game or during downtime, Tiger always had a wall up, behind which I'd long imagined there was some kind of personal turmoil. His scandal brought home the uneasy sense of pressure building that I'd always had around Tiger. On some deep level, I'd been expecting something to break.

As I reflected back, I realized that I'd never thought of Tiger as happy. Whether with friends, business associates, other players, his mother, or his wife—indeed, with just about everyone except an audience of kids at one of his clinics—he seemed to keep the atmosphere around him emotionally arid. Part of it was the insane drive that was vital to his greatness. It seemed the longer he was the best, the more isolated and lonely he became.

No golfer had ever played in a bubble of fame like Tiger's, so when his scandal occurred, my first reaction was sympathy. I began to think of Tiger as belonging to a group that included such figures as Michael Jackson and Britney Spears—public superstars whose ways of escaping pressure became self-destructive. I began to understand that Tiger's burden had been even heavier than I'd thought.

Once the news was out, I tried to contact Tiger by text but didn't hear back. On December 23, I sent him a longer message that offered support:

> Tiger,
>
> I just wanted you to know that I will always be your friend, bud. I am sure you feel bad about everything that has happened. The fact is that everyone makes mistakes and you can't undo something that has already been done. All you can ever do is live in the present and then plan for the future. Like I always say, the great thing about yesterday is that it is

> never going to happen again. A great man once said this: "The lessons I learn today I will apply tomorrow, and I will be better." That great man is you. It is obvious that you have a long road, but short road or long road you handle it the same way, one step at a time. If I can ever help in any way I am always available. I just wanted to let you know that I am thinking of you. Hang in there.
> Hank

He didn't e-mail back, but right after Christmas, he called. His first words were, "Well, I finally got my phone working," which was a line he'd used before when he hadn't returned a call for a while. He had a lot of problems with his phone, in part because he changed his number so often. His voice was flat, as if nothing had happened since the last time we spoke, which had been about six weeks before, just after he won the Australian Masters. But when I ventured to ask how he was doing, his answer—"About as good as I can"—was somber.

He didn't volunteer anything else. The only reference he made to his situation was, "God, the media is pounding me. They're such vultures." At the end of the conversation he said, "I'm going to be gone for a while." He didn't say where he was going, and I didn't ask. But I figured it was somewhere to disappear from view, and maybe to get some help.

During the month he spent at a Mississippi clinic, I didn't hear from him. I received texted updates and reports from Mark and Tiger's longtime friend Bryon Bell, but they had their hands full with the aftermath of the scandal, and there were no details. I heard only that Tiger was OK, but that he wasn't taking any calls as he underwent treatment.

After Tiger got out of inpatient treatment in early February, he called me at home in Dallas. He sounded better and was more forthcoming. He described his therapy as "horrible, the worst experience I've ever been through" and "the hardest thing I've ever done," but he didn't offer any details. When I asked about Elin, who'd participated in some couples therapy with him, he said, "We're trying. But I don't know if she is buying all this stuff." He added, "She wants me to not play golf for two years. Right now, I don't know." The call lasted about ten minutes.

On February 19, I watched Tiger give his televised apology from the PGA Tour's headquarters in Ponte Vedra Beach, Florida. I didn't attend because I was in Cabo San Lucas, where I'd picked up a bad case of bronchitis. Mark Steinberg had called me two days before to ask me if I could get to Florida right away. Because it was such short notice and because my bronchitis made me apprehensive about getting on a long flight, I declined, and Mark didn't pressure me to change my mind.

Watching Tiger deliver his apology in front of that blue curtain was depressing. He looked more wrung out than I'd ever seen him. I was disappointed that he chose to read from a prepared statement. I found myself wanting to hear him speak more naturally, more from the heart, and even take some questions. I'd hoped that he'd come out of treatment trying to be more open.

To be supportive, I sent him a text message telling him he did a good job. To my surprise, he got right back, texting, "Thanks. Appreciate it." A few minutes later, he called.

It seemed as if giving the speech had lightened his load, because he sounded upbeat. He was almost talkative, and at one point actually dropped his guard. "I learned one thing for sure," he said with conviction. "When I play golf again, I'm going to play for myself. I'm not going to play for my dad, or my mom, or Mark Steinberg, or Steve Williams, or Nike, or my foundation, or you, or the fans. Only for myself."

It was the most intimate and revealing thing he'd ever said to me. It was the first time he'd suggested that he was actually conflicted about his upbringing. I'd never heard him publicly or privately question the way he'd been raised. Both his parents had consistently maintained that Tiger was never pushed to play golf—that he'd loved the game as a toddler and constantly wanted to go to the golf course. As Tiger became a prolific winner in junior golf, both he and his parents publicly held to the line that the game was never put before his education or a normal life. I'd never heard Tiger mention his father's oft-quoted statements that his son would be more influential than Gandhi or that he was a better person than he was a golfer. I'd never heard him question a public image that carried the dual expectation of superstar-level golf playing and flawless public behavior, or express resentment about his responsibilities as an employer or head of a foundation. But it was clear from the forcefulness of Tiger's tone that he'd learned that the obligations imposed on him had exacted a considerable toll.

I thought, *This is a good start. He's really looking at himself.* It gave me hope that Tiger was on his way to becoming a more self-aware and contented person. In his public apology, he'd vowed to go back to the Buddhist values that his mother had taught him in childhood. "Buddhism teaches that a craving of things outside ourselves causes an unhappy and pointless search for security," Tiger said. "It teaches me to stop following every impulse and to learn restraint. Obviously, I lost track of what I was taught."

I'd never seen Tiger meditate or talk about Buddhism, but the ideals made sense. Tiger seemed to be talking about a radical change, which made me wonder about how altering the Package would affect his golf. Tiger's intense sense of mission when he played gave him his fire, his focus, and his incredible ability to find something extra at the most urgent moments. For all the success this had given him, what if that mission had helped mess up his life? If Tiger was asking himself that question, was he going to be reluctant to keep putting his whole identity on the line when he played? If golf didn't mean as much to him anymore, then he'd probably win less often. If that happened, I thought it might make him more enjoyable to coach and be around. Going forward, that was a trade-off I would take.

After going uncharacteristically deep, Tiger backed off and

changed the subject. "Anyway," he said, "I have a lot of work to do." But he continued the personal tone when he told me that the night before, he had walked out onto the practice range across from his house and, in the pitch dark, had hit five full shots with a sand wedge. "First swings since all this shit happened," he said. I asked, maybe a little too earnestly, "So, how did you hit them?" He probably heard in my voice a slight worry that his ordeal might have completely erased his aptitude for the game, because he kind of chuckled and said, "Oh, they were solid." Then before hanging up he said, "I'm getting ready to start back up. Once I get going, I want you to come down here, and we'll start working."

From my perspective, there was an obvious question: When was Tiger coming back to competition? In his apology, he'd said, "I do plan to return to golf one day. I just don't know when that day will be. I don't rule out that it will be this year." The choice of words suggested later rather than sooner. But I didn't want to press Tiger in a delicate moment, so I refrained from asking if he had a date in mind.

A week later, he called and said he was ready for me to come to Isleworth to begin rebuilding his game. "You can stay in the house as long as you want," he said, adding that Elin and the two children had moved to a rented home nearby. "It's just me." On March 8, the same date I began as his coach six years before, I flew from Dallas to Orlando and again rented a car. On the drive to Isleworth, I decided I would stay as low-key as I could. I figured Tiger would be in a pretty fragile state, and I didn't want to appear to be forcing anything. But as I drove up to the country club's guardhouse, gave my name, and was allowed through the gates, I couldn't help being a little nervous.

As I pulled into Tiger's driveway, I saw that he was already on the practice range hitting balls. When I walked across the street onto the long hitting area, I was taken aback by the sight of Elin standing nearby with the two kids. As I got closer, Tiger stepped toward me and gave me a man-hug that was quick and a little awkward.

"How you doin', bud?" I said, and he answered, "Good to see you." He seemed determined to keep things as normal as possible.

I then approached Elin. It was a difficult moment, but at the same time I didn't feel any dread. I was at peace because, after everything happened, I'd texted her with some messages of concern, and made it clear that I hadn't known about Tiger's activities. And Tiger had told me in our last phone call, "Elin knows that you and Stevie weren't involved or knew anything." The look on her face was sad, and she hugged me a little longer than usual.

I sensed a force field up between Tiger and Elin, who didn't speak directly to each other. After a bit of small talk about how the kids were growing, she gave a wave and said she was taking them to a playground. After she left, Tiger was visibly relieved. When our eyes met, I said, "That seemed a little icy. How's it going?" In a resigned voice, he said, "Yeah, pretty slow. We're trying."

Tiger was definitely subdued. Our usual topics of conversation on the practice range might be the latest tour gossip or some development involving another player, but there was none of that. He seemed to be carrying himself gingerly, like a person who's been beaten up. It hit me that for six weeks he'd been in a confined, highly controlled place with expert counselors who know how to break a person down. He might have been the toughest patient they ever faced, but there'd been an effect. I wondered about a loss of self-confidence and what all that therapy would do to his killer instinct. I actually flashed on the sensation I got as a kid the first time I watched *The Wizard of Oz* and saw the curtain being pulled back.

As Tiger hit balls and we talked a bit about how his swing felt, I didn't sense that he was highly excited about golf. He didn't say he'd missed it or that he was more motivated than ever or how he couldn't wait to prove his critics wrong. It seemed instead that he was easing himself back into something familiar, something he knew he could do well, something that allowed him to feel a little better about himself.

His swing was bad but not terrible. His ball control was poor, with a lot of curve to his shots. He'd told me on the phone that he was hitting the ball farther, and that was always a red flag to me. It meant his club was flattening out too much on the downswing, creating a slinging motion with his hands that is not a reliable way for him to hit straight, controlled shots. As was usually the case when he took a break from the game, he'd thought up a new swing idea that had to do with creating more power by increasing the wrist cock in his downswing, and he was trying it out. He knew I wouldn't be thrilled with him going off plan. I never approved of that move, but he didn't say anything about it, and I didn't either.

Even as I watched the erratic ball flight, I offered only encouragement. It felt too early to impose much structure or a plan. He said he'd watched some tournaments on television, and he commented on how much he liked the backswing of Justin Rose, who'd just switched to instructor Sean Foley.

After about an hour of full shots, followed by some short-game and putting practice, we walked back to the house. Inside, it was less furnished than I remembered it and strangely dark for daytime. That's when I noticed that all the outside windows were covered with butcher paper to prevent photographers from taking pictures of anyone inside the house—a real possibility because it was hard for security to keep paparazzi from taking boats on the lake behind the property. I also noticed a few self-help books on the kitchen counter. Tiger told me he hadn't been outside the gates of Isleworth since coming back from rehab a month earlier. In the four days I stayed, either we ordered meals from the club, or I went out and picked up food at a nearby Boston Market. Tiger always had the turkey dinner with sides of steamed vegetables and mashed potatoes.

One night he said, "We're going to eat in the clubhouse. It's family night. Elin and the kids are going." Inwardly, I cringed. I told him I felt as if I'd be imposing, but he insisted. I knew it was going to be awkward, and it was. We sat at a big table, and the conversation was either forced or nonexistent. It was a buffet, and though other members were pleasant and polite to Tiger and Elin as they got their food, when they sat down, I could feel the stares. I guess Tiger wanted me there as a buffer, but after I made a couple of attempts to start conversation with little success, I felt kind of helpless and just waited out the ordeal.

When Tiger began to play practice rounds, it was in a threesome with me and Corey Carroll. At the hardest time of his life, it appeared to me that he was closer to Corey than anyone else.

Mark O'Meara had once held a similar place. But since the scandal, Mark had been hurt that Tiger had not returned his calls. "I've tried to contact him a few times to let him know I'm thinking about him and his family," Mark told writers in February. "My phone is always on." Shortly after, Tiger referred to the quote and commented, "I guess Mark is pretty disappointed in me." I thought it was a sign of Tiger becoming more empathetic, but only to a point, because when I spoke to Mark weeks later, he said Tiger had still not gotten back to him.

Mark had been one of the few touring pros that Tiger practiced with at Isleworth. After Mark had moved to Houston a couple of years earlier and John Cook had gone back to California, only Arjun Atwal, among the touring pros who lived at the club, was a regular playing partner. Arjun is two years older than Tiger and originally from India. His friendship with Tiger had grown in 2007 after Arjun had been involved in a car accident in which another driver was killed when both cars went off the road. Witnesses claimed the two men were street racing, but Arjun denied those claims. For eleven months, Arjun's career was on hold as law enforcement considered charging him with vehicular homicide, but ultimately no criminal charges were brought. At Isleworth, other pros seemed to shy away from Arjun during this period, but Tiger, perhaps feeling a kinship with another outsider, invited him to hit balls and practice with him. Tiger seemed comfortable with Arjun's low-key personality, and Arjun had a nice way of working hard on his game while still deferring to Tiger. O'Meara and Cook were the same way. Even when Mark won two major championships in 1998, he was never a threat to Tiger, and neither was Arjun.

It got more complicated for players to be Tiger's practice partners after the scandal. Extreme discretion was implicitly demanded. Mark and John had been interviewed about Tiger many times over the years, but both had a way of saying things about the "private" Tiger without giving anything away. Arjun played it even safer, giving only the most general of answers. It was easy for a quote to backfire, as another pro, Ben Curtis, found out the hard way.

When Tiger started practicing again, he agreed to play a couple of rounds with Ben at Isleworth as a favor to Steve Johnson, my partner in my instruction schools and Ben's teacher. Tiger didn't play very well, but he was nice to Ben, a quiet guy who was very respectful. Tiger even helped Ben with his game. The gesture suggested that Tiger was being more considerate of others since emerging from therapy, and I complimented him on it. But a few days later, after it got out that Ben had practiced with Tiger, some reporters at the Bay Hill tournament asked Ben his impressions of Tiger's game. Despite having won the 2003 British Open, Ben is not that media savvy, so quite innocently, he said something about Tiger appearing nervous and his game looking a bit rusty. It was a poor choice of words, considering how much attention another player's assessment of Tiger's game would get, and it led to news stories portraying Tiger as fragile in the wake of the scandal. Ben hadn't meant to criticize Tiger, but that didn't matter. The next time I saw Tiger, he mentioned Ben's quotes and said, "I'll never play with that guy again."

Actually, "rusty" was a gentle description of Tiger's game. He simply didn't have his old command. His body speed seemed slower, and for the first time that I'd ever observed, he was mis-hitting a lot of shots. In my experience, even when Tiger hit the ball off line, he would always hit it in the middle of the club. I knew this by the sound and also because when I'd clean off his irons during his practice sessions at Isleworth the only impact mark on the face was always right on the sweet spot. Now he was catching irons too much toward the top of the ball—"thin"—as well as hitting the ground behind the ball—"fat." Both Corey and I kept encouraging him, but it was obvious Tiger was struggling. One day, Corey quietly said, "Hank, he's just not as good as he was."

Tiger had plenty of distractions, including meetings with a team of public-relations experts who specialized in emergency damage control. He gave whatever energy he could muster to his golf game, but he seemed to tire more quickly, physically and mentally. At night, we'd sometimes talk about his swing, but mostly we watched sports on television. He was going to bed a lot earlier, around nine p.m. He said one of the best things that had come from his therapy was new medication that allowed him to sleep better. He'd long complained about being a light sleeper, one who usually had a hard time getting more than five hours, but now he claimed to be getting a solid eight.

There was also less conversation during our practice and playing sessions, and even during our downtime. After Tiger got out of therapy, Mark Steinberg told me, "Hank, he needs us really badly right now. Be as positive as you can be." But even in Tiger's best years, it was awkward trying to say anything motivational to him. I might acknowledge a good work session by saying something like, "Your dad would be really proud of the way you worked today." But about the most such a comment would get would be a nod. It was why I preferred texting Tiger when I wanted to impart something substantial.

There were a couple of times when I was at his house when Tiger *did* talk a bit about his situation. He knew I understood the language of therapy, and he knew I believed that sex addiction was a legitimate condition. He opened up a little, telling a few stories about some of the people he'd met in his group without ever saying who they were. There was one guy about his age who was also trying to save his marriage after having multiple affairs, and another man whose problems had started as a child when he was molested by a priest.

He said nothing about the root of his problems, though he did speculate about what the future held. "There are some girls who are going to be after me even more now, especially the wild ones," he said. "But what I learned is that for the rest of my life I can't have sex with someone unless I genuinely feel something for them. If I do, I'm putting myself in jeopardy."

It was a statement that hinted at his lack of confidence in the future of his marriage. When I asked how things were going, he admitted he wasn't sure Elin could ever overcome feeling betrayed. I told Tiger, "It's normal that she feels it was all somehow about *her.* It's going to take time for her to understand that it was about *you.* You did this to yourself and, unfortunately, Elin was really hurt in the process."

I knew I'd ventured into sensitive territory with that statement, so I waited for Tiger to respond. Again, he just nodded. I guessed he agreed with me, but as was so often the case, I wasn't really sure.

When I got back to Dallas, I thought a lot about Tiger and how I could help him. I probably doubled the rate at which I sent him text messages. I put a lot of thought into them because I was trying to demonstrate friendship. I hoped I could get him to be more in touch with his feelings and be able to express them. But I never got a response.

It was right before my next trip to Isleworth a week later, on March 16, that I learned that Tiger had decided to end his hiatus from competition at the Masters, which was less than a month away. I wasn't consulted on the decision, and I was disappointed to hear the news. I thought it was a bad game plan. Too soon, too much pressure, too easy to have a confidence-killing disaster. Normally after a long absence, six weeks was the time that Tiger needed to get ready. With all he'd been through and the way he'd been holed up indoors for so long, I figured that, ideally, he should put in ten weeks before testing his game in a tournament. It was going to be a rush job. Still, I didn't argue against the decision. I was fairly certain I wouldn't change Tiger's mind, and I didn't want to be considered unsupportive at a sensitive time. He made the public announcement the next day.

From a selfish perspective, I wanted him to take a much longer break, even to the point of skipping all four majors. It would lessen the pressure on me in general, particularly because of what was coming up. The U.S. Open was at Pebble Beach, where ten years before, Tiger had won by 15 strokes in what is commonly considered the greatest major-championship performance of all time. A month later, the British Open would be played at St. Andrews, where it would be the ten-year anniversary of his eight-stroke victory. Returning to the scenes of that double would mean an endless media diet of "Tiger then" versus "Tiger now"—the peak of the Butch Harmon era versus the possible nadir of the Hank Haney era. It wasn't something I was looking forward to.

When I returned to Isleworth a few days after the announcement, Tiger's game was still erratic. Two weeks before the Monday of Masters week, Corey and I joined him on a trip to Augusta. Corey was actually a late fill-in. Tiger had originally invited one of his rehab friends to play—another thoughtful gesture—but at the last minute, the guy had canceled. On the early-morning drive to the airport, I asked Tiger how he felt to be outside Isleworth for the first time in six weeks. "Good," he said, but nothing more, and the conversation stopped there. Just as his life was about to become public again, he seemed to be retreating deeper into himself.

To make sure there were no photo opportunities, Tiger drove his Escalade into the hangar where his Gulfstream G550, which he now owned, was being parked. After landing in Augusta, the plane was towed into the hangar, where a van from the Augusta National awaited us.

The club rules mandated that we had to play with a member, and our host was a former Augusta National club champion.

Though Tiger's game had been bad at Isleworth, it got worse at Augusta. I'd never seen him look as helpless on a golf course, as he sprayed several drives into the trees and mis-hit a bunch of irons. Rather than show anger, he got sullen and discouraged. When we got to the ninth hole, he decided not to hit his tee shot. At first I didn't know what he was doing, so when I showed puzzlement, he said, "I'm not going to play for a couple of holes." He proceeded to walk along with us on the ninth, tenth, and part of the eleventh hole without hitting a shot. It was a first. Before, when he played badly in practice, he'd get hot, but he'd also get motivated and play better. Now he was moping and quitting. Obviously, he was loaded down with thoughts.

We all stayed in one of the club's cabins that night. Even though Tiger is considered a member of Augusta because he's won the Masters, he isn't a regular member, and club rules dictate that the regular member who was hosting us had to stay in the cabin as well. The next morning, the weather was cold and damp, making it hard to make the cleanest contact off the wet, tight turf. As I warmed up on the range, I could hear Tiger hitting balls behind me. I could tell from the slapping sound his clubhead was making at impact that he was repeatedly hitting iron shots fat. It didn't get much better on the course. There was no way that, counting his first ball on every hole, Tiger broke 80. It was ugly, and though I still believed focused practice would bring his game back to a respectable level in time for the Masters, I was also starting to wonder whether Tiger would ever be the same player again.

The following week, we returned to Augusta. This time I didn't play and focused totally on helping Tiger get ready. Tiger shot somewhere in the mid-70s in both his rounds and was still struggling.

The time had come for me to be assertive. Tiger was subdued on the ride back to the airport for the return flight. There was still plenty of daylight when we got to Orlando, so as we drove back to Isleworth, I went strong.

"Look, Tiger," I said. "Just give me thirty minutes on the range.

We can fix what you're doing wrong, and we've got to fix it because you're going to have no chance at the Masters if we don't. And in these thirty minutes, I don't want to hear how far you're hitting it, or any of that shit. I just want you to try what I'm going to tell you."

I got his attention. He didn't protest, just said OK. I got his clubs onto his cart and we drove over to the practice tee. Right away, I focused on the bad habit that had gotten worse, dropping his head down and away from the target on the downswing. It was a tendency Tiger fell into when he became consumed with hitting the ball farther, which had happened more often in recent years as more and more young players outdrove him. To steady his downswing, I stood facing him as he took his address position, my right arm outstretched and holding the top of his head with my hand. Immediately he hit the ball better, and he continued to after I stepped away. To prove to him how much better his swing looked, I filmed him with my iPhone and showed him—something I rarely did, because I usually wanted the emphasis of our analysis to be based on ball flight. He agreed that he was hitting the ball with more control, but he also added, "Yeah, but it doesn't go as far." That frustrated me, especially when I saw that over the next few minutes of hitting more balls, he gradually returned to moving his head down and back and slinging his arms through impact. It was Tiger the student at his most stubborn.

There was another problem: Steve Williams. Since the scandal broke, I'd been in touch with Steve, who'd been in New Zealand. Steve is a tough customer who lives by an old-school code of behavior, and he was upset that Tiger hadn't called him or returned his calls. He was particularly upset that Tiger hadn't made it clear publicly that Steve hadn't been involved in the womanizing in any way—didn't even know about it, in fact. Steve told me the scandal had hurt his reputation in his home country and even caused some tension in his marriage. He'd even made public comments that Tiger had to "earn back my respect."

In our phone conversations, Steve told me he was very eager to have a long talk with Tiger when he came to caddie at the Masters. He wanted to discuss his salary as well as ask that Tiger show him more appreciation verbally. And what he really wanted from Tiger was an apology.

I told Mark Steinberg that Tiger had to have a talk with Steve before Masters week, or their relationship was going to be damaged, perhaps irreparably. As much as he didn't want to, Tiger first called Steve's wife, Kirsty, in New Zealand. Kirsty was a good friend of Elin's, so Tiger knew the conversation was going to be uncomfortable. Tiger said he told her that Steve was blameless. He also tried to get her to understand that his actions hadn't been aimed at Elin but instead were a compulsion that had gotten out of control. I asked Tiger how that conversation went, and he shook his head. "I don't know," he said. "She was still mad, and she didn't really understand."

Meanwhile, Steve wanted a face-to-face meeting with Tiger, and he was told by Mark it would happen Saturday after Steve landed in Orlando and came to Isleworth. But when Steve went to Tiger's house to see him, all he got was a lukewarm greeting. Tiger was preoccupied, and he told Steve he had to go somewhere and that they'd talk later.

Steve was upset. "The guy couldn't even look me in the eye," he told me. "He hasn't changed one bit." His frustration spilled over when he saw the state of Tiger's game later that day on the practice tee. "I don't even know why we're going to Augusta," he told me. "He can't make the cut hitting it like this. It's horrible."

Steve seemed to be right in his assessment of Tiger's golf. That evening, on the eighteenth fairway at Isleworth, I made a final plea that was calm but loaded with urgency. "Tiger, you have no chance the way you're swinging," I said. "I don't know what new ideas you've been trying, but they haven't worked, and they won't work. Here's what you have to do." I then reiterated the basic things we'd always worked on, except that I wanted him to exaggerate them to make sure he didn't fall into the destructive tendencies that had impeded his preparation so far. It meant that he'd have to employ a slightly outside-to-in swing path that would produce a left-to-right ball curve on his shots. It would cost him distance off the tee but keep his missed shots from straying as far off-line. I also knew it was a swing path that would improve his iron play. "You've got to eliminate the big miss off the tee," I told him. "Let's get the ball in play, where you can rely on your irons."

Tiger knew time was running out, so he not only listened, he put what I said into practice, almost immediately hitting the ball with more control. It was not a great session. The truth is, we never had a great session in preparation for the 2010 Masters. But now he had a plan and something that he could at least repeat. It had been the logical path all along, and I lamented all the lost time his stubbornness had cost him. Still, I respected that no one had a better track record of being ready for big moments. Maybe he'd be ready again.

As we loaded up to go to the airport the next morning, I didn't sense a lot of energy coming from Tiger. The only time I'd seen him in a similar state was during the 2006 U.S. Open at Winged Foot, which took place less than six weeks after his father had died, and where Tiger missed the cut for the first time at a major in his professional career. Before the 2008 U.S. Open at Torrey Pines, Tiger had projected total determination. I wasn't sensing anything similar now.

I had to drop off a rental car, so Tiger and Steve rode to the airport alone. It still wasn't the face-to-face encounter that Steve had wanted so badly, as Tiger was wearing wrap-around sunglasses and was looking at the road as he drove. But at least they talked, and Steve told me on the plane that he felt better about going forward. All Tiger said to me was, "I talked to Stevie. Can you believe he asked me for a raise?"

Tiger moved into his rented house, along with Steve and a couple of staffers. I'd stayed in the house with Tiger before, but there was so much extra going on that there weren't any more rooms, so my wife, Suzanne, and I went to a hotel.

On Sunday afternoon, Tiger surprised Steve and me by playing well. That was important because he was facing a big press conference at the club on Monday, the first time he'd be taking questions from reporters about the scandal and its aftermath, and we had been worried the stress could set him back. He was also unsure about how he'd be received by the fans. At his rental house, I heard Mark Steinberg repeatedly telling Tiger that all he had to do was perform well and people would forgive and forget, as they'd done with Kobe Bryant and Michael Vick. Tiger didn't say much in return, but I got the feeling he didn't believe it. Later on, Tiger prepared for his press conference with his team, fielding hypothetical questions and discussing possible answers.

Rather than trying to ignore what was being written and said about him, Tiger was taking it in. While we were in Augusta driving back and forth to the course, Tiger sat in the front passenger seat while I sat in the back, and I could see as he surfed the Web on his phone that he was searching for stories about himself on the gossip sites. A couple of times he suddenly said, "Uh-oh, here's another story," before immersing himself in it. Worse, he was reading the comments from readers, many of them vicious cheap shots. I was thinking there was no way that could be helping his frame of mind.

When I saw that he chose to play his practice rounds wearing sunglasses, I was disappointed. Tiger legitimately has terrible allergies, and they really affect him at Augusta in early spring. In fact, in each of his four Masters victories, it had rained sometime during the week, lessening the pollen count. The shades helped ease the irritation, but I still thought it was a mistake as far as the first impression he was making. People needed to see Tiger's eyes.

He played his practice round on Monday with Fred Couples, someone he has always felt comfortable with and who has always been one of Tiger's biggest supporters among the players. I know

Fred well, and he's very adept at acting as if everything is fine even when there's a lot of chaos in his life. He and Tiger saw each other on the practice tee for the first time since the scandal, and Fred greeted him with an easy casualness, putting his hand on Tiger's shoulder. Tiger's game improved, which seemed to calm him before going to the dreaded press conference.

It went better than the apology from Ponte Vedra. Without a script, his answers were credible, and he stayed poised in the line of fire. A couple of times I thought his choice of words revealed the profound pain he'd experienced, as when he said that because he forgot his core values, "I lost my life in the process."

Afterward, Tiger seemed unburdened, and his practice play got better each day leading up to the tournament. He was staying with our swing plan, and I gradually began to believe that he had a decent chance to turn in a respectable performance.

In our last two practice rounds, a couple of men Tiger had gone to rehab with followed us. Tiger had gotten them tickets, and he thoughtfully went over to talk to them along the ropes of the practice area. Tiger introduced me, and the three of us talked quite a bit as we followed Tiger on the course. They were hopeful about Tiger, and I thought, *This is good. He's got some new friends.* I knew that rehab counselors encourage patients to shed enablers. Although I realized that it would always be complicated for Tiger to trust anyone outside his inner circle, I thought he'd benefit from developing confidants beyond those who worked for him.

But as we talked, I learned that Tiger hadn't kept in touch with these guys or others he'd met in therapy, even though the clinic encouraged staying in contact. I heard later that Tiger had gone back only once for aftercare treatment, a week or so after his inpatient care had ended.

On Wednesday, Tiger got publicly slammed by Augusta National chairman Billy Payne, who said, "He disappointed all of us." When asked about it, Tiger took the high road, saying, "I disappointed myself." Privately, I didn't hear him complain about what

Payne had said. On the ride from the course back to his house, I expressed my view that I thought Payne had unnecessarily piled on, saying, "Man, how about Billy Payne?" All Tiger said was "Yeah," but he didn't look like he was suppressing any anger. I thought that on the eve of the tournament, he didn't want to waste any energy and was homing in mentally.

Still, I really had no idea how Tiger would react once play began on Thursday. I was nervous for him when he got on the first tee, which was more jammed with people than I'd ever seen it. The reception he got after being announced was respectful and supportive, but the air was tense. I was really proud of Tiger when he rose to the occasion. He smoked a driver down the middle with a little cut, just as he'd been practicing. Considering the occasion, I believe it's one of the best shots he ever hit.

As he walked down the fairway, a plane with a banner that read TIGER: DID YOU MEAN BOOTYISM? flew overhead. There was no way of knowing if Tiger saw it, because his eyes were still hidden by sunglasses. I was grateful, though, that I didn't hear any other negative comments from fans during the round.

Tiger started well, then hit a couple of loose shots that led to bogeys, but he made eagles on two par 5s, the eighth and the fifteenth. His 68 was the lowest score he ever shot in the first round of a Masters, and it could have been lower if he'd converted short birdie putts on the last two holes. The missed five-footer on eighteen was concerning because Tiger was always conscious of the importance of ending rounds on a positive note and was usually deadly with short putts on the last hole. Especially worrisome was the way he missed—hitting the ball too hard and pulling it to the left with a clearly anxious stroke. But overall, he'd dug very deep and once again found a way to meet the moment.

Friday he hit the ball even better but had three three-putts to shoot 70. The three-putts were a bad sign. Even for Tiger, it was very hard to win a tournament if he had more than three three-putts over 72 holes. He was two shots behind the leaders.

He shot another 70 on Saturday. It wasn't a perfect round, but a pretty darn good one. He'd hit 15 of 18 greens in regulation, and though he'd hit a couple of errant drives and one or two poor iron shots, I thought the good far outweighed the bad. He'd ended the round with a birdie after stiffing a 6-iron on the eighteenth hole. He was trailing leader Lee Westwood by four shots and Phil Mickelson by three. Considering where Tiger had started from a month earlier, I was amazed.

Tiger's reaction was just the opposite. Losing ground to the leaders put him in a bad mood. Rather than the 33 putts he'd taken, he focused on blaming his swing. "I warmed up terrible," he told the media. "I didn't have control of the ball." He also complained of a "two-way miss." Even though he had, from my perspective, hit the ball better than he had since beginning his comeback, Tiger made a point of telling the media that, for the first time all week, he was going to hit balls after his round. Before meeting Tiger on the range, I got a warning from Mark Steinberg, who said, "Be careful, he's really pissed."

When Tiger got to the practice area, he was at his most sullen. Almost under his breath, he said, "I hit it like shit." It was so contrary to what I saw that I simply said, "Tiger, no you didn't." He didn't respond. He'd said he hit it bad and I was his swing coach, and he wanted me to chew on that.

Tiger hit a bunch of irons in silence. He wasn't going through the Nine Shots, but he actually hit the ball quite well. Clearly, though, he was steaming, and I decided it wasn't a good time to engage him. The year before at Augusta he'd come off the course angry and I'd tried to calm him down, which only led to his snapping at me loudly enough for other players and even some spectators and golf writers to notice. About ten minutes later, he semi-apologized, saying, "Sometimes you've just got to let me get hot and get over it." So that's what I did this time. I thought then that his tantrum had been for effect, and I thought the same thing this time. *Why* remained unclear.

After he cooled down, Tiger went to the practice green to do some work on his putting. It was the first time at this Masters that he'd putted after one of his rounds. For the tournament, he put in less cumulative putting practice than at any other major I could remember—a continuation of the lessening short-game practice trend that had begun in 2007.

Tiger putted for about 15 minutes, and when we left, he seemed in a better mood. He gave Suzanne and me a ride back to the hotel, and before dropping us off, said, "We're only four back. We can make that up on the front nine." Somehow, though, I didn't sense a lot of conviction in his words.

The next day, Tiger seemed tense on the ride to the course. That made the mile-long crawl along traffic-choked Washington Road feel especially long. I tried a standard "How you feeling, bud?" but all Tiger said was, "Yeah, feel good." He stayed silent as we parked and he walked to the clubhouse.

After he had lunch and changed his shoes, he walked out to meet me on the range. While warming up with an 8-iron early in his session, he suddenly complained, "I can't draw the ball."

I was taken aback. We'd decided that his compressed preparation for this Masters made it necessary to rely on a left-to-right fade for the length of the tournament. Now he wanted to hit the ball right to left, the draw that is considered advantageous off the tee on several holes at the Augusta National. But attempting the draw caused him to fall into the destructive swing habits that had made his play in the weeks leading up to the Masters so poor.

I calmly said, "Tiger, we talked about this, right?" He didn't answer, and that's when he began hitting faster and not giving a good effort. A lot of the shots were low. I stayed quiet for a long time, but knowing this was my last chance to have some input on his performance, I decided to break the silence.

"Tiger, are you open?" It was the language of rehab. Tiger looked up at me, and with a hard look said, "Yeah, I'm open."

"You just have to get the ball up in the air." This was something

I'd often said to him, and it was like code. It essentially meant making his downswing plane more upright, so that the club came down in front of him rather than more behind him, opening the clubface and thus increasing the loft at impact.

It was an instruction that I had given him countless times over the years, and it always got immediate results. But this time, Tiger looked at me and said, "What do you mean by that?"

It was no time for me to escalate the conflict, so I explained what I meant specifically. But he kept hitting the ball low. More than not doing what I was asking, he wasn't really trying. That had never happened before.

And it suddenly hit me: a very strong feeling that this would be the last time I ever worked for Tiger Woods.

I was stoic, but inside I was churning. For a moment I stood outside myself and wondered, *Is this how I really feel?* I thought, *Wow. You're done with the greatest coaching job ever? You're going to walk away from the most interesting and rewarding player to teach, probably in history? The guy you've studied endlessly and whose game you've woken up every morning thinking about. Really?* But that didn't change my mind. Something inside me had snapped and made all the things I sought when I took the job seem no longer worth it.

For six years, I'd adapted to the way Tiger chose to be, even when I found him difficult. I had much to gain. I wanted to be part of golf history. I wanted to better understand what it took to be great. I wanted to contribute to greatness.

I also genuinely cared about Tiger as a person and knew his life wasn't easy. I sensed that despite the assumption that he'd followed his dream, he hadn't chosen his life as much as it had chosen him. Giving himself over to golf instead of a more normal life had many advantages, but being a well-adjusted, fulfilled person wasn't one of them. I admired tremendously the way he held up his end of the bargain to produce excellence. But I'd seen close-up the cost of so much single-mindedness, and I wondered, *As much as Tiger has gained in wealth and glory, is it possible that he feels used?*

In that moment I realized that a big part of the emotional exhaustion I was feeling was Tiger's concept of friendship. I always thought of Tiger as my friend, and he often referred to me as his friend. Mark Steinberg would often say that Tiger considered me one of his best friends. But Tiger threw the term around so liberally, using it to describe his relationship with people he barely interacted with, that I had to reassess what "friendship" really meant in my case. An old confidant of mine, Sam Ainsley, once asked me during one of our discussions about Tiger, "Hank, was friendship even *available*?" And the hard truth was—even after his treatment—it wasn't.

This whole interpersonal calculation was feeding into my desire to resign. There was also a pragmatic side to consider. I'd seen slippage in Tiger's commitment to practice even before the scandal, particularly in regard to his short game and putting. There was also the possibility that his injuries would be chronic. Although I believed—and still believe—that Tiger could come back to be great again, I sensed that because of the new complications from the scandal, the road back would be difficult. And I realized that I didn't want to take it.

I also couldn't deny the possibility that Tiger's behavior at this Masters was a sign that he wanted to fire me. I always knew that day could come. I'd observed from afar the way Tiger had ended relationships with ex-caddie Mike "Fluff" Cowan and my predecessor, Butch Harmon. In both cases the process had been dragged out, with Tiger being vague in public statements and seemingly constitutionally unable to cut things clean. I wasn't willing to be left hanging in a similar way.

But even as I was contemplating my exit, part of me stayed in coaching mode. Time in the warm-up was running out, but I encouraged Tiger to literally restart by again hitting his shorter clubs and trying a fresh approach. On a couple of occasions when he'd had bad warm-ups in the past, I'd suggested this, and it had worked. But this time Tiger's attitude was worse and his ball striking didn't improve. Steve, who rarely said much when Tiger hit balls, offered some encouragement, but it didn't improve Tiger's mood.

After Tiger had finished his range work, I followed him as he wordlessly headed to the putting green for a final few strokes before teeing off. I realized that despite everything, he still had a shot at winning this Masters and once again making golf history. I wanted to leave him with a positive thought, so after he hit some putts and got ready to go to the first tee, I said, "You know what we talked about. Do that, and you'll be all right." He gave me a nod, and I said, "Good luck." It was the last contact I'd ever have with Tiger on a golf course as his coach.

I stayed to watch Tiger hit his opening drive, not feeling good about the prospects. I was worried about him succumbing to his issues with first-tee drivers, but it was the negative attitude from his warm-up that really left me uncertain. Sure enough, he pulled his drive a good 80 yards, a shot far more crooked than anything he'd hit on the range, the ball nearly going through the adjoining ninth fairway. Because I knew he still had a shot from over there, and because of all my conflicted feelings about Tiger, I wondered if he was conspiring against me. Did he want to establish that his Hank Haney swing was so bad that his only chance to win would be to rescue himself with an improvised fix? I'd eventually dismiss such thoughts, but that they even occurred told me a lot about the dysfunction in our situation.

Tiger's round was tumultuous. He bogeyed the first hole after a poor chip, and was three over par after five holes, seven shots behind the leader. Then he miraculously holed an 8-iron from 160 yards on the seventh hole for an eagle, and he birdied the eighth and ninth holes to get back with a chance. On the par-4 fourteenth, Tiger missed a seven-foot birdie putt and then rushed the 20-inch tap-in, the resulting bogey effectively ending his chances. He eagled the fifteenth and birdied the eighteenth to play the last 12 holes six under, but after a 69 he still finished five strokes behind Mickelson.

The big picture? Considering the mental load Tiger was carrying, his performance was phenomenal. But he was in no shape to see it that way. The crowd was cheering loudly for Mickelson coming up the 72nd hole when Peter Kostis of CBS interviewed Tiger a few yards behind the green. Rather than take the opportunity to be gracious and win friends and support, he was curt. Later, Tiger told reporters, "I had another terrible warm-up today. I've got to be able to shape the ball both ways. I felt very uneasy over every shot I hit out there."

I didn't wait around to see him. Suzanne and I walked back to the hotel along Washington Road, which was still crammed with traffic. We could overhear people celebrating Phil's victory and wondering about Tiger's future. A couple of people recognized me, one saying, "Nice try, Hank." We stopped at a Subway to get a couple of sandwiches for the road, and after checking out, headed to Hilton Head, 350 miles away, where I was going to spend several days at my junior academy.

Before long we were on moonlit, tree-lined country roads in the middle of South Carolina, which put me in a reflective mood. "Holy shit," I said out loud. "Am I crazy?" There were tears in my eyes, but both of us were laughing. Then I turned serious again and said to Suzanne, "Maybe I am. But I just can't do it anymore."

Filled with that thought and knowing it wasn't the right time to talk to Tiger, I decided to call Mark Steinberg to air my feelings. "Mark, I'm finished," I said. "I've had enough. I've put everything into this. I've been a good team player. But I'm just done."

Mark and I had talked often about the pressure of serving Tiger, the constant scrutiny and criticism from the media, and Tiger's moody ways. He knew the effort I'd put into getting Tiger ready for the Masters, and how disappointed I'd been that Tiger hadn't come away from therapy an easier person to work with. So I doubt Mark was shocked that I was unhappy. Still, he reacted strongly.

"Hank, you can't do this," he said. "You can't do this to him. This is the toughest time of his life. You're one of his best friends.

You understand him. He needs you. Whatever you do, don't abandon him now."

I'd never heard my role valued quite that much, and it made me pause. I told Mark that I was too emotional to make a decision at that moment. I told him I'd think about it and call him in the morning.

By the time I called back, I'd calmed down and taken Mark's pleadings to heart. If Tiger truly needed me as much as he said, quitting now was not the right thing to do. I told Mark I'd delay my decision and see how things developed. "I won't leave him hanging," I said. "I'll be there for him."

Four days later, I'd gotten more comfortable with the idea of continuing to coach Tiger. I sent him a five-page e-mail—with a cc to Mark—that critiqued his Masters performance and proposed a plan for his game going forward. The e-mail was more extensive and candid than anything I'd written to him since 2005. I felt I had nothing to lose and got some things off my chest.

The e-mail included the following passages:

> You have great knowledge of the golf swing and the parts of the golf swing, but at times you are all over the place with what you are working on. It is as if you are doing what a lot of people do that don't know anything, looking for the secret. I mean, in the weeks leading up to Augusta it seemed like you had musical swing thoughts going on. First I heard it was get the club more inside and around, then it was get the left arm up, stand closer, posture through the ball, some kind of release I hadn't seen before and the list seemed to go on and on. Corey says it is sometimes like you have swing ADD.

> I thought your attitude on the golf course was incredibly good. You were so great with the fans, and I truly believe it had a positive impact on your preparation and ultimately

on how well you did in the opening round. I know you will kind of laugh at that last notion.

Sunday was not a good day from start to finish. In your warm up . . . it didn't seem like you gave yourself much of a chance to get something going because you were so upset and negative about how you were hitting it. This to me is a waste of energy and talent. One of your greatest attributes is that you can figure things out, you can come up with something that will work, but when you get so upset it really makes it hard to get something going.

Not only does your head tilt with the longer clubs but it drops way down in the downswing and hangs back. If your head drops your posture changes, and if your head lays back your body has no chance to move in sync together. You have got to fix that mistake. IF YOU WOULD COMMIT YOURSELF TO FIXING THAT MISTAKE YOU WILL BE THE GREATEST BALL-STRIKER OF ALL TIME.

One last thought. Every time you get done with a round and talk about how terrible you hit the ball it is a direct knock on me. I know you are frustrated, and rightfully so. I also can take it, but I could take it a lot better if I really felt you were committed to the things that I believe in that I think would really help you. I know in my mind I have helped you learn more about the swing and playing the game, and I know that the best of your golf is yet to come. You have had a terrible time in your personal life and have handled it in a manner that I totally respect you for. As I have told you before, you are on the climb back up now and not the slide down and I am always on your side. Hang in there and get working on your game.

As usual, Tiger didn't respond to my e-mail. Given that I'd just spent fourteen days in a row with him and that Mark had probably told him that I'd threatened to quit, I thought that this time he might get back to me right away. Instead, more than two weeks went by before he called me the night before the first round of the Quail Hollow Championship in Charlotte, which I didn't attend.

He didn't acknowledge receiving the e-mail and opened the conversation as if everything was normal. He greeted me with a customary "What's up?" and went on to talk about the NBA and baseball and even the weather. For the 20 minutes we talked, he didn't mention golf. When I brought up his game, he changed the subject. He told me he hadn't slept well and was considering withdrawing. He admitted being worried about a woman who was claiming that he'd fathered her child. He said the claim couldn't be true because the timeline was wrong, but he knew it was going to lead to taking another hit in the media. At the end of the call, I asked him how he was doing overall, and he said, "I'm hanging in there."

That call turned my mind back toward leaving Tiger. The lack of acknowledgment of my e-mail or any of the subjects in it bothered me, because if he'd actually read it, it would have been impossible not to notice that I'd given it a lot of time and thought and that the tone carried some urgency. If he *hadn't* read it, that obviously told me something, but if he *had* and decided to blow it off, that was revealing as well. I realized he was under a lot of pressure and had a lot on his mind—soon he would miss the cut at Charlotte with scores of 74 and 79—but at a time when I needed Tiger to acknowledge some things about our partnership, he just didn't.

Tiger played the following week at the Players Championship, which he hadn't asked me to attend. At his Tuesday press conference, he told the media, "Hank and I talk every day, so nothing's changed. According to the press, I've fired him five times by now."

He lied. That pissed me off, because we *didn't* talk every day. We had talked once since the Masters, and not about golf. I was getting the feeling that Tiger wanted to string me along, keep me as his coach mostly to take the blame for his "bad" swing but listen to me less and less.

Tiger's first three rounds at the Stadium Course left him eight strokes back. He called me on Sunday morning before the last round. It was mostly 20 minutes of small talk. His main concern was his neck. He said he feared he had a herniated disk. In what I took as a passive-aggressive suggestion that my swing instruction might have been the cause of his pain, he said, "It's weird. It only hurts when I play golf."

When we hung up, I'd made up my mind. I'd been giving my exit a lot of thought and had prepared some statements and even what I would say to Tiger when the time came. I intended to resign on Sunday, but when Tiger withdrew on the seventh hole because of his neck, I thought it might seem like piling on, and I also didn't want to take attention away from the final day of the tournament.

As if I needed any more reasons to quit, Johnny Miller took a shot at me during the NBC telecast of the final round, saying of Tiger, "This might be a little harsh, but I really believe he needs to, every night, watch the U.S. Open in the year 2000 at Pebble and just copy that swing and forget the Haney stuff. That was the best golf anybody has ever played in history." Just as it was with Tiger, it seemed that whatever I'd accomplished as his coach was never going to be good enough.

On Monday morning, I called Jim Gray, who had been a friend and mentor at ESPN but who now worked for the Golf Channel, to tell him I'd be resigning as Tiger's coach. Because I also had a contract with the Golf Channel, I felt an obligation to give them the news first. I sent Jim a prepared statement and asked them to wait a few hours before breaking the story.

Then I sent a text to Tiger saying we needed to talk. He texted back, "I can't talk today. I'm with my kids." The wheels were already in motion, so I put everything I was going to say in a text and sent it to Tiger. It said:

> Tiger, in every instance when I am asked about Tiger Woods, I always answer in the best interests of Tiger Woods. Every time you are asked about Hank Haney, you never answer in the best interests of Hank Haney. It bothers me. It hurts me. If anybody should understand the value of friends at this point in their life, it should be you. I feel like I've been a great friend to you. I don't feel I've gotten that in return.

He texted me back right away:

> I always tell people you're my coach. You take criticism of my game way too seriously. And maybe it's time that we just take a little break.

I had another text ready. I thought, *How am I going to feel when I press the Send button?* It was definitely a big moment in my life. I pressed that Send button, and immediately felt a huge sense of relief. I sort of checked to make sure I wasn't deluding myself, and realized that my emotion was genuine. I thought, *Oh my God, I can't believe I feel this good.*

The message said:

> Tiger, I appreciate everything you did for me. The incredible opportunity I had to work with you. It's been an unbelievable six years. You've won a lot of tournaments, we've had a lot of great times. It's taken me to a place in my profession that I would never ever have hoped to have been. I can't tell you how grateful I am for the opportunity, but it's time for you to find another coach.

He responded,

> Thanks, Hank. But we're still going to work together.

I was surprised, but I wasn't going to waver. I answered,

> No we're not. It's finished. Done. Over. I'm no longer your coach.

A few seconds later, Tiger texted,

> We'll talk in the morning.

Amazingly, I later learned that Tiger did a telephone press conference in the afternoon supporting the AT&T National in which he referred to me as his coach while talking about how his neck injury affected his swing. "I talked to Hank about some of the stuff," he said. "We're still working on it. We have a lot of work to do."

Not long afterward, the Golf Channel read my prepared statement, which I also posted on my website. It said, in part:

> I have informed Tiger Woods this evening that I will no longer be his coach. I would like to thank Tiger for the opportunity that I have had to work with him over the past six-plus years. Tiger Woods has done the work to achieve a level of greatness I believe the game of golf has never seen before and I will always appreciate the opportunity that I have had to contribute to his successes. . . . It has been a great learning experience, and along the way Tiger has elevated me in my profession to a level that I never thought I would achieve before I had the opportunity to work with him.

I made sure to add,

> Just so there is no confusion, I would like to make clear that this is my decision.

The next morning, Mark Steinberg called me. He said, "Hank, you handled everything well. Your statement was classy. Tiger's fine about it. He's going to issue a statement and say it was a joint decision."

I said, "What? Mark, that's bullshit."

He said, "What do you mean?"

"That's not what happened," I said. "And you *know* that's not what happened." I was hot, and I just let go as I never had with Mark before. "That's something that can get you in trouble with the media, telling a lie. That's not what happened. And if you say it was, I'm not going to go along with it. I tell the truth."

There was silence for a few seconds, before Mark said, "OK, OK." Still, when Tiger's statement came out, it didn't acknowledge that I resigned. Instead, it said:

> Hank Haney and I have agreed that he will no longer be my coach. Hank is an outstanding teacher and has been a great help to me, but equally important he is a friend. That will not change. I would like to thank him for all he has done for me the past six years.

That afternoon, Tiger called me. I felt and probably sounded emotional, and I'm sure he could sense it. He sort of reiterated his official statement, saying, "Thanks, Hank, so much for everything you've done. I felt like my game got so much better with you helping me. We have been great friends and the most important thing is to remain great friends. You know, we're still going to work together."

For some reason that I still can't figure out, he just didn't want to let go. "Tiger," I said, "if you ever want me to watch you or help you with an opinion, as a friend I'll be happy to do it. But we're not going to work together. I'm never going to be your coach again."

"We're still going to work together," he said again.

And I answered, "No, we're not." He kind of chuckled, and we said good-bye.

A few days later, Jim Gray came to my home in Dallas to do a long sit-down interview for the Golf Channel. When Jim asked me about whether I'd ever known Tiger to take performance-enhancing drugs, I said very firmly that even when I witnessed Tiger's injections from Dr. Galea, I never saw anything suspicious, and I didn't believe Tiger ever took any kind of PEDs. I added, "The only thing I knew about was his issue with the sex addiction."

After the interview aired, I got a text from Tiger that said, "Thanks for telling everyone that I was in sex-addiction treatment." I felt bad, because I'd intended to exonerate Tiger, and I'd assumed his sex therapy was common knowledge, since it had been widely reported. But he'd never actually publicly confirmed that he'd been treated for sex addiction.

The next morning, Mark Steinberg called me, fuming. "How could you do that?" he said, raising his voice. "How could you say that? How can he raise any money? This will kill his foundation."

I said that I was sincerely sorry. "I tried to be very positive in that interview," I said. "I didn't mean to hurt him or cause him any problems. I apologize if I did."

Mark didn't let up, saying, "You better not be doing any more interviews."

That hit me wrong. "Mark," I said, "you don't control me anymore. I'm going to talk to who I want to talk to."

I hadn't wanted there to be any bad blood, but now it appeared there might be. I figured my next meeting with Tiger would be awkward. I was pretty much done traveling to tournaments, so I didn't expect to see him soon. But then I learned that he'd be playing at J. P. McManus's pro-am in Ireland in July, where I was scheduled to do a clinic. I was nervous on the way to the event, hoping I wouldn't have to see Tiger. There was a chance I wouldn't, depending on when Tiger played on the two days I'd be there. Because he usually skipped pro-am dinners, I didn't expect to see him there. But when Suzanne and I walked into the dining room the first night, there was Tiger at a table with J.P.

I sucked it up and walked right to him. When Tiger saw me, he stood up with a big smile and hugged me. "How you doin', bud?" I asked. "Good as I can do," he said. I told him to hang in there, and he said, "I'm making it." I don't know what Tiger said about me when I left, but while I was there, he was gracious. Except that doesn't describe it exactly. I guess you could say that he was the same as always—warm and cold at the same time.

It was the last contact I've had with Tiger.

My departure was complicated, but I'm proud of the way I managed it. The analogy the whole experience brings to mind is that of a frog in a pot of water. When a frog is thrown into an already boiling pot, it will jump out. But when a frog is placed into water that is tepid, it will stay in. And if the temperature is raised gradually, it will stay in until it's too late.

I guess I'd felt the water getting warmer, but until I hit that Send button, I hadn't realized how hot it really was.

8

Adding It Up

On the television screen, Tiger is studying a six-foot putt to win the Chevron World Challenge in December 2011. For nearly two years, he's missed from this distance more than he ever did before. But something has shifted. On the previous hole, Tiger had made a birdie putt to tie for the lead, and now his face has the calm intensity that erases the doubt I've felt over every important shot he's faced since the scandal. When the ball goes into the center, he's once again simply Tiger, the guy who can make the last putt.

It means that Tiger has won his first tournament in the 27 he has played since hitting the fire hydrant on November 29, 2009. The Chevron isn't an official event, but rather a select field invitational with only 18 players who get a nice payday and the Southern California star treatment before the holidays. Tiger has hosted the event as a way to raise money for his foundation, and in the ten times it has been held at Sherwood CC in Thousand Oaks, California, he has won five times and been second four times.

But the soft setup doesn't diminish the victory as one of the most important of his career. Tiger has been in the wilderness since returning to competition at the 2010 Masters—mentally lost, injured, uncertain with his golf swing and tentative with the putter. After ranking number one in the Official World Golf Rankings for 667 of 723 weeks since January 1998—and never falling below number two during that time—Tiger dropped as low as 58th in 2011. Many said he'd never be back.

But something special is still in there, under the rubble. Whereas postscandal he'd responded to the few times he'd gotten in contention by backing up, now he doesn't. He is clutch again. Tiger reacts with an unrestrained fist pump and yell, but a few minutes later he's eerily matter-of-fact in his interview. The governor on his emotions is there to send a message: This is just another win, and winning is what I do. It's that quality of self-belief, that implicit faith in his own specialness, that tells me Tiger shouldn't be counted out yet in his bid to catch Jack Nicklaus's major-championship record. It's as if he's wearing a sandwich board that says CONDUCTING BUSINESS AS USUAL. Perhaps he believes that if he says it enough times, and walks the walk, the scandal and the victory drought that followed in its wake will simply fade away. Maybe he is right.

Meanwhile, there is an outpouring of pent-up pro-Tiger sentiment. As Tiger has gradually played better, fans and commentators, a lot of the same ones who've been bashing him, clearly want him back. There are retrospectives of Tiger's journey. A topic of continuous speculation is whether Tiger can ever regain his best golf of the early 2000s.

It hits a nerve. I wonder, will that always be history's verdict?

Three days after resigning as Tiger's coach in May 2010, I decided to do some research of my own. As I sat down at my computer in my office in Dallas, I was nervous. For a change, it wasn't because of what I might see on websites and blogs about how I'd messed up Tiger's swing. And I'd taken relatively few hits for leaving Tiger; few saw it as the abandonment of a friend in a time of need. There *was* some unfounded but not unreasonable speculation that I'd made a preemptive strike before being fired, but most of the coverage was on my side. It was as if the revelations about Tiger had made it clear that being his coach was a wearing job, and that—as a cabinet member often bids adieu after a president's troubled first term—it was time to move on.

But to achieve closure, there was still something I needed to do: add up the score.

In the last few years of my tenure, I'd resisted the urge to closely track the record Tiger had built with me as his coach. I knew he'd won a lot of tournaments in our last three years together. I had a strong sense that he'd achieved more consistency than ever. But I didn't really want to know how I stood.

Like Tiger, I was avoiding self-congratulation. Just as any sports psychologist would advise, I wanted to stay in the moment, take one tournament at a time, and just keep working hard. I also had to admit that the negative shots I'd taken from commentators had me a little gun-shy, and there was a part of me that was afraid that a hard look at the numbers might support my detractors.

I knew the source of the criticism: Tiger's time with Butch Harmon. Throughout my own run there was a widely held assumption that Tiger's record with me would never measure up to his record with Butch. It was implied whenever anyone questioned why Tiger would ever want to change the teacher who taught him the swing that won four straight majors, seven out of eleven majors, and the U.S. Open by fifteen shots.

I'd gone into the job anticipating that Butch's record as Tiger's coach would very likely be unbeatable. When I left, with Tiger having won six majors during my tenure as compared to eight with Butch, I figured that the same ratio would extend to Tiger's overall record with each of us.

Butch's coaching monument was the 2000 season. It was the year that Tiger's nine victories included the first three legs of the Tiger Slam, the year he gave golf a Secretariat moment by winning the U.S. Open and British Open by a combined 23 strokes. With the possible exception of Byron Nelson's 1945 performance, when he won 11 straight tournaments and 18 overall, Tiger's 2000 is probably the greatest season by a player in history. And although golf statistics are not as definitive as those of baseball or football, Tiger's were so overwhelming in 2000 that they received a lot of notice. He was second in driving distance and 54th in driving accuracy, which made him the leader in total driving. He led in greens in regulation with a career best of 75.20 percent, in ball striking, in the all-around category, and in scoring, with a career-low average of 67.79, which broke Byron Nelson's record. On par 5s, his birdie-or-better percentage was an off-the-charts 61.89. Basically, Tiger's 2000 was the equivalent of baseball's Triple Crown or a running back leading the NFL in rushing *and* receiving yards or an NBA forward leading in scoring *and* rebounding.

The best driving stats Tiger ever achieved with me were in 2009, when he finished 12th in total driving and 86th in driving accuracy. His performance in the year 2000 supported the idea that he'd not only swung his best under Butch, but that it was the swing he should be going back to.

Still, something nagged at me. *What about wins?* I asked myself. With whom did Tiger have a greater winning percentage, Butch or me? Shouldn't that *also* be a valid measure of whether I helped Tiger get better?

I took a breath and opened two websites, the PGA Tour's and Tiger's, both of which documented Tiger's professional playing record through the years. Then I started clicking the calculator. I tabulated Butch's tenure first, beginning with Tiger's professional debut in August 1996, though they'd actually started together in 1993. While there was never really a hard date when Butch stopped working with Tiger, I decided the end of 2002 seemed reasonable. Much has been made of Tiger telling Butch he didn't want him to work with him on the practice tee at the PGA Championship in 2002, but Butch remained under contract through 2002. He later said he didn't renew his contract in 2003.

Although prior to that afternoon, I'd been prepared to defer to Butch's record, I now felt my competitive instincts kick in. I winced inwardly when I saw that Tiger had notched eight victories in 1999 and nine more in 2000. But I was a little less daunted when I saw only five Tiger victories in both 2001 and 2002. The final tally: In the 127 official PGA Tour events that Tiger played as a professional with Butch as his coach, he won 34 times—just under 27 percent of his starts.

Now more hopeful about what I might find, I checked the record of my time with Tiger. It was discouraging to tally no official wins in 2004, but then the victories came more steadily. I got excited as I saw that Tiger won exactly half of his last 46 official events with me as his coach.

For the entire six years that I was officially his swing instructor, from Bay Hill of 2004 through the Masters of 2010, Tiger played in 91 official PGA tour events. He won 31 of them—34 percent.

I was surprised. As measured by victory percentage, Tiger had performed better with me than he had with Butch. My respect for Butch would keep me from gloating. But I felt good that in the future those numbers would empower me when answering my critics.

I then broke it down further. In my time with Tiger, he was in the top ten in 66 of his 91 events (73 percent). He was in the top three 52 times, which is 57 percent. With Butch, he was in the top ten 82 times in 127 events, which is 65 percent. His top-three finishes were 55 out of 127, or 43 percent.

Subtracting our swing transition years—1998 for Butch, 2004 for me—I also came out ahead. From 1999 through 2002, Butch's last year, Tiger played in 78 official PGA Tour events and won 27 (35 percent). From 2005 up through the 2010 Players Championship, Tiger played in 78 official tournaments and won 31 (40 percent). In Butch's period, Tiger had 55 top tens (71 percent). In my period, he had 57, or 73 percent.

I realize that there's a good argument that Tiger *should have* won more with me. Tiger was a 20-year-old rookie when he turned pro under Butch, and he had much to learn. With me, he had more experience and maturity, and at 28—the age when we started in 2004—he was entering prime years. Even among those who would concede that Tiger improved with me, some would say he didn't improve enough.

What's hard to gauge is whether the older Tiger, with more pressure concentrated on him and a greater sense of restlessness robbing him of his focus, was a more difficult athlete to coach when I encountered him. Comparing age-specific psychological states is pretty much guesswork. But still, since most students—golf or otherwise—tend to veer toward independence with greater maturity, it's rational to argue that the teaching challenge is distinctly different as the years unfold.

Some will say none of that matters—Tiger won more majors with Butch than he did with me, period. True, but I'm proud of the greater consistency Tiger achieved with me in the majors. With Butch, Tiger played in 24 majors as a professional. In those, he had 15 top tens, 12 top fives, and 11 top threes. In the 23 majors he played with me as his coach, Tiger posted 17 top tens, 14 top fives, and 12 top threes. He also had five runner-up finishes in his majors with me compared to one with Butch. Winning is the bottom line, but with me Tiger was in the hunt more often.

I don't mean to sound as if I'm taking credit for Tiger's record. Neither Butch nor I hit a shot. I bring all this up not to run down Butch in any way, but rather to once and for all refute the argument that I hurt Tiger or retarded his progress. The numbers simply don't support that view. People are entitled to their own opinions, but they're not entitled to their own facts. Bottom line: I like what the facts say about my time with Tiger.

People have continued to ask me if I miss coaching him. It's a legitimate question. How could someone of my training and mind-set *not* wish he was coaching the greatest player of all time? I tell them truthfully that I've been happier not working for Tiger than, toward the end of our partnership, I had been working for him.

The greatest gratification I received from working with Tiger came during the times when I knew I'd helped him. Those moments occurred throughout our six years, but they were more concentrated in our first two. The most productive learning invariably occurred in our preparation sessions, often under a very hot Florida sun, alone on the practice tee at Isleworth. There's no doubt that Tiger could be a difficult student, but I took that more as a teaching challenge than as an annoyance, and when I did get through to him, I felt proud.

It was the reason I never got as big a charge out of coaching Tiger at tournament sites. I actually felt awkward being on the "stage" of the practice tee, because at that point, I was usually doing more monitoring than teaching, and my role really wasn't that important. The limelight never excited me much, which is why I came to prefer traveling to fewer tournaments—and even when I did go, I often left before the first round. For me, the sensation of being famous or part of the action wasn't an incentive to stay.

I've never regretted my decision to leave Tiger. But I've often wondered how things could have been different. If I had a wish list, here's what it would include:

I wish Tiger's game during his time with me hadn't always been compared to his game in the year 2000, but rather to his game in 2003 and early 2004, the period just before I started.

I wish Tiger had been less reckless in partaking in workout regimens and military-training activities that further damaged his knee.

I wish Tiger had postponed his knee surgery in April 2008 until after the final major of that year. My guess is that while he would have continued to play with pain and might not have won at Torrey Pines, he would have played well enough with a torn ACL to be a legitimate threat to win not only the U.S. Open but also the British Open and PGA. More important, by postponing the operation, he would have kept himself from rushing back to competition and hurting himself again. And he wouldn't have had to deal with the motivational issues that came from having climbed the ultimate mountain with his victory at Torrey Pines.

I wish Tiger had been more open to a lower-maintenance coaching relationship in which he essentially monitored himself and just called me when he needed me.

I wish Tiger had come back from rehab a different person. Not a *lot* different, just a little warmer and more open. It could have started with something as simple as offering me a popsicle. I realize now that as hard as I tried to understand Tiger, he tried just as hard not to let me.

I wish we could have been better friends. I haven't communicated with Tiger since I saw him in Ireland in July 2010. Another pro, Pat Perez, told me that Tiger had complained that I hadn't called him. My feeling was that because he'd just taken on a new coach, Tiger could have easily misconstrued my reasons for calling. And as I told Pat, there was nothing keeping Tiger from calling me. Now, my guess is that the publication of this book won't bring us closer. As much as Tiger and I went through, and as much as I cared about him and still do, I consider the distance between us a big miss for both of us.

All that said, I'll always be thankful for my experience with Tiger. In so many ways, it's the best thing that ever happened to me.

Probably the most valuable gift I took away from that experience was the insight I gained into the phenomenon of greatness. Studying Tiger was like taking a survey course on all the best players who ever lived, because he epitomizes every essential quality of a champion. I firmly believe that no one has ever played the game of golf as well as Tiger Woods. Not Jack Nicklaus, not Ben Hogan, not Byron Nelson, not Bobby Jones. Even with deeper competition than ever, Tiger's total career winning percentage of 26 percent from 1996 through 2011 is more than twice that of Jack's 12 percent. The career winning percentage closest to Tiger's belongs to Ben Hogan, who won 20.7 percent of his official events (61 of 294). Tiger is even more dominant when it comes to closing out tournaments. He's gone on to win after holding or sharing the lead going into the final round of official events 48 out of 52 times, an off-the-charts conversion rate of 92 percent that is probably his most admired record among his peers and past greats.

More than any other player, Tiger has expanded the idea of what is possible. Before Tiger, there was a presumption that no golfer could have it all—be long and straight with the driver, creative and accurate with the irons, masterful with the short game, and a deadly putter. Well, when Tiger was perceived as a good driver of the ball and won four straight majors, he created the impression of having it all, or at least being more capable of it than anyone ever. Even when driving deficiencies cropped up later, Tiger's mental gifts of focus and toughness under pressure still brought him closer to the ideal than anyone else.

I've closely followed Tiger's progress since we parted ways. About a month after I quit, his much anticipated return to the U.S. Open at Pebble Beach became electric when he closed with a 31 on Saturday to get within five shots of the lead. But he faltered on Sunday with a 75 to finish tied for fourth. It seemed to take something out of him, because he wasn't as good at the British Open at St. Andrews, where he'd won two of his British Opens. He opened with a 67 that was spoiled by a weak finish, and then faded to tie for 23rd. With that, his much anticipated return to the sites of his historic Open double in 2000 ended, and it seemed that the effects of coming back too early after his scandal kicked in.

A lot of things were hitting him at once. His divorce became final in August. Corey Carroll told me that Tiger seemed depressed and was barely practicing at Isleworth. One day when Tiger seemed particularly down, Corey expressed concern. "He looked at me," Corey told me, "and just said, 'I'm tired.' It was sad because I'd never heard that kind of defeat in his voice before."

In August, Tiger hit what looked like bottom at the WGC Bridgestone Invitational at Firestone. At a tournament and course where he'd won six times, Tiger shot 18 over par in the no-cut event to finish next to last, 30 strokes behind the winner. It was after a ragged third-round 75 that Tiger called swing coach Sean Foley to inquire about working with him.

The next week at the PGA Championship at Whistling Straits, where Tiger finished in a tie for 28th, Sean worked with Tiger on the practice range, and Tiger acknowledged that he had a new coach. Naturally, this led to comparisons between Tiger's "old" swing and the changes he was making. I was disappointed that Sean was critical of me in interviews, telling Fox Sports in September 2010, "Let's be honest about this, it's not like he was flushing the ball with Hank. I think he hasn't been happy with the way he's hit it for a very long time." A few months later, Sean would say of my work with Tiger, "There was nothing about what he was doing in his previous swing that made any sense to me."

I was irritated, but my lasting thought was that Sean hadn't yet learned that Tiger had some difficult swing issues and that simply imposing what Sean believed was a biomechanically "correct" swing might not be the solution. In other words, Sean didn't know what he was dealing with. As Butch had once told me, coaching Tiger was harder than it looked.

In taking on Sean after working with me, Tiger committed himself to making a bigger conceptual swing change than he had when he'd gone from Butch to me. At first, Sean expressed confidence that within a relatively short time Tiger would incorporate the changes easily because they were so "correct." Sixteen months later, though, Tiger was still hitting wild shots, driving the ball more poorly than at any other time in his career, and still hadn't won. And Sean was saying Tiger needed more reps.

I have no doubt that Sean is a very good teacher. I agree with a lot of his beliefs about the golf swing. To me, Tiger's overall motion looks good. But the facts show that Tiger has gone backward with what was already his weakness—his tee shots, particularly with the driver.

In nine official events on the 2011 PGA Tour, Tiger hit only 48.9 percent of his fairways, a career-low number in driving accuracy that ranked him 186th on the tour. The drop would have been less striking if Tiger's driving distance had gone up, but it, too, dropped to a career-low 71st on the tour, with an average of 293.7 yards.

What stood out to me was how often Tiger started missing to the left. For right-handed tour players, especially power hitters, left is where the big miss most often occurs, because a hooked ball that curves right to left is "hotter" and is more likely to run farther into trouble than a softer-landing, left-to-right-curving fade. When I coached Tiger, he hated missing to the left so much that his bail-out shot when he was uncomfortable became a high-spinning fade that usually expired in the right rough. It was a shot that I took a lot of heat for, even as I worked to get Tiger to stop relying on it, but at least it got him around the golf course in a way that still allowed him to win a lot of tournaments.

When Sean made Tiger's grip even stronger (by having Tiger turn his left hand more clockwise) than it had been when I began working with him in 2004, I thought it was risky. While I understood that the goal was a more powerful position that produced more solid and longer shots and that many top players have played and do play with such a grip, I felt it was a radical change for a player in his mid-30s. If Tiger's hands ever reverted to their old position in the hitting area, it meant the face would close and the ball would head left. Tiger indeed began hitting more such shots, and I noticed that by the fall of 2011 his grip had moved back to a weaker position.

Sean also emphasized having Tiger lean the shaft more toward the target with his irons at impact. Again, this produced longer distances on his shots and also a more solid feeling of contact, and Tiger several times commented on how much more he felt he was "compressing" the ball. The problem with emphasizing such a position is that it can create issues with distance control. Shots tend to explode off the face of the club when the shaft is significantly leaned forward, and will often go farther than anticipated. In his first year with Sean, I noticed that Tiger was too often long with his irons. When he was leading the tour in greens in regulation, the hallmark of his iron play was that he was so often pin high. Again, I thought Tiger had reduced some of this shaft lean when his iron play regained some of its precision in the fall of 2011.

With his mental game undoubtedly shaken by the aftermath of the scandal, the swing changes made for a greater rate of big misses than Tiger had ever produced. At the end of 2010, he took a four-stroke lead into the final round at the Chevron at Sherwood. In his pro career, he'd never lost a tournament with such a lead on the last day. But he got shaky on the back nine and fell behind Graeme McDowell. While Tiger made a courageous birdie on the final hole to get into a playoff, he lost when McDowell answered with a long birdie on the first hole of sudden death.

The loss seemed a bad omen for 2011. In the WGC-Accenture Match Play Championship, Tiger tied his first-round opponent, Thomas Bjorn, after 18 holes. On the first extra hole, Tiger pushed his 3-wood tee shot into the desert and lost the match. It was the first time I'd ever seen Tiger lose an official event because of a drive into trouble on the last hole.

At the Masters two months later, Tiger made a tremendous Sunday charge, shooting 31 on the front nine. Tied for the lead on the twelfth hole, he ran a 25-foot birdie putt less than three feet past the hole and missed the par putt. It was shocking, because the twelfth is perhaps the flattest green on the course, and Tiger's purpose was to make sure of par so he could assault the two short par 5s ahead of him and take control of the tournament. Instead, he made the kind of error that he was renowned for never making when he was in the lead. With his momentum stalled, he didn't birdie the par-5 thirteenth even though he had only a 6-iron for his second shot, and the Masters slipped away.

After the tournament, Tiger said he'd hurt his left knee and Achilles tendon hitting a shot from under a tree on the seventeenth hole on Saturday. It was a surprising claim, because he'd played so well on Sunday and with no apparent limp. A few weeks later, he withdrew from the Players Championship after a front-nine 42, again claiming left leg problems, and he eventually took a break from the game that included missing the U.S. Open and the British Open. Whatever the state of his injury, in my opinion a break was what he needed.

In July, Tiger fired Steve Williams, who'd been his caddie since 1999. I wasn't shocked. Steve had been upset when Tiger had neglected to inform him that he was pulling out of the 2011 U.S. Open at Congressional outside Washington, D.C., causing Steve to fly all the way from New Zealand, only to find out he wouldn't be working. Steve then asked Tiger if he could caddie in the championship for Adam Scott instead. Tiger approved it, but he didn't like it, especially when Steve continued to caddie for Adam. At the AT&T National at Aronimink near Philadelphia, where Tiger wasn't playing but was still acting as tournament host, he met with Steve in the clubhouse. It was reported that Tiger told Steve he'd been "disloyal" and that he'd been "overcaddying"—tour jargon for giving the player too much advice—and ended their relationship. The whole thing infuriated Steve, especially the idea that he hadn't been loyal. Steve is old-school, and he was bent on revenge. In August, when Adam won at Firestone, Steve used the occasion to go on national television and take a shot at Tiger by calling the win his greatest victory. Although it made Steve feel good, caddies are supposed to keep a low profile, and Steve was perceived as grandstanding as well as kicking Tiger when he was down. Later,

Steve made an unfortunate "black arsehole" remark about Tiger. I thought it was a sign of maturity that Tiger made it clear he didn't believe Steve was a racist, which probably saved his career as a caddie.

While Steve's time with Tiger may have run its course, just as mine did, I doubt that Tiger will ever have a better caddie. Steve's record as a caddie is the greatest in the history of golf, and he was tremendous under pressure, as Tiger always acknowledged. Joe LaCava, the guy now carrying Tiger's bag, is experienced and respected, but I don't see anyone who'll ever again have the authority with Tiger that Steve had.

When Tiger came back to play at the 2011 PGA Championship in Atlanta, his substitute caddie was boyhood friend Bryon Bell, who works in Tiger's office. On a course that required a lot of drivers off the tee, Tiger's golf was abysmal. In 36 holes, he hit four balls into the water, landed in 22 bunkers, and made five double bogeys, shooting 150 to miss the cut by six. It was surreally bad, and Tiger cited more injuries and took another break from competition.

By then Tiger had moved from Orlando to a home he and Elin had designed on Jupiter Island. It was a period when Tiger's future as a golfer was in serious question, but he gathered himself and went back to the one thing in his life that had always stood him in good stead: hard work on his game.

By all accounts, he started practicing intensely at a new home course, the Medalist, shooting some low rounds and telling people he was finally healthy physically and again able to practice and work out. When Fred Couples made him an early captain's pick for the 2011 Presidents Cup, that served as further motivation. Tiger did a good job of convincing the media that his problems had been due mostly to injuries, which had prevented him from getting sufficient "reps." It was a plausible story, and it allowed him to avoid acknowledging the psychological toll the scandal and divorce might have had on him. To ease back into competition, he entered a smaller PGA Tour event in early October, the Frys.com Open, and played erratically. But he showed some progress at the Australian Open, where he took the lead after two rounds. It had been a while since Tiger had led a tournament, and he opened the third round with three straight bogeys on his way to a 75 that took him out of serious contention.

The next week at the Presidents Cup, at fast and firm Royal Melbourne, Tiger was more solid and won his Sunday singles match impressively. He controlled his approaches very well in the wind, and because the course was playing short, it required very few drivers. Tiger was able to find a lot of fairways hitting low-flighted long irons off the tee, a shot he was gaining confidence with. He relied on them again at the Chevron, as he played Sherwood, a course with five par 5s, more defensively from the tee than he ever had. Zach Johnson outplayed him for 16 holes on the final day, but when Tiger came up big to birdie the last two holes, it was the best medicine to regenerate confidence. He was openly optimistic about 2012, and most of the golf world, clearly missing the pre-scandal Tiger, was rooting for him.

The most asked question about Tiger is whether he'll break Jack Nicklaus's record for major championships. Jack has 18, and Tiger, who had 14 going into the 2012 Masters, needs five more. Getting there will require the most sustained battle of Tiger's career.

Even after going winless in 14 majors since his victory at the 2008 U.S. Open, Tiger is still 14 for 56 in the majors he has played in. If he keeps that rate up, he'll get the five he needs in the next 18, a few months before he turns 40. But that seems like a very fast track now. If his rate slows, it means he will have to get those last wins in his 40s. And considering that Tiger has been winning national titles since he was eight, along with the turmoil of the last two years, in golf years he is an old 36.

Certainly, there are questions of health, psyche, and technique to consider, but to me the most important issue is desire.

Tiger for the longest time had more than anyone else. He may still. Certainly, he likes to prove people wrong, and with the majority view being that he'll never be as good as he was, nor ever catch Nicklaus, he has plenty of motivation. He seemed to regain his work ethic in late 2011, but it's yet to be seen whether he can sustain the effort. If he does, it will again make him different. I've never known a player who lost his hunger for practice to regain that same level of hunger. Usually he or she will show spurts of intensity, but if those aren't rewarded with good play, older players will tend to go back to struggling with their motivation. Nick Faldo, who in his prime was one of the most diligent and intense workers the game has ever seen, said that after he won the 1996 Masters, he lost the drive to practice. He tried to regain it but it never came back, and that drop-off marked the end of his career as a champion.

Jack Nicklaus called the energy it takes to be a champion his juice. "You only have so much juice," he once said. "You try to save what you've got so you can use it when it means the most." Tiger had a tremendous amount, and no doubt he had an inner sense of how he was going to allocate it long-term. But the scandal forced him to use emergency reserves, and it's natural now to wonder whether he has enough left.

If Tiger can keep his work ethic strong, he'll sort out his golf swing. Whatever theory he's using, he'll find a way—either in concert with Sean Foley or another teacher or by finding his own accommodation of their theories. However, I don't think simply solidifying his technique alone will fix his problem with the driver. There is a mental issue there that needs to be addressed, and the odds are against it ever being completely resolved.

It's a weakness that tells the most in majors. It's why, unless he finds some kind of late-career fix with the driver, Tiger's best chances in majors will come on courses with firm, fast-running fairways that will allow him to hit irons off the tee. Of the four majors, the British Open best fits this profile.

I'm not sure what to make of Tiger's putting problems. Technically, he still looks good over the ball and has a textbook stroke. But putting is undone by the smallest and most mysterious of errors, and players rarely improve their putting after their mid-30s. The short par putt Tiger missed on the twelfth hole after tying for the lead in the final round of the 2011 Masters stays in my mind. His putting, both his ability to lag long ones close and his solidness in holing from within six feet, was the foundation of Tiger's ability to close out victories when he had the lead. But postscandal, expecting him to keep up a 90 percent conversion rate when holding the 54th-hole leads seems unrealistic.

Before closing, a player has to get in or near the lead on Sunday, and Tiger also did this at a greater rate than anyone else, including Nicklaus. In order to win five more majors, Tiger is going to have to contend quite a bit. There are exceptions either way, but historically players who have won more than three majors have won about one out of three times they've gotten into serious contention down the stretch. Jack Nicklaus's conversion rate was just above that, with 19 second-place finishes and nine thirds in majors to go with his 18 victories.

Tiger has been even better at converting. He was superefficient with Butch, seriously contending on Sunday 11 times out of 24 majors and winning eight. In the 23 majors Tiger played with me, he seriously contended in 12 of them, winning six. By that formula, Tiger will have to be in contention about 10 more times to get the five majors he needs to pass Jack. But if he's not quite the same kind of closer, or not quite as fortunate as he's been, it could take 15 or more of such opportunities. It seems like a tall order for the Tiger who enters 2012.

Chances are it will mean that he'll eventually have to do something he has never done before: come from behind in the last round to win a major. As good as he's been mentally, it will take a slightly improved mind-set—more patience and acceptance of imperfection—than he's normally displayed.

A final factor to consider is that, whereas Jack Nicklaus's final few majors were won in a historical vacuum and were essentially padding to his record, Tiger will face ever mounting pressure and scrutiny the closer he gets to number 19. Assuming the erosion of age, for Tiger, the sooner he can get to 18, the better.

To propel the chase forward, I believe Tiger has got to get a major in 2012. Without one, his winless streak in Grand Slam events will stretch to 18, which will force him to feel he has to go faster at a time when age is slowing him down. Nicklaus was able to win four majors after turning 36, but three of them came by age 40, with the last one, at age 46, a miracle even to Jack. Bottom line: The odds don't currently favor Tiger catching or passing Jack. But he can make them better than even with a major in 2012. If Tiger again gets good enough to win one major, he'll be good enough to win a few more.

The part of me that believes in his genius still thinks he can do it. A study of geniuses through history shows their most distinguishing characteristic was a willingness to pay any price until the goal was achieved. Tiger had that. The question is whether he still does.

Unlike the Tiger who in his 20s and early 30s was virtually indomitable, today's Tiger has discovered that in life real disaster lurks. Plans don't come true. Things can go wrong. That realization creates doubt, and in competitive golf doubt is a killer. I'm sure what Tiger went through will mature him as a person, but there's no guarantee that it will help him as a golfer. The big miss found its way into his life. If it's ingrained, primed to emerge at moments of crisis, his march toward golf history is over.

The game at the very highest level is a mystery. I thought working with Tiger might provide the key to solving it, but he was too inwardly directed to share it. Of course, he may not have understood the source or the nature of his own gift. Genius is delicate, and it doesn't come with an instruction manual.

Recently, I was watching Arnold Palmer being interviewed by Charlie Rose. Naturally, Arnold was asked whether he thought Tiger would come back, and I was struck by the depth and passion in his answer. Arnold has always been a big supporter of Tiger's, but he didn't sugarcoat the verdict.

"Not sure about that," he said. "Once you vary, and you lose that thing—what is it? Sometimes it's hard to put in place. What is it? I'm not sure I know. I'm not sure Jack [Nicklaus] knows. . . . When you have a disturbance in your life that's major, can you get it back, can you get that thing you can't put your finger on and get hold of it and choke it and keep it? Boy, that's a tough deal. . . . It could be a psychological thing. You say, 'Well, I've done it.' Then you say, 'I want to do it again.' But it isn't there. You can't find it. You can't grasp it. You can't hold on to it."

No other golfer or athlete has seen more slip through his grasp than Tiger. But the biggest miss of all gives him a chance for the biggest recovery. It's a destiny that would match his greatness.

I wish him well.

ACKNOWLEDGMENTS

My sincerest thanks to:

Jim Hardy, whose interest in a young golfer on a very cold day in Chicago inspired me to be a teacher.

John Jacobs, the finest and most important teacher in the history of golf, for the example he set, and for his time and encouragement.

Mark O'Meara, the greatest student and friend any instructor could ever have, who changed my life by allowing me to teach him for 25 years.

Corey Carroll, for his friendship and insight.

Tiger Woods, for an incredibly rewarding six years.

Jeremy Aisenberg, a tireless agent with great judgment.

Steve Johnson, a loyal and always reliable business partner.

Rick Horgan, a wise and artful editor.

Nathan Roberson, for his patience with revisions to the manuscript.

Tammy Blake, for her guidance through the marketplace.

Tina Constable, Crown Archetype's dynamic publisher, whose vision gave this project life.

Jerry Tarde, Mike O'Malley, and Kathy Stachura of *Golf Digest*, Geoff Russell of *Golf World*, and Sam Weinman of Golfdigest.com, for their support and assistance on this project.

Finally, to Jaime Diaz, my collaborator, for his dedication and skill in helping me put this book together.

TIGER WOODS'S WORLDWIDE PERFORMANCE RECORD WHILE HANK HANEY WAS HIS COACH

March 2004 to May 2010

	Scores	Total	Position	Margin	Earnings
2004					
Bay Hill Invitational	67 74 74 73	**288**	T-46	Minus 18	$65,855
The Players Championship	75 69 68 73	**285**	T-16	Minus 9	$116,000
Masters Tournament	75 69 75 71	**290**	T-22	Minus 11	$70,000
Wachovia Championship	69 66 75 68	**278**	T-3	Minus 1	$324,800
EDS Byron Nelson Championship	65 67 70 69	**271**	T-4	Minus 1	$239,733
Memorial Tournament	72 68 67 69	**276**	3rd	Minus 6	$367,000
U.S. Open (Shinnecock Hills)	72 69 73 76	**290**	T-17	Minus 14	$98,477
Cialis Western Open	70 73 65 71	**279**	T-7	Minus 5	$144,600
British Open (Troon)	70 71 68 72	**281**	T-9	Minus 7	$167,598
Buick Open	67 68 66 66	**267**	3rd	Minus 2	$261,000
PGA Championship (Whistling Straits)	75 69 69 73	**286**	T-24	Minus 6	$46,714
WGC NEC Invitational	68 66 70 69	**273**	T-2	Minus 4	$552,500
Deutsche Bank Championship	65 68 69 69	**271**	T-2	Minus 3	$440,000
WGC American Express	68 70 70 70	**278**	9th	Minus 8	$155,000
Tour Championship	72 64 65 72	**273**	2nd	Minus 4	$648,000
Dunlop Phoenix	65 67 65 67	**264**	1st	Plus 8	$388,080
Merrill Lynch Skins Game	5 Skins		2nd		$310,000
Target World Challenge	67 66 69 66	**268**	1st	Plus 2	$1,250,000
2005					
Mercedes Championship	68 68 69 68	**273**	T-3	Minus 2	$350,000
Buick Invitational	69 63 72 68	**272**	1st	Plus 3	$864,000
Nissan Open	67 70	**137**	T-13	Minus 4	$77,333
WGC-Accenture Match Play	T-17 (lost to Nick O'Hern in second round)				$85,000

	Scores				Total	Position	Margin	Earnings
Ford Championship	65	70	63	66	**264**	1st	Plus 1	$990,000
Bay Hill Invitational	71	70	74	72	**287**	T-23	Minus 11	$42,143
The Players Championship	70	73	75	75	**293**	T-53	Minus 14	$18,613
Masters Tournament	74	66	65	71	**276**	1st	Playoff	$1,260,000
Wachovia Championship	70	72	73	71	**286**	T-11	Minus 10	$127,200
EDS Byron Nelson Championship	69	72			**141**	MC (missed cut)		
Memorial Tournament	69	68	71	68	**276**	T-3	Minus 4	$286,000
U.S. Open (Pinehurst)	70	71	72	69	**282**	2nd	Minus 2	$700,000
Cialis Western Open	73	66	67	66	**272**	2nd	Minus 2	$540,000
British Open (St. Andrews)	66	67	71	70	**274**	1st	Plus 5	$1,261,584
Buick Open	71	61	70	66	**268**	T-2	Minus 4	$404,800
PGA Championship (Baltusrol)	75	69	66	68	**278**	T-4	Minus 2	$286,000
WGC NEC Invitational	66	70	67	71	**274**	1st	Plus 1	$1,300,000
Deutsche Bank Championship	65	73	72	71	**281**	T-40	Minus 11	$20,350
WGC American Express	67	68	68	67	**270**	1st	Playoff	$1,300,000
Funai Classic at Disney World	68	73			**141**	MC		
Tour Championship	66	67	67	69	**269**	2nd	Minus 6	$715,000
HSBC Champions	65	69	67	70	**271**	2nd	Minus 3	$550,995
Dunlop Phoenix	65	67	68	72	**272**	1st	Playoff	$336,920
PGA Grand Slam	67	64			**131**	1st	Plus 7	$400,000
Merrill Lynch Skins Game	3 Skins					2nd		$75,000
Target World Challenge	72	72	69	73	**286**	T-14	Minus 14	$167,500
2006								
Buick Invitational	71	68	67	72	**278**	1st	Playoff	$918,000
Dubai Desert Classic	67	66	67	69	**269**	1st	Playoff	$396,405
Nissan Open	69	74			**143**	WD (Illness)		
WGC-Accenture Match Play	T-9 (lost to Chad Campbell in third round)							$125,000
Ford Championship	64	67	68	69	**268**	1st	Plus 1	$990,000
Bay Hill Invitational	70	71	71	72	**284**	T-20	Minus 10	$59,583
The Players Championship	72	69	73	75	**289**	T-22	Minus 15	$76,800
Masters Tournament	72	71	71	70	**284**	T-3	Minus 3	$315,700
U.S. Open (Winged Foot)	76	76			**152**	MC		
Cialis Western Open	72	67	66	68	**273**	T-2	Minus 2	$440,000
British Open (Hoylake)	67	65	71	67	**270**	1st	Plus 2	$1,338,480
Buick Open	66	66	66	66	**264**	1st	Plus 3	$864,000
PGA Championship (Medinah)	69	68	65	68	**270**	1st	Plus 5	$1,224,000

	Scores				Total	Position	Margin	Earnings
WGC-Bridgestone Invitational	67	64	71	68	**270**	1st	Playoff	$1,300,000
HSBC World Match Play	T-9 (lost to Shaun Micheel in first round)							$112,000
WGC American Express	63	64	67	67	**261**	1st	Plus 8	$1,300,000
HSBC Champions	72	64	73	67	**276**	2nd	Minus 2	$555,550
Dunlop Phoenix	67	65	72	67	**271**	2nd	Playoff	$169,840
PGA Grand Slam	70	66			**136**	1st	Plus 2	$500,000
Target World Challenge	68	68	70	66	**272**	1st	Plus 4	$1,350,000
2007								
Buick Invitational	66	72	69	66	**273**	1st	Plus 2	$936,000
Dubai Desert Classic	68	67	67	69	**271**	T-3	Minus 2	$135,654
WGC-Accenture Match Play	T-9 (lost to Nick O'Hern in third round)							$130,000
Arnold Palmer Invitational	64	73	70	76	**283**	T-22	Minus 11	$51,058
WGC-CA Championship	71	66	68	73	**278**	1st	Plus 2	$1,350,000
Masters Tournament	73	74	72	72	**291**	T-2	Minus 2	$541,333
Wachovia Championship	70	68	68	69	**275**	1st	Plus 2	$1,134,000
The Players Championship	75	73	73	67	**288**	T-37	Minus 11	$38,700
Memorial Tournament	70	72	70	67	**279**	T-15	Minus 8	$93,000
U.S. Open (Oakmont)	71	74	69	72	**286**	T-2	Minus 1	$611,336
AT&T National	73	66	69	70	**278**	T-6	Minus 7	$208,500
British Open (Carnoustie)	69	74	69	70	**282**	T-12	Minus 5	$120,458
WGC-Bridgestone Invitational	68	70	69	65	**272**	1st	Plus 8	$1,350,000
PGA Championship (Southern Hills)	71	63	69	69	**272**	1st	Plus 2	$1,260,000
Deutsche Bank Championship	72	64	67	67	**270**	T-2	Minus 2	$522,667
BMW Championship	67	67	65	63	**262**	1st	Plus 2	$1,260,000
Tour Championship	64	63	64	66	**257**	1st	Plus 8	$1,260,000
Target World Challenge	69	62	67	68	**266**	1st	Plus 7	$1,350,000
2008								
Buick Invitational	67	65	66	71	**269**	1st	Plus 8	$936,000
Dubai Desert Classic	65	71	73	65	**274**	1st	Plus 1	$421,717
WGC-Accenture Match Play	1st (defeated Stewart Cink in final)							$1,350,000
Arnold Palmer Invitational	70	68	66	66	**270**	1st	Plus 1	$1,044,000
WGC-CA Championship	67	66	72	68	**273**	5th	Minus 2	$285,000
Masters Tournament	72	71	68	72	**283**	2nd	Minus 3	$810,000
U.S. Open (Torrey Pines)	72	68	70	73	**283**	1st	Playoff	$1,350,000

	Scores				Total	Position	Margin	Earnings
2009								
WGC-Accenture Match Play	T-17 (lost to Tim Clark in second round)							$95,000
WGC-CA Championship	71	70	68	68	**277**	T-9	Minus 8	$95,000
Arnold Palmer Invitational	68	69	71	67	**275**	1st	Plus 3	$1,080,000
Masters Tournament	70	72	70	68	**280**	T-6	Minus 4	$242,813
Quail Hollow Championship	65	72	70	72	**279**	4th	Minus 2	$312,000
The Players Championship	71	69	70	73	**283**	8th	Minus 7	$294,500
Memorial Tournament	69	74	68	65	**276**	1st	Plus 1	$1,080,000
U.S. Open (Bethpage)	74	69	68	69	**280**	T-6	Minus 4	$233,350
AT&T National	64	66	70	67	**267**	1st	Plus 1	$1,080,000
British Open (Turnberry)	71	74			**145**	MC		
Buick Open	71	63	65	69	**268**	1st	Plus 3	$918,000
WGC-Bridgestone Invitational	68	70	65	65	**268**	1st	Plus 4	$1,400,000
PGA Championship (Hazeltine)	67	70	71	75	**283**	2nd	Minus 3	$810,000
The Barclays	70	72	67	67	**276**	T-2	Minus 3	$495,000
Deutsche Bank Championship	70	67	72	63	**272**	T-11	Minus 5	$165,000
BMW Championship	68	67	62	68	**265**	1st	Plus 8	$1,350,000
Tour Championship	67	68	69	70	**274**	2nd	Minus 3	$810,000
WGC-HSBC Champions	67	67	70	72	**276**	T-6	Minus 5	$190,000
JBWere Masters	66	68	72	68	**274**	1st	Plus 2	$270,000
2010								
Masters Tournament	68	70	70	69	**277**	T-4	Minus 5	$330,000
Quail Hollow Championship	74	79			**153**	MC		
The Players Championship	70	71	71		**212**	WD (injury)		

GLOSSARY OF GOLF TERMS

Across the Line

With the clubshaft parallel to the ground at the top of the backswing, and looking down the target line from behind a right-handed golfer, the clubshaft points to the right of the target, is therefore "across the line." From this position, the tendency would be for the golfer to swing on an "in to out" path, producing either a shot that curves from right to left or a push to the right. When I first began working with Tiger, he was slightly across the line at the top of his swing.

Draw

A shot, when hit by a right-handed golfer, that curves slightly from right to left. Because a draw carries less backspin than a fade, it tends to hit the ground harder and roll farther, making it the ideal shot for distance. Powerful players tend to be wary of regularly playing a draw because a misdirected draw can roll farther into trouble. Short hitters tend to favor a draw as a way to gain needed distance. A shot with significantly greater right-to-left curve is called a *hook*.

Fade

A shot that, when hit by a right-handed golfer, curves slightly from left to right. A fade is often favored by the most powerful touring professionals because, while it sacrifices some distance due to the relatively high backspin it carries, it tends to be the best shot for control due to the softness and backspin with which it lands. A shot with significantly greater left-to-right curve is called a *slice*.

Hook

See *Draw.*

Laid Off

The opposite of *across the line.* Looking down the target line from behind a right-handed golfer, the club shaft points to the left of the target, thus is "laid off." From this position, the tendency would be for the golfer to swing on an "out to in" path, producing either a shot that curves from left to right or a pull to the left. I wanted Tiger to always err more toward a laid-off position at the top of his swing.

Links Course

Links courses are located almost exclusively in the British Isles. Each year, the British Open is held in either Scotland or England on one of nine classic links courses. The term *links* refers to the relatively thin strips of land—often amid dunes—that "link" the sea with more fertile growing areas. Links are where golf began several centuries ago. The characteristics of links golf include firm, fast-draining turf that allows for a lot of roll, nearly constant wind, gentle undulations, and few trees. There are fewer than 200 true links courses in the world.

On Plane

In an ideal swing, the correct swing plane retains the angle of the shaft at address. An important distinction in an "on plane" swing is that the shaft actually travels along multiple parallel planes. On the backswing, it travels above—but parallel to—the original plane angle established at address, and on the downswing it travels below but parallel to the original plane angle. When Tiger's swing was at its best, he was on plane.

Pull

A shot that, when hit by a right-handed golfer, does not curve but is hit straight and left of the target. It is typically caused by moving the upper body more quickly than the lower, causing the right-handed player to pull the shot left.

Push

A shot that behaves opposite of a pull. It does not curve but goes straight and right of the target. It may be caused by moving the upper body too slowly, resulting in a shot that is pushed out to the right.

Saw Across

A term Tiger and I used that refers to an intentional "out to in" downswing path that produces a controlled fade or slice, primarily to reduce the possibility of a "big miss." I recommended that Tiger use this technique with his driver in particular whenever he felt uncomfortable or lacked confidence on a tee shot. Although playing the shot meant sacrificing distance, even when it missed the fairway, it usually wasn't by much.

Slice

See *Fade*.

Stinger

A term coined to describe the low-flying tee shot that Tiger favored when getting the ball in the fairway was the priority. The shot was particularly effective for him in the windy conditions and fast-running fairways found at the British Open. Tiger performed the shot best with his 2- and 3-irons, but he was also proficient with his 5-wood and 3-wood. My unfulfilled goal was to get Tiger to confidently and consistently perform the shot with a driver.

Strong Grip

Marked primarily by a left-hand position (in a right-handed golfer) in which the thumb rests on the right side of the club handle. At address, the golfer would look down and see at least two knuckles showing on his left hand. In a strong grip, the club tends to be held more in the fingers. A strong grip is good for creating power, but because it allows the hands more play to turn counterclockwise through impact, it carries more potential for wild shots to the left.

Stuck

The position that occurs on the downswing when the lower body gets too far ahead of the upper body, leaving the arms and hands behind. The club can then no longer be released to square with a simple rotation of the body, but must be "caught up" with compensating arm and hand actions in the hitting area. Highly gifted players like Tiger can often "save" shots in this manner, but not with real consistency. A more reliable downswing would have the hands and arms coming down more "in front" of the body. Players who are *across the line* at the top of the backswing are more likely to get *stuck* than those who are *laid off.*

Weak Grip

When the left thumb rests more on the top of the club handle (in a right-handed golfer). At address, the golfer would look down and see fewer than two knuckles, and in an extremely weak grip, barely one knuckle. In a weak grip, the club tends to be held more in the palms. Because such a grip restricts hand rotation through the ball, it tends to be favored by players who are seeking accuracy more than power. Tiger weakened his grip shortly after I became his coach.

Up and Down

The act of taking two strokes to hole out from areas within about 50 yards of the putting surface, including sand bunkers. For a professional golfer "getting up and down" usually means "saving" a par, but it can also produce a birdie on a par 5 after a player has gotten near the green in two shots. Getting up and down consistently requires both skill and creativity with short shots, and a sure putting stroke.

INDEX OF NAMES

Ainsley, Sam, 217
Ames, Stephen, 73, 156
Anselmo, John, 38
Armstrong, Lance, 184
Atwal, Arjun, 202–3

Baddeley, Aaron, 156
Bailey, Donovan, 184
Baker-Finch, Ian, 25, 64
Ballesteros, Seve, 25, 64
Barkley, Charles, 71–72
Barton, Tom, 155
Begay, Notah, 72, 154
Bell, Bryon, 72, 196, 242
Bird, Larry, 116
Bjorn, Thomas, 240
Bon Jovi, Jon, 183
Bryant, Kobe, 211

Cabrera, Angel, 156
Calcavecchia, Mark, 154
Campbell, Joe, 14
Campbell, Michael, 113
Carmichael, Sam, 14, 105
Carroll, Corey, 71, 72, 141, 142, 143, 150, 151, 185, 202, 204, 206, 237–38
Cink, Stewart, 146
Clark, Tim, 186
Clarke, Doug, 11
Cleland, John, 16
Colvin, Geoff, 100
Cook, John, 11, 55, 70, 202–3
Couples, Fred, 50, 91, 211–12, 242
Cowan, Mike "Fluff," 217
Crenshaw, Ben, 20
Crow, Ken, 18
Curtis, Ben, 203

Daly, John, 31
Davis, Al, 47
Desmond, Dermot, 81
DiMarco, Chris, 107, 108, 109, 129
Donald, Luke, 129
Doyle, Allen, 105
Druckenmiller, Stan, 155
Durant, Joe, 65
Duval, David, 25, 64, 115, 149
Dye, Pete, 99

Eastwood, Clint, 73
Edison, Thomas, 115
Elkington, Steve, 105
Els, Ernie, 90, 113

Faldo, Nick, 13, 19–20, 85, 117, 244
Federer, Roger, 45, 109, 184
Feherty, David, 91
Flick, Jim, 18
Floyd, Raymond, 6, 56, 59
Foley, Sean, 201, 238–40, 244
Frey, Glen, 183
Furyk, Jim, 59, 74, 116

Galea, Anthony, 185–86, 227
Garcia, Sergio, 92, 111, 129
Gladwell, Malcolm, 11
Glenn, Vencie, 152
Glover, Lucas, 189
Goosen, Retief, 82, 113
Gray, Jim, 186, 223, 227
Grout, Jack, 20, 162
Gruden, Jon, 78

Haas, Jay, 14, 36, 91
Haney, Jerilynn, 162
Haney, Jim, 20–21, 37, 40
Haney, Suzanne, 211, 215, 219, 228
Hardy, Jim, 15–17, 38, 49
Harmon, Billy, 36
Harmon, Butch, 6, 11, 13, 16, 19, 29, 30, 31, 32–34, 35, 36, 38–39, 41, 44, 50, 51, 52–53, 54, 55, 57–58, 60, 66, 84, 98, 115, 150, 206, 217, 231–34, 238, 245
Harrington, Padraig, 97
Hitchcock, Ken, 144
Hogan, Ben, 4, 15, 23, 49, 61, 76, 90, 99–100, 105, 117, 125, 132, 181, 191, 237
Holmes, Larry, 53

Jackson, Michael, 195
Jacobs, John, 16–17, 29
James, Kevin, 184
Jeter, Derek, 152
Johnson, Steve, 203
Johnson, Zach, 73, 148, 243
Jones, Bobby, 50, 132, 237
Jordan, Michael, 71–72, 92, 109, 133, 140, 144, 184

Kaminski, Janusz, 123
Kite, Tom, 20
Klein, Emilee, 23
Kleven, Keith, 3, 53, 81, 138, 144, 145, 150, 152, 154, 165, 174–76, 177–78, 180, 184–85
Knowles, Bill, 185
Kostis, Peter, 18, 219
Kuehne, Ernie, 8–9, 11, 20
Kuehne, Hank, 8, 10, 11, 20, 96
Kuehne, Kelli, 8, 10, 20
Kuehne, Pam, 8, 20
Kuehne, Trip, 8–9, 10, 20

LaCava, Joe, 242
Leadbetter, David, 13, 16, 19–20, 32, 55
Lehman, Tom, 73

Lietzke, Bruce, 17
Lindsay, Mark, 184–85
Locke, Bobby, 17, 61
Love, Davis, Jr., 18

McDowell, Graeme, 240
McGinley, Paul, 36
McLean, Jim, 16
McManus, J. P., 81, 228
McNamara, Rob, 72
Mahan, Hunter, 105
Malik, Peter, 36
Mandela, Nelson, 183
Mediate, Rocco, 178, 180
Mickelson, Amy, 93
Mickelson, Phil, 2, 5, 52, 75, 81, 83, 90–94, 111, 113, 114, 120, 123–24, 187, 214, 218–19
Miller, Johnny, 104, 117–18, 223

Nelson, Byron, 23, 105, 116–17, 131–32, 136, 191, 232, 237
Nicklaus, Jack, 2, 4, 7, 20, 40, 61, 87, 90, 105, 114, 116, 117, 119, 124, 132, 135, 137, 138, 143–44, 162, 163, 169, 182, 190, 230, 237, 243, 244, 245, 247
Norman, Greg, 6, 13, 32, 59, 114
Norman, Moe, 25, 67, 117

Obama, Barack, 183
O'Hair, Sean, 91
O'Hern, Nick, 134–35
Oliver, Carl, 15
O'Meara, Mark, 11, 13, 18–20, 23, 24, 26–29, 30–33, 34–36, 39, 41, 42, 44, 49, 51, 52, 53, 54, 56, 62, 67, 70, 71, 76, 82, 88, 115, 146, 202–3
O'Neal, Shaquille, 153

Palmer, Arnold, 17, 76, 90, 246
Parnevik, Jesper and Mia, 86
Payne, Billy, 212–13
Penick, Harvey, 20
Perez, Pat, 236
Player, Gary, 137
Poulter, Ian, 74
Price, Nick, 117

Reis, Henri, 65
Rodriguez, Alex, 184
Rose, Charlie, 246
Rose, Justin, 201
Rosenberg, Thomas, 154, 165, 168–69, 170–71, 181, 182
Rucker, Darius, 184
Runyan, Paul, 18

Sabbatini, Rory, 148, 161
Sanders, Mike, 17–18
Scott, Adam, 241
Servick, Todd, 83
Singh, Vijay, 80–81, 92, 94, 104–5, 113, 129–30
Sluman, Jeff, 91
Smith, Rick, 93
Smoltz, John, 71
Snead, Sam, 17, 49, 87, 90
Sörenstam, Annika, 65, 115

Spears, Britney, 195
Steinberg, Mark, 53–54, 56, 72, 144, 145, 153, 161, 172, 177, 193, 196, 197, 204, 209, 211, 214, 217, 219–20, 222, 226, 227
Stewart, James, 184
Stewart, Payne, 135
Streck, Ron, 15
Stricker, Steve, 74
Sutton, Hal, 92

Tillman, Pat, 140
Torrance, Bob, 55
Toski, Bob, 18
Trevino, Lee, 59, 61, 117, 137, 191

Vardon, Harry, 132
Vedra, Ponte, 212
Vick, Michael, 211

Waite, Grant, 184
Ward, Hines, 185
Watson, Bubba, 96
Watson, Tom, 114
Westwood, Lee, 2, 178, 214
Wiley, C. J., 104
Williams, Kirsty, 209
Williams, Steve, 6–7, 56–57, 59, 63, 80, 86–87, 114, 120, 131, 141, 144, 147, 150, 153, 157, 158, 160, 161, 165, 174, 177–78, 197, 200, 208–9, 210, 218, 241–42
Woodland, Gary, 96
Woods, Charlie, 93, 157, 199–200, 201
Woods, Earl, 8–9, 10, 12, 38, 58, 69, 81, 90, 99, 103, 110, 122, 123, 125, 132, 133, 138, 139, 141, 144–45, 153, 157, 183, 197, 198, 210
Woods, Elin, 5, 45–46, 75, 81, 82–83, 84, 86, 93, 106, 121–22, 126, 140, 144, 155, 157, 164, 167, 193, 197, 199–200, 201–2, 205, 209, 242
Woods, Sam, 157, 199–200, 201
Woods, Tida, 12, 110–11, 197

Yang, Y. E., 189